S0-AGY-767

Women, Men, Work and Family in Europe

DISCARD

DISCARD

Women, Men, Work and Family in Europe

Edited by

Rosemary Crompton,
City University, UK

Suzan Lewis
Middlesex University, UK

Clare Lyonette
City University, UK

Selection and editorial matter © Rosemary Crompton, Suzan Lewis and
Clare Lyonette   2007
Chapters © their authors   2007

All rights reserved. No reproduction, copy or transmission of this
publication may be made without written permission.

No paragraph of this publication may be reproduced, copied or transmitted
save with written permission or in accordance with the provisions of the
Copyright, Designs and Patents Act 1988, or under the terms of any licence
permitting limited copying issued by the Copyright Licensing Agency, 90
Tottenham Court Road, London W1T 4LP.

Any person who does any unauthorised act in relation to this publication
may be liable to criminal prosecution and civil claims for damages.

The authors have asserted their rights to be identified as the authors of this
work in accordance with the Copyright, Designs and Patents Act 1988.

First published 2007 by
PALGRAVE MACMILLAN

Houndmills, Basingstoke, Hampshire RG21 6XS and
175 Fifth Avenue, New York, N.Y. 10010

Companies and representatives throughout the world

PALGRAVE MACMILLAN is the global academic imprint of the Palgrave
Macmillan division of St. Martin's Press, LLC and of Palgrave Macmillan Ltd.

Macmillan® is a registered trademark in the United States, United Kingdom
and other countries. Palgrave is a registered trademark in the European
Union and other countries.

ISBN-13: 978–1–4039–8719–8   hardback
ISBN-10: 1–4039–8719–X   hardback

This book is printed on paper suitable for recycling and made from fully
managed and sustained forest sources.

A catalogue record for this book is available from the British Library.

Library of Congress Cataloging-in-Publication Data

Women, men, work, and family in Europe / edited by Rosemary Crompton,
    Suzan Lewis, and Clare Lyonette.
        p. cm.
    Includes bibliographical references (p.) and index.
    ISBN-13: 978-1-4039-8719-8 (hardback)
    ISBN-10: 1-4039-8719-X (hardback)
        1. Work and family–Europe–Cross-cultural studies. 2. Sexual division
of labor–Europe–Cross-cultural studies. I. Crompton, Rosemary. II. Lewis,
Suzan. III. Lyonette, Clare, 1960–

    HD4904.25.W6545 2007
    306.3'6094–dc22

                                                                2006050198

10   9   8   7   6   5   4
16   15   14   13   12   11   10   09   08

Printed and bound in Great Britain by
Antony Rowe Ltd, Chippenham and Eastbourne

Contents

List of Tables

List of Figures

Acknowledgements

This book originated at a seminar held at City University, London in April 2004. The participants were working on three main research projects. These included two projects funded by the Economic and Social Research Council, entitled 'Employment and the Family' (research grant number R000239727) and also 'Families, Employment and Work–life integration in Britain and Europe' (research grant number RES000220106), as well as a series of projects entitled 'Transitions', funded by the European Commission (2003–2005). The authors would like to thank all those who participated in the seminar, many of whom have contributed to this book.

Notes on the Contributors

Anneli Anttonen is a Professor in the Department of Social Policy and Social Work, University of Tampere, Finland. She heads the research group *Care and Social Policy*. Among her latest publications are *The Young, the Old and the State: Social Care Systems in Five Industrial Nations* (2003), and 'Empowering social policy: the role of social care services in modern welfare states', in Olli Kangas and Joakim Palme (eds) *Social Policy and Economic Development in the Nordic Countries* (2005).

Margareta Bäck-Wiklund is a Professor of Social Work and Family Policy at Göteborg University, Sweden. She heads the research programme *Parenting and Childhood in Modern Family Cultures*. Among her publications are *The Modern Parenthood. Family and Gender in Transition* (*Det moderna Föräldraskapet*) (1997, 2002, 2005); *The Network Family* (*Nätverksfamiljen*) (ed., 2004); 'New trends in the time bind – the Swedish case', in M. Jacobssen and J. Tonboe (eds), *The Work Society* (*Arbeidssamfundet*) (2004).

Rosemary Crompton is a Professor of Sociology at City University, London, UK. She and Clare Lyonette are currently working on a project in the ESRC Gender Network which involves both qualitative and quantitative methods to map the work and family careers of men and women in four different occupational sectors. Her latest book is *Employment and the Family* (2006).

Maria das Dores Guerreiro is at CIES-ISCTE, Lisbon, Portugal. She and **Inês Pereira** have been working in TRANSITIONS – Gender, Parenthood and the Changing European Workplace, a European project involving case studies in both the public and private sectors, and biographical interviews with young parents in several countries, as well as in a national study on the policies for work–family balance in Portuguese companies. Her latest book is on young people's transition to the labour market: *Os Jovens e o Mercado de Trabalho* (co-author, 2006).

Laura den Dulk is a senior researcher at the Department of Sociology, Utrecht University, the Netherlands. Her main area of expertise is cross-national research regarding work–life policies in organisations in different welfare state regimes. In 1999 she co-edited a book on work–family arrangements in Europe. Her latest co-edited book is *Flexible Working, Organizational Change and the Integration of Work and Personal Life* (2005). Current research interests include the attitudes, opinions and behaviour of top managers towards work/life policies and social quality in European workplaces. She participates in various EC research projects: 'Quality of Life in a Changing Europe' (QUALITY) and 'Gender, Parenthood and the Changing European Workplace: young adults negotiating the work–family boundary' (TRANSITIONS).

Colette Fagan is a Professor in the Department of Sociology and Co-Director of the European Work and Employment Research Centre at the University of Manchester, UK. Her research focuses on gender relations in employment and domestic life, with a particular interest in international comparative analysis and working time. She is a coordinator of the European Commission's Expert Group on Gender, Social Inclusion and Employment. Her recent publications include the co-edited volume *Gender Divisions and Working Time in the New Economy: Public Policy and Changing Patterns of Work in Europe and North America* (2006) and contributions to J. Messenger (ed.) *Finding Balance: Work Time and Workers' Needs and Preferences* (2004).

Jeanne Fagnani has been a Senior Research Fellow at CNRS (National Centre for Scientific Research) since 1981. From 1991 to 2001, she also worked at the National Family Allowance Fund (CNAF). She has conducted many comparative research projects funded by the European Commission, particularly on interactions between family policies, female employment and labour markets. She is currently involved in cross-national research (coordinated by Prof. J. Bradshaw from York University; 2006–2007) on child-benefit packages in 17 countries. She is also conducting comparative research on family policies in France and Germany, funded by CNAF.

Richenda Gambles is a Lecturer in the Department of Social Policy and Social Work, University of Oxford, UK. As well as being an Associate of the Work–Life Research Centre, she has been involved with the Institute of Family and Environmental Research and has worked at the Open University as an Associate Lecturer. She has recently co-authored *The Myth of Work–Life Balance* (2006) with Suzan Lewis and Rhona Rapoport.

Hana Hašková, a sociologist, works in the Department of Gender and Sociology, Institute of Sociology, Academy of Sciences in the Czech Republic. She has completed research on Czech obstetrics, work–life balance and women's civic and political participation in Central and Eastern Europe. Currently she is coordinating research on childlessness. She is the co-author of *Women's Civic and Political Participation in the Czech Republic and the Role of the European Union Gender Equality and Accession Policies and Relations and Changes of Gender Differences in Czech Society in the 1990s* (2003).

Nicky Le Feuvre is a Professor of Sociology at Toulouse-Le Mirail University in France, where she is Director of the SAGESSE gender studies research centre. She has carried out several cross-national comparative research projects on women's labour market experiences, particularly in the professions (medicine, law, pharmacy, speech therapy). Her recent publications include *Employment Opportunities for Women in Europe* (2004, with Muriel Andriocci) and a contribution in G. Griffin (ed.) *Doing Women's Studies: Equal Opportunities, Personal Impacts and Social Consequences* (2005).

Clotilde Lemarchant is an Assistant Professor of Sociology at the University of Caen, Normandy, France. She is a member of Centre Maurice Halbwachs, a laboratory of the CNRS (National Centre of Scientific Research). She has been working in the field of kinship and gender and social politics. She is author of *Belles-filles: Avec les beaux-parents trouver la bonne distance* (1999).

Suzan Lewis is Professor of Organisational Psychology at Middlesex University, UK. She coordinated a recently completed EU Framework Five project, Gender, Parenthood and the Changing Workplace (TRANSITIONS) and is a partner in a new EU project on Quality of Life in a Changing Europe.

Clare Lyonette is a Research Officer at City University, London, UK. She and Rosemary Crompton are currently working on a project in the ESRC Gender Network which involves both qualitative and quantitative methods to map the work and family careers of men and women in four different occupational sectors.

Linda McDowell is Professor of Human Geography, University of Oxford, UK. She is a member of the ESRC-funded Gender Equality Network and is currently working on a project on labour market segmentation in the service sector in Greater London. Her most recent book is *Hard Labour: the Forgotten Voices of Latvian 'Volunteer' Workers* (2005).

Diane Perrons is Director of the Gender Institute, London School of Economics, UK. She is co-author of *Globalisation and Social Change* (2005) and co-editor of *Gender Divisions and Working Time in the New Economy: Changing Patterns of Work, Care and Public Policy in Europe and North America* (2006). She is currently working on employment change and complex inequalities.

Lars Plantin is Senior Lecturer at Health and Society, Department for Social Work at the University of Malmö, Sweden. His main area of expertise is family sociology with a special focus on fatherhood. He is the author of *Men, Family Life and Parenthood* (2001) (*Man, familjeliv och foraldraskap*) and is currently starting a project on fatherhood and reproductive health with a focus on fathers from the Middle East living in Sweden.

Rhona Rapoport was, until recently, Director of the Institute of Family and Environmental Research, London, UK. For twenty years, she was a consultant to the Ford Foundation working on affirmative action programmes in the United States and in developing countries and on work and family issues. She has numerous publications, many with her late husband, Robert, including pioneering work–family literature such as 'Work and family in contemporary society,' (1965, *American Sociological Review*, 30) and *Dual Career Families* (1971). In 2002, she published *Beyond Work–Family Balance: Advancing Gender Equity and Workplace Performance* (co-authored with L. Bailyn, J. K. Fletcher and B. Pruitt). For the past three years she has been involved in a project entitled 'Work–Personal Life Integration – Looking Backwards to Go Forward' in seven countries. This has now been published as *The Myth of Work-Life Balance* (2006) with her colleagues Professor Suzan Lewis and Richenda Gambles.

Kath Ray is a Research Fellow at the Policy Studies Institute, London, UK. Her current work focuses on the employment–family interface and work–life balance issues, and changing racisms/identities in contemporary Britain. She is co-editor of *Gender Divisions and Working Time in the New Economy* (2006) and co-author of *Ethnic Minority Perceptions and Experiences of Jobcentre Plus*, DWP research report, no. 349 (2006).

Jorma Sipilä is in the Department of Social Policy and Social Work, University of Tampere, Finland. He was editor-in chief of *Janus* 1996–97 (the journal of the Social Policy Association in Finland). His main areas of interest include social care, the welfare state and comparative research. He has published six books and two edited books in Finnish, three edited books in English and one in Japanese. In addition to texts published in Finnish, he has also authored about 40 articles, chapters or reports in English plus some in Swedish, Spanish, Italian and Estonian.

Anneke van Doorne-Huiskes is emeritus Professor of Sociology at the Department of Sociology and ICS Research School of Utrecht University. Her major research interests lie in the areas of welfare states, labour market and gender, gender and organisation, organisational culture and work–life balance. She has written numerous articles on these topics and is co-editor (with Jacques van Hoof and Ellie Roelofs) of *Women and the European Labour Markets* (1995), (with Susan Baker of Cardiff University) *Women and Public Policies: the Shifting Boundaries between the Public and the Private Spheres* (1999), *Work–Family Arrangements in Europe* (1999), and *Flexible Working and Organisational Change* (2005). She has recently been engaged in the international research project 'TRANSITIONS: Gender, Parenthood and the Changing European Workplace'. She also participates in QUALITY, an internationally comparative project on the quality of life and work of European citizens, financed by the European Commission (2006–2009).

Karin Wall is a Sociologist and Senior Research Fellow at the Institute of Social Sciences (ICS) of the University of Lisbon, Portugal. She coordinates the Research Network on Sociology of Families and Intimate Lives at ESA and has carried out national and cross-national research on family policies in Europe, family patterns and interactions, gender and family, work and family life, migrant women and families. She is currently working on three projects, involving both qualitative and quantitative methods: men's roles and identities in different kinds of families; family trajectories and social networks; the politics of leave policies. She recently published *Famílias em Portugal* (2005).

Kevin Ward is a Reader in Geography, School of Environment and Development at the University of Manchester, UK. He is co-author of a number of books including *Spaces of Work: Global Capitalism and the Geographies of Labour* (2004, with Noel Castree, Neil Coe and Michael Samers), and *Managing Employment Change: the New Realities of Work* (2002, with Huw Beynon, Damian Grimshaw and Jill Rubery). His research interests focus on state spatiality, the politics of urban development and social reproduction and labour market restructuring.

1
Introduction: The Unravelling of the 'Male Breadwinner' Model – and Some of its Consequences

Rosemary Crompton, Suzan Lewis and Clare Lyonette

Introduction

The trends underlying the issues that are the major focus of this book are well known. These include rising employment amongst women, particularly mothers, and thus an increase in dual-earner households, increasing instability in interpersonal relationships, and declining fertility together with a growing recognition of the problems of work–life 'balance'. They have been gathering pace since the second half of the twentieth century, and indeed a further increase in the level of women's employment is now enshrined as a European policy objective. The most usual template against which these changes are evaluated is the male breadwinner/female caregiver model of the articulation of employment and family life. This work–family arrangement reached its peak in the mid twentieth century, and indeed, an earlier generation of sociologists assumed this model not only to be 'natural', but also to represent a positive functional adaptation to the requirements of 'industrial society' (Parsons, 1949) However, it may be argued that it has not been fully appreciated, either in the recent past or in the present, that this 'golden age' of the (nuclear) family covered in fact only a very short period in human history (Seccombe, 1993).

In the eighteenth and nineteenth centuries, in less well-off households in newly industrialising countries such as Britain, during the early stages of capitalism all members of the family – even children – were expected to make an economic contribution. In the coalfields and in the cotton mills, whole families were engaged, via the male household head, to carry out a diverse range of productive tasks. Working and living conditions were hard and dangerous, and social reformers campaigned for, and achieved, protective legislation for women and children in particular (Humphries,

1

1984). Further reforms, including the introduction of compulsory education during the nineteenth century, moved children from being an economic benefit to an economic cost (Irwin, 2003), and increasingly, working age men came to predominate in the labour force. Seccombe argues that these changes in labour use were in large part a consequence of economic and technological developments as capitalism developed from the 'extensive' exploitation of labour, using relatively simple techniques and considerable labour inputs, to 'intensive' exploitation, requiring more complex technologies and a greater level of work intensity from a labour force that was increasingly (although never completely) masculine.

The 'breadwinner wage' – that is, an income sufficient to support a working man and his family – became a major objective of the trade union movement (Humphries, 1982). In relation to women, there were also accompanying changes in gender ideology. Women had always been regarded as the 'natural' inferiors of men, but during the nineteenth century, the notion that women (particularly wives and mothers) were, 'naturally', *morally* superior increasingly took root. Women became 'the angels of the house' and its nurturing and moral centre. The 'ideology of domesticity' (Williams, 1991) assigned caring and domestic work uniquely to women and indeed, the contribution of women to household management and domestic production was often essential to family prosperity.

However between the two world wars:

> The advent of mass production for consumption . . . redrew the boundary [*i.e., between the household and the wider economy*] and resulted in a transformation of the relation between the two spheres. The shift to production for consumption pulled the household economy much more fully into the orbit of the market economy . . . leading to . . . less insulation and a greater integration between them. At the same time, the possibility of domestic tasks being undertaken on the basis of purchased commodities . . . and on a less labour-intensive basis . . . resulted in a long-term shift of labour out of the household economy and into the wage economy. (Glucksmann, 1995: 71)

These changes had their major impact on younger women, as married women were still not expected to go 'out to work' – unless enforced to do so by economic necessity. Indeed, in Britain, in many occupations and industries, a marriage bar was in operation between the two world wars, persisting, in some cases, until after the Second World War. There has in fact been considerable variation both in the timing and extent of the shift of (women's) labour out of the household economy. Later industrialisation, as in some of the Scandinavian countries, led to a later historical shift of labour out of the household economy. In some countries, most notably in Eastern Europe, after the Second World War, women were drafted into paid labour as a national duty (Einhorn, 1993) and much of the labour of care provided by the state. Moreover, Pfau-Effinger (2004) has argued that the emergence of the housewife model of the male breadwinner family was crucially dependent not on industrialisation, but on the extent of the development and influence of the urban bourgeoisie (see also Davidoff & Hall, 1987). In some societies, therefore, such as the Netherlands, the housewife model was established even before industrialisation, whilst in others, including Finland, it was never the norm. Thus as Esping-Andersen and others have argued, national 'path dependency' is likely to have had a discernible impact on the characteristic manner of articulation between employment and family life.

Nevertheless, in Western Europe, the male breadwinner gender/welfare arrangement came to underpin the 'mid [20th] century social compromise' (Crouch, 1999: 53). Men in full-time employment received a 'family wage' and related benefits, women gained benefits, often indirectly, as wives and mothers (Pateman, 1989). These arrangements were in a broad sense a class 'compromise'. Governments of left and right supported social protections and increasing welfare, and left parties and their representatives did not seek to radically destabilise existing social arrangements. The 'breadwinner' model was buttressed by the institutional separation of women from both the political, and much of the economic, spheres of human activity. During the course of the twentieth century, the consolidation of the 'male breadwinner' model was accompanied by institutional developments and arrangements that reflected its basic assumptions, from school hours to pensions and the delivery of health and welfare services (Esping-Andersen, 1990, 2002; Sainsbury (ed.), 1994).

In the later decades of the twentieth century, the 'male breadwinner' model of the articulation of employment and family life began to unravel. In the 1960s and 1970s, some kind of paid employment for married women without small children became the norm, and women increasingly returned to work once their youngest child had reached school age. By the 1980s and 1990s, even mothers of small children were staying in the labour market (although there is considerable cross-national variation in this respect). However, the gendered ideology of domesticity, that holds women responsible for the domestic sphere, together with its accompanying (implicit or explicit) gender essentialism, has proved to have deeper roots. Nevertheless, the major shift in gender relations and associated norms and attitudes that is currently in process raises a series of important issues that will be explored in the chapters in this book. How is the work of caring to be accomplished, given that it can no longer be automatically assumed that it will be undertaken (unpaid) within the family? How may sets of institutions, moulded to the contours of the 'male breadwinner' arrangement, be reconstructed in order to accommodate to new realities? How do families adjust to these changing circumstances and what is to be done about the growing conflict between paid employment and the demands of family life? Will social and economic inequalities, between women and men, as well as between different social classes, be ameliorated or intensified by these recent changes?

Explaining change in gender and employment relations

The complex nature of the changes that are under way means that single factor explanations are not likely to take our understandings very far. Very schematically, the elements contributing to work–family articulation may be divided into two broad categories: 'structural' and 'relational'. Structural elements include national 'welfare regimes', and the kinds of supports they offer to employed mothers and dual-earner families, together with wider national economic and social policies such as labour market regulation (particularly in respect of working hours). Other structural elements include employer policies, not only in respect of the work–life entitlements they offer to their employees (employer policies and state policies are closely linked; see Evans, 2001), but also employee management strategies, such as 'high commitment' management, that have been demonstrated to have an impact on work to family 'spillover' (White et al., 2003; Crompton, 2003). At the level of individual families, the extent and level of social and material resources available to the household will obviously have an impact. Thus we might expect there to be more or less systematic class differences in the strategies whereby individual families combine employment and family life.

Relational elements will include, above all, those between men and women. The precise nature of every heterosexual (and same-sex) partnership is of course unique, but will be, nevertheless, shaped by the normative context in which it is embedded. Attitudes to gender relations, and gender roles, have been changing in parallel with the erosion of the breadwinner model, but nevertheless, women are still held to be largely responsible for caring and domestic work. That is, despite the fact that it is increasingly accepted (indeed, expected) that women should be in paid employment, they are also likely to shoulder the major responsibility for 'work' within the domestic sphere. The extent to which partners share responsibility for domestic and caring work will have an important impact on the extent to which a positive articulation of employment and family life is achieved by individual families. Individual attitudes will vary, and a range of evidence suggests that educational level, the extent of the woman's employment, age and social class are all factors that contribute to both more 'liberal' gender role attitudes and a greater extent of the sharing of domestic work between the sexes (Crompton, 2006). However, there are also national variations, in both attitudes to gender roles, and the advisability of mother's employment, (particularly when children are young), as well as on wider normative questions such as what constitutes 'good mothering'.

Pfau-Effinger (2004), for example, has argued that whereas in Germany, 'good mothering' is seen as requiring sole and direct maternal input, in Finland, mothering is seen as a societal responsibility in which the state should play an active role. Ideals of 'masculinity' and 'femininity' also vary, both nationally as well as between different classes and ethnic groups (Connell, 1995). As market and domestic work have become so closely associated with men and women respectively, the nature of the domestic division of labour will be influenced by dominant masculine and feminine identities, and some men (and women) consider it inappropriate for men to carry out domestic work (West & Zimmerman, 1987). In a similar vein, organisational cultures may express particular kinds of masculinities and femininities, (McDowell, 1997), as well as shaping a more or less sympathetic environment for men and women with caring responsibilities (Lewis & Lewis, 1996).

One way of understanding work–life articulation outcomes at the relational level might be to view them as deriving from structural elements – the economic context, state, labour market and employer policies – but crucially filtered by varying norms and values at the national, group and individual levels. This is not to imply that beliefs, norms and values are 'determined' by structural factors, as institutions are themselves shaped by beliefs, norms and values. For example, structures of labour market regulation will vary according to the extent that governments are influenced by neo-liberal or neo-Keynesian economic policies. Policies in relation to working mothers will be similarly affected. In Britain, for example, a network of state funded nurseries was created during the Second World War in order that mothers might contribute to wartime production. This network was wound up during the post-war period, an era which also happened to coincide with the zenith of the male bread-winner model in theory and practice. Thus there is a reciprocal relationship between norms, values and institutions, but for the purposes of analysis, it is useful to begin at a particular point on this loop. Our discussion below, therefore, will begin by examining a major structural factor shaping capacities for work–life articulation – that is, the role of the state.

National variations

The increase in women's employment has been under way in all 'late modern' societies – that is, it is a notable area of cross-national continuity. In this book, our major focus is on the consequences of this increase, rather than its cause. Economic and technological change, including the decline of heavy industry and the growth of service sector employment, together with the development of efficient contraception and, not least, the rising aspirations of women themselves (as expressed through 'second-wave' feminism), have all contributed to the growth of women's employment, but we will not be dealing with these topics here. Other areas of cross-national continuity include a range of factors that impact on the nature of gender relations and the domestic division of labour – class, level of education, and ethnic differences. Despite these continuities, however, there are also systematic cross-national variations in both structural and relational elements impacting on work–life articulation.

State policies

One of the most significant structural sources of variation is in national welfare regimes. As is well established (Esping-Anderson, 1990; Korpi, 2000; Lewis, 1992), there are considerable differences in the extent to which states support employed mothers and dual-earner families. Supports may be direct – as in, for example, state provided and/or subsidised child and elder care, or cash allowances for family caring. Other supports include statutory parental (maternity and paternity) and carers' leaves, and tax allowances for childcare costs. In general, it is the social democratic (Scandinavian or Nordic) welfare regimes that provide the highest levels of these supports. These countries are also characterised by relatively low levels of class and gender inequality (Korpi, 2000), and the level of women's employment is generally high. In these countries, the principle of universalism means that all citizens qualify for welfare benefits. At the other extreme are the liberal welfare regimes that characteristically provide only a 'safety net' for those in direst need. Neo-liberal policies dictate only a low level of public spending, thus few state resources are assigned to support the caregiving that has been tradition-ally provided by families. However, other aspects of neo-liberal policies (for example, little or minimal wage or employment protections) will operate so as to pull women into the labour market because of economic need, and levels of women's employment are relatively high. 'Corporatist' (or conservative) welfare regimes have historically evolved along Bismarckian principles, and welfare benefits have been closely tied to the 'breadwinner' wage. Generous supports for those in employment have carried with them the assumption that care will be provided within the family, to which welfare resources are directed. Standard 'male breadwinner' jobs have been protected, and the provision of non-family state care rather limited. Thus women's employment levels tend to be relatively low. A further regime category that has been identified is the 'familialist', in which it is assumed that care will be the responsibility of private households, and alternative state supports are minimal or even non-existent.

In this book, the countries under discussion include examples of all the regime types discussed above. Finland and Norway would both be considered to be examples of Scandinavian or social democratic welfare regimes, and Britain as an example of a liberal regime. France and the Netherlands are examples of conservative regimes, although as we shall see, France is relatively unusual amongst corporatist welfare states in having relatively high levels of historic support for working mothers. Portugal might be described as a mixed corporatist/familialist welfare regime. Finally, we also include discussion of eastern European ex-state socialist countries, once characterised by universal state provision but, since the late 1980s and early 1990s, now making the (often uncomfort-able) transition to market capitalism.

Another major source of structural variation that impacts on capaci-ties for work–life articulation are different patterns of labour market regulation. As we have already noted, conservative regimes have often sought to protect full-time 'breadwinner' jobs, resulting, it has been argued, in rather inflexible labour markets. At the other extreme, neo-liberal policies place a high premium on labour market flexibility, controls are few and both 'long' and 'short' hours jobs are common. It is also a fea-ture of neo-liberal policies that there are few restrictions on working hours. In fact, average hours of work show considerable national variation. Amongst the countries discussed in this book, for example, Britain has a partial 'opt-out' from European legislation that restricts working hours to 48 a week (and incidentally, has the second longest average working hours in Europe for full-time men), whereas France has introduced a statutory 35-hour working week.

Employer policies

Employing organisations can affect capacities for work–life articulation in respect of both the demands they make on their employees, as well as in the concrete work–life entitlements they offer (enhanced maternity leaves, opportunities for flexible working, etc.). Hours of work are crucial here (although working hours are also very sensitive to national regulation). In countries in which state provision for dual-earner families is not particularly generous, one government strategy has often been to give enthusiastic support and encouragement to employers to develop 'family friendly' policies (e.g. Department of Trade and Industry, 2003). However, the evidence suggests that such 'voluntary' employer provision falls far behind that of the more generous (i.e. social democratic) welfare states (Evans, 2001). The level of employer provision is generally higher in 'corporatist' welfare states than in neo-liberal countries, but the level of state provision in the Scandinavian countries means that employers provide little by way of 'extra' policies.

In the management of their workforces, employers may make demands that mean that employees find it necessary to work beyond their contracted hours (for example, by setting targets for sales or completed transactions). More particularly, it is often expected that an employee who wishes to be promoted has to demonstrate 'commitment' (and thus promotability) by working longer hours than contracted. Although flexible working is often advocated as a major measure whereby work–life 'balance' may be achieved, employer-led flexible working may often result in work intensification. For example, an employee may be required to carry out weekend or 'non-standard' hours work without an overtime premium, and to take hours off during the 'standard' working week. Such measures decrease the 'porosity' of the working day (Rubery et al., 2003) and, as far as the employer is concerned, increase the profitable use of labour time.

Thus 'positive' work–life and/or family-friendly policies offered by the employer may co-exist uneasily with other organisational values (Lewis, 1997). Managers may place a greater value on employees who do not allow family commitments to intrude in their working lives, and long hours in the workplace may be seen as an indication of organisational commitment. Lewis identifies two major barriers to a culture change in a family-friendly direction: subjective senses of entitlement, and organisational discourses of time. In her research (in a manufacturing company, a public sector organisation, and an accountancy firm), family-friendly provisions were often seen as being 'perks' rather than a basic right (women were more likely than men to feel 'entitled' to these provisions but less likely to feel 'entitled' to a career), and long hours working was seen as a measure of commitment to the organisation. Individual managerial and supervisory discretion (both *de jure* and *de facto*) is often central to the implementation of policies such as short-term leave, or the ability to change or reduce working hours (Yeandle et al., 2003, Valcour & Batt, 2003). Thus, even if an organisation has policies available, supervisory discretion means that they may not be equally available to all employees.

Lewis (1996; see also Bailyn, 1993) argues, therefore, that the most significant change necessary to achieve a positive work–life 'balance' is to change organisational 'cultures'. This will involve efforts to 'challenge and modify all organisational practices based on assumed separation between work and family lives so as to empower men and women to make optimum contributions in both spheres . . . to adapt organisational policies and structures to enable people to manage multiple demands in work and family with maximum satisfaction and minimum stress' (Lewis, 1996: 9). However, the question may be raised as to whether the kinds of workplace pressures that inhibit individual empowerment and create pressures for family life are best described as 'cultural' (and therefore, in theory, amenable to normative transformation). It is true that the normative assignment of caring work to women, and thus their felt 'entitlement' to family-friendly provisions, may be described as 'cultural', as is the sense that men should have career preference – both of these may be seen as deriving from the normative assumptions that underpin the 'breadwinner' model. However, other aspects of organisational demands, including the consequences of work intensification and pressures to work long hours, derive from managerial practices that have a very clear material basis.

Recent changes in the way in which employees are managed, it is argued, have 'forced' individuals to develop 'enterprising selves' in which they engage in a constant process of identity construction and reconstruction (Rose, 1989; Du Gay, 1996; McDowell, 1997). In particular, 'high commitment' managerial techniques, together with focused attempts to build positive organisational 'cultures of excellence', have become increasingly influential. We do not need 'hands' in today's organisations, it is argued, but 'hearts and minds' instead (Thompson & Warhurst, 1998). Organisations seek to develop 'cultures of excellence' that work to establish 'that ensemble of norms and techniques of conduct that enables the self-actualising capacities of individuals to become aligned with the goals and objectives of the organisation for which they work' (Du Gay & Pryke, 2002: 1). As Du Gay (1996: 72) has argued, such projects of 'excellence' mesh positively with neo-liberal ideas as they seek to establish a connection between the self-fulfilling desires of individuals and the achievement of organisational objectives. The person becomes a neo-liberal 'entrepreneur of the self', autonomous, responsible, free, choice-making, and through these individual actions, organisational goals are achieved.

However, the setting of individual targets for even lower-level employees, as well as the kinds of changes to the working day described above, suggests that a culture of entrepreneurship is not just a matter of changing hearts and minds, but has material consequences for the nature of workers' jobs. What may be described as 'top-down' entrepreneurship may be in direct conflict with other company policies that ostensibly attempt to enable employees to better accommodate their family lives. Taking a carer's day may mean that targets are not met, for example, and pay may be affected. More particularly, replacement staff are rarely made available for absent colleagues, whose work has to be covered by others – often first-line supervisors as well as immediate workmates (Crompton, 2006) – leading to further work pressures. Thus, it may be argued, a positive change of organisational cultures in a more 'family-friendly' direction will also have to involve a change in managerial practices of employee control.

Management strategies and policies tend to be developed and offered as universal nostrums, although they do vary cross-nationally (Edwards et al., 1996). However, the pressures of competitive capitalism (and the individual career development that is its inevitable accompaniment) may cut across national institutions. For example, Hojgaard's (1997) case studies of three Danish organisations found that men felt constrained to 'put in the hours' if they wished to develop their careers, and Crompton and Birkelund's (2000) comparative study of banking in Norway and Britain found that career-minded men (and women) in Norway tended not to take full advantage of the policies available for fear of affecting their career development.

There are, therefore, convergent, as well as nationally divergent, tendencies as far as work–family articulation is concerned. National variations in welfare regimes as well as in the institutions of labour market regulation have a demonstrable impact on capacities for positive work–life 'balance' as far as families are concerned. For example, Gornick and Meyers (2003) have demonstrated that in those countries that have good dual-earner family supports, family and child poverty is relatively low, as is the impact of children on mother's employment. However, the pressures of competitive capitalism and modern managerial techniques can have a negative impact on individuals with caring responsibilities, whatever the national institutional context. Abstractly, it is the case that capitalism undermines the family form via its indifference to the 'private' lives of the labour power it purchases (Seccombe, 1993: 19), and as Beck has remarked, 'The market subject is ultimately the single individual, "unhindered" by a relationship, marriage, or family' (1992: 116). Historically, the 'male breadwinner' model emerged as part of a range of measures designed to ameliorate the worst excesses of capitalist development. Our brief review has suggested that, with the entry of women into the labour force, it will be necessary to re-regulate the employment relationship if a positive work–life 'balance' (to say nothing of women's equality) is to be achieved.

Relational factors

It has been emphasised that institutions are shaped by prevailing norms and values, as well as vice versa. As Korpi (2000) has demonstrated, cultural and religious factors (particularly the influence of the Catholic church) have been significant in shaping family policies in Europe. Although in all 'western' countries, gender role attitudes are becoming more 'liberal' over time, there are still considerable cross-national variations. For example, amongst the countries discussed in this volume, the percentages of respondents to similar national surveys[1] 'agreeing' that 'a man's job is to earn money, a woman's job is to look after the home and family' were only 10 per cent in Norway, and 12 per cent in Finland, but 18 per cent in Britain, 22 per cent in France and 34 per cent in Portugal (Crompton, 2006: 145). It is, of course, not only institutions that are shaped by norms and values at the national and local levels, but also interpersonal relations between men and women, and within families and households.

Norms and values do not necessarily have a direct impact on individual behaviour. For example, in aggregate, Portugal is one of the more gender conservative countries discussed in this volume, and attitudes to mother's employment, particularly when children are young, are rather negative (Lyonette et al., forthcoming 2007). Nevertheless, the level of mother's employment in Portugal, particularly full-time employment, is relatively high (largely because of economic need; see OECD, 2004).

However, changing attitudes to gender roles have not only had an impact on whether or not women 'go out to work', but also on the division of labour between men and women within the household.

As noted above, despite the widespread entry of women into employment, women are still held largely responsible for, and carry out the majority of, caring and domestic work, although the situation has changed since the mid twentieth century. Cross-national data, as well as detailed information for the US (Bianchi et al., 2000; Sullivan & Gershuny, 2001), indicates that women's hours of household work declined considerably from the 1960s to the 1980s. In the US: 'women spent about 30 hours doing unpaid household work in 1965, over six times the 4.9 hours men spent in housework. Women's housework hours dropped to 23.7 hours per week in 1975, 19.7 hours per week in 1985, and reached a low of 17.5 hours per week by 1995. Men's hours increased to 7.2 hours in 1975, 9.8 hours in 1985, and levelled off at 10.0 hours in 1995' (Bianchi et al., 2000: 206). Thus, there has been a considerable convergence between men and women in the hours spent on housework, but this has been largely as a consequence of women reducing their domestic work hours. Data from a range of other countries shows a similar trend, that is, a considerable reduction in the hours devoted to housework by women, together with a (smaller) increase in housework hours amongst men (Sullivan & Gershuny, 2001; Baxter et al., 2004; Gershuny et al., 1994).

To a considerable extent, the extent to which men participate in domestic work is a consequence of both the earning power, and number of hours worked, by their partners. That is, as women generate more material resources and thus enhance their economic power, so men carry out more of the tasks by tradition allocated to women (Blood & Wolfe, 1960) – although a completely gender egalitarian division of domestic work is still relatively rare. However, feminists have argued that the allocation of the primary responsibility for housework to women itself constitutes a symbolic re-enactment of gender relations, as the roles of wife and mother are intimately tied to expectations for doing housework (West & Zimmerman, 1987). Thus, order and cleanliness within the home are reflections on women's competence as a 'wife and mother' – but not on men's competence as a 'husband and father' (Bianchi et al., 2000: 195). According to these arguments, given that the construction and reconstruction of gendered identities is the major factor in the determination of who does domestic work, its allocation is not necessarily rational and women will almost invariably do more of it, even when in full-time employment.

Nevertheless, attitudes to gender roles, and gendered identities, are changing. Higher educational levels, and more liberal gender role attitudes, are both associated with a less traditional division of domestic labour within households. Thus, as a general rule, countries characterised by more 'liberal' gender role attitudes are also characterised by a less traditional division of domestic labour (Crompton & Lyonette, 2006b; Crompton, 2006). However, it should not be forgotten that even though more men may be taking the view that they should be sharing domestic and caring work with their partners, the demands of full-time paid employment – particularly if work intensification is on the increase (Burchell et al., 2002) – may mean that many men are physically unable to share equally in the work of the household.

Summary of chapters

In Chapter 2, Gambles et al. develop further the themes introduced in this chapter in their three-country (Netherlands, Norway and the UK) exploration of progress towards gender equitable divisions of paid work and care. They argue that related changes are needed at individual, relational, workplace and societal levels. One factor they emphasise is the increasing demands on 'ideal' (i.e., full-time, long-term) workers that make it so problematic to move from a 'modified male breadwinner' towards a 'universal caregiver' (Fraser, 1994) or 'dual earner/dual carer (Crompton, 1999) model. In Chapter 3, den Dulk and Doorne-Huiskes examine in greater depth the impact of the major structural factor that has been identified as shaping capacities for work–life articulation – social policies or 'welfare regimes'. They demonstrate, as anticipated, that the social democratic model offers the best conditions for equality between men and women, but also that the 'gender logic' – what we have described as the 'ideology of domesticity' is deeply engrained across Europe. Thus, the gender pay gap, and gender inequality in managerial positions, persists across Europe, despite variations in institutional regimes.

As is well known, the increase in women's employment has been accompanied by declining rates of fertility. In Chapter 4, Fagnani carries out a comparative analysis of six countries (Norway, Sweden, UK, the Netherlands, France and Portugal) in order to explore the impact of institutional factors on fertility rates. She finds that in the three countries – Norway, Sweden and France – where affordable, high-quality childcare is available, fertility is higher than in the other countries, where societal supports for combining work and family responsibilities are lower. This debate is carried over into Chapter 5, in which Hašková argues that a gender equity approach is the best model via which to understand the recent decline in fertility, and postponement of childbearing, amongst the countries of Central and Eastern Europe.

Chapter 6 has a primary emphasis on the normative dimension, and Wall explores the complexities of attitudes to motherhood, employment and family life across Europe. Although attitudes are affected by systematic variations in factors such as institutional arrangements, and traditions such as full or part-time working, her analysis reveals a considerable plurality of attitudes, suggesting that despite 'homogenising' tendencies (most notably, EU membership), national variations in attitudes are likely to persist.

The comparative theme continues in Chapter 7, in which Crompton and Lyonette examine in some depth the relationship between occupational class, country and the domestic division of labour in Finland, Norway, Britain, France and Portugal. They find that in all countries, professional and managerial women receive greater assistance with household tasks, either from partners or via 'outsourcing' – i.e., marketised domestic work. Although assistance from partners is associated with less family stress in all countries, the impact of 'outsourcing' reveals a rather more complex picture. The significance of class is also emphasised in Chapter 8 by Perrons et al. Their qualitative study of two British localities – London and Manchester – illustrates the complex logistics whereby families (more usually women) manage caring, employment and family life. They demonstrate the considerable importance of changing and variable proximate factors – such as the availability of transport, and/or family help – in mothers' decisions relating to their employment.

This emphasis on the importance of proximate circumstances in shaping work–life articulation is reflected in the concept of 'care capital' – time, capability, money and good social relationships – which is explored in Norway and Finland by Antonnen and Sipilä in Chapter 9. They found that the central dimensions of care capital – time, money, and other people – were all connected with scores of stress and satisfaction, but not in a direct way. The next two chapters focus more directly on workplace relationships and their impact on work–life articulation. In Chapter 10, Bäck-Wiklund and Plantin explore the organisational workings of universal and generous Swedish work–life policies in two workplaces. They find that although these policies are designed at the national level to facilitate the autonomy of the individual, in practice, working mothers are not always able to use them because of workplace constraints. In a similar vein (and in a very different national context), Guerreiro and Pereira's case studies of Portuguese organisations in

Chapter 11 emphasise the importance of collective (i.e. trade union) presence in establishing work–life entitlements beyond those of basic labour law, as well as the persistence of gendered assumptions that hold women responsible for caring work even when in employment.

In Chapter 12, Le Feuvre and Lemarchant explore the case of France, a country with a history of active (and changing) family policies that have had varying impacts on mother's employment. Their careful examination suggests that working-class women have benefited least from recent reforms, a situation that is exacerbated by the rather low level of participation in domestic and caring work by French men.

Conclusions

In the Introduction to this chapter, we have emphasised that although the male breadwinner/female caregiver model of work–life articulation was for decades seen as being 'natural', it represented what was in fact only a relatively short period of 'western' history. As Folbre (1994) has remarked, although this division of labour between men and women was hardly 'fair', it did at least serve to underwrite human reproduction. As many of the chapters in this book will demonstrate, a 'mutated version' of the ideology of domesticity (Williams, 2000) persists, despite the widespread entry of women into the labour market, and thus gender equality is very far from having been achieved in any material sense. As many have argued, gender equality is most likely to be achieved in 'dual earner/dual carer' societies (Crompton, 1999, 2006; Gornick & Meyers, 2003), but the institutional and normative frameworks that would facilitate this model of work–life articulation have yet to be fully developed.

Nevertheless, as women's employment becomes, increasingly, a fact of modern life, institutional shifts that adjust to the new realities are under way. This book describes considerable national variations in national institutional arrangements that are likely to persist. Our comparisons will enable us to judge, nevertheless, which national institutional arrangements facilitate the most positive work–life adjustments, and this will be a major focus of our final chapter. However, the impact of national policies, as well as prevailing cultural norms, are institutionally, organisationally and individually mediated.

In particular, there would seem to be a growing body of evidence to the effect that contemporary strategies of employee management in contemporary capitalism are making it more, rather than less, problematic to combine employment and family life in dual-earner households. Individual hours of paid work are not necessarily growing, but nevertheless, the increase in dual-earner families will mean that the hours of paid work undertaken by households are on the increase (Moen, 2003). Moreover, the current intensification of paid employment associated with organisational 'cultures of excellence' and 'high-commitment' management is likely to lead to greater work–family conflict and stress, and make employees feel reluctant to make use of positive work–family policies even if they are available (Crompton et al., 2003; Gallie, 2002). These kinds of pressures from within the workplace will in turn have an impact on capacities for domestic sharing between men and women, and although gender role attitudes are certainly in the process of transformation, a combination of material constraints and workplace pressures may seriously inhibit their capacities for realisation in any practical sense.

Note

1. This was the International Social Survey Programme (ISSP) 'Family 2002' module that has been drawn upon in a number of chapters in this volume. For a description of the ISSP programme, see Jowell et al. (1993).

2
Evolutions and Approaches to Equitable Divisions of Paid Work and Care in Three European Countries: a Multi-level Challenge

Richenda Gambles, Suzan Lewis and Rhona Rapoport

Despite growing numbers of women in the labour force, and varying national policies and workplace policies developed to support the reconciliation of paid work and family life, progress towards gender equity remains uneven and painfully slow across Europe. In this chapter we define gender equity in terms of a fair distribution of paid and unpaid work and of both opportunities and constraints, between men and women (Rapoport & Rapoport, 1971, 1975).[1] We conceptualise progress (or lack of it) towards gender equity as part of an evolutionary process of change that takes place at many levels and proceeds in different ways and at different rates across national contexts. National policies are an essential part of the process but are not sufficient. Related changes are needed at individual, relational, workplace and wider societal levels. At the workplace level there is now much evidence that policies alone do not bring about changes in structures, cultures and practices needed to enable equitable sharing of paid work and care among men and women (Brandth & Kvande, 2001, 2002; Crompton, 1999; Haas & Hwang, 1995; Lewis, 1997, 2001; Rapoport et al., 2002). At the individual and relational levels, research tends to focus on the division of domestic labour (see Oakley, 1974 for an early example), but less attention has been paid to the evolutionary and multi-level process of reciprocal change between men and women. By this, we mean the process whereby women's behaviour has changed in recent decades, requiring reciprocal change in men, which in turn will require further reciprocal change in women, and so on, in a cycle of continual adaptation and change. In this chapter we focus on barriers to reciprocal changes between men and women, in the context of national policy and workplace practices in Norway, the Netherlands and the UK, drawing upon a wider cross-national qualitative research project.

It is also important to situate an analysis of experiences and concerns about work, family and gender equity within the wider international context, as experiences in Europe cannot be divorced from experiences more globally (Bauman, 1998). We begin at the policy level, by discussing some relevant European policy debates about combining paid work with other parts of life and discuss models that are useful for conceptualising degrees and types of change towards gender equity. After briefly describing our study, we then locate evolving national policy and workplace contexts in Norway, the Netherlands and the UK, in relation to these models, and discuss implications for reciprocal changes between men and women. We then draw on qualitative data to explore some current tensions and barriers to more fundamental shifts and 'mindset' changes with regard to gender equity in paid work and other parts of life in the three countries.

Policy issues

Against a backdrop of changing patterns of working and caring and concern about population ageing, welfare 'dependency' of lone mothers, and child poverty or well-being, work–family reconciliation has risen firmly up the policy agenda in many European countries during a period in which many other policy areas have seen more retrenchment or cutbacks (Daly, 2004; OECD, 2001). Policy developments include, for example, various care leave entitlements and the development of care services or cash benefits for children and the frail elderly, although there is much diversity in generosity and scope in different countries (Gornick & Meyers, 2003; Daly & Rake, 2003). These policy developments have occurred in response to – but have also impacted upon – the changes men and women are making in terms of their involvement in paid and unpaid work and care. Although women still undertake the majority of unpaid work and care activities in countries across Europe, there is evidence that men are beginning to change and that their involvement in unpaid work is gradually increasing (Gershuny, 2000; OECD, 2001).

There has been a noticeable shift in policy rhetoric, in many contexts, towards an adult worker model in which men and women are increasingly assumed to be active in paid work (Lewis, J., 2001), and growing discussion about the role of fathers (Stanley, 2005; Burgess & Russell, 2003; Hobson, 2002). Yet the complexities surrounding gender relations and reciprocal shifts between men and women in relation to unpaid care within the home receive much less discussion than the rhetoric and strategies geared at enhancing women's paid employment. If an adult worker model is assumed without policy frameworks that support care provision or considers thorny issues of gender relations and responsibilities, only an *illusion* of progress is achieved (Lewis, 2002: 333).

In terms of policy, workplace and wider societal responses, Nancy Fraser (1997) sets out three different ideal models that approach gender equity in varying ways and to different degrees. The first is a universal bread-winner model in which care services are commodified and available to all. This is designed to enable men and women to participate equally as paid workers. The second is a caregiver parity model in which leaves and part time working are made available (for women) and rewarded suffi-ciently to render care costless. Fraser finds both these models problem-atic. The first requires women to adapt to a male worker norm, but even if care services are comprehensive and available, there may be problems of a deficit of time available for care and women will continue to suffer second shift problems (see Pateman, 1989; Hochschild, 1989). The second model enables women to participate in paid work to a lesser degree than men currently do. This model further reinforces assumptions about gen-der differences and continues to position women as making adaptations against a male ideal in workplaces (see Pateman, 1989; Lewis, 1997, 2001). The problems with both models, Fraser contends, are that neither requires men to change. The very factors that serve to make many women more vulnerable to time poverty and workplace marginalisation simul-taneously prevent men from changing their behaviour. Structural and cul-tural barriers that make it difficult for women and men to actually change their behaviour are not addressed.

Fraser therefore develops a third model: a universal caregiver model (similar to the dual-earner/dual carer model discussed by Crompton, 1999; and Gornick & Meyers, 2003) in which men and women are *both* expected and enabled to participate in paid and unpaid activities. This would be reflected in reduced working hours – to free up time and energy for both men and women to participate in a range of paid and unpaid activities – alongside a range of supports for care activities. This model envisages change in the structure and culture of workplace organisa-tions, as well as within the family and society more generally, so that those with care responsibilities are not seen as 'unusual' but rather the norm: hence the universal caregiver. It also focuses on gender relations and a more equitable sharing of activities between women *and* men (Fraser, 1997; see also Lister, 2003), which, in turn, depends on changes and initia-tives at multiple levels of society. Fraser notes that a universal caregiver model requires a complete restructuring of the entire gender order (1997: 61). There can be no quick fixes, but we suggest that an evolutionary multi-layered approach to gender equity, that focuses on structural, cultural and mindset shifts to support reciprocal changes between men and women, may help to foster change in that direction.

However, much European policy still tends to be thought about in traditional ways. The reconciliation of employment and family life or 'work–life balance' continues to be viewed as much more of a problem for women than for men (reflecting rather than challenging ongoing trends). If taken-for-granted assumptions about the nature and demands of paid work and gender roles are not challenged, then workers making use of 'work–family' or 'work–life' policies – overwhelmingly women – will continue to be marginalised in the workplace and men will continue to be marginalised as carers (Lewis, 1997; Burgess & Russell, 2003). The crucial issue of reciprocal change between men and women is also virtually absent from policy discussions, beyond some consideration of fathers' caring roles.

The research

In this chapter we draw upon data from a recent qualitative cross-national project, *Looking Backwards to Go Forwards: The Integration of Paid Work and other Parts of Life*.[2] The grant for this study was given to support a 'think' piece about progress towards gender equity in relation to paid work and other parts of life in various societies, using an evolutionary framework. The aim was to explore the evolutions of men–women relationships towards gender equity in working and caring as they occur at different times and are experienced in different ways, in different national contexts. We explored the ways in which debates, policies and practices relating to paid work and personal life, including care activities, have evolved during the past half century, current debates and concerns, and implications for future change initiatives in a range of countries. An important objective was to identify levers for change as well as barriers and resistances to shifts towards gender equity, as conceptualised within a universal caregiver model. Countries in the wider study included India, Japan, South Africa, the US, the Netherlands, Norway, and the UK. These were chosen to include diverse contexts with varying levels and types of government and/or workplace policy support and reflecting different stages of economic 'development'. In this chapter we focus on experiences and concerns in the three European countries in our study: the UK, the Netherlands and Norway.

In the course of the research we held *country meetings* organised and convened by local colleagues to explore the experiences, perspectives and reflections of a range of 'experts' connected with issues about combining or harmonising paid work with other parts of life as: academics and researchers; as politicians or policy makers; as people working at various levels in formal workplace organisations, including in the public and private sectors and NGOs; as external consultants; trade union officials; and as journalists. The meetings constituted a form of focus group in which public accounts of work–personal life dilemmas and perspectives on associated debates provide some insight into the national context (Smithson, 2000, 2006). Our participants offered their own grounded insights from the experience, research and individual understandings of their own countries, workplaces, families and personal circumstances and collaborated with us in the process of mutual enquiry. In addition, 60 in-depth interviews were conducted across the seven countries to generate personal stories and engage in deeper level discussions and thinking about work and the rest of life. The interview and group data were contextualised within *country timelines*, developed with the help of local participants, to capture something of the history and shifting evolutions of combining paid work with other parts of life over the last 50 years, focusing on relevant government policy, workplace policies and practices and potential and emerging social forces for change.

In the next section we explore evolutions towards a universal caregiver/gender equitable model, making links with reciprocal change between men and women in the three European countries in our study.

Country contexts

The country timelines highlighted the ways in which various social and economic forces, such as the growing numbers of women in paid work, advances in technology, economic developments and ageing populations, became potential levers for change towards greater gender equity. However, these forces affect different countries at different phases in their social evolutions and lead to different responses and supports for combining paid and unpaid work. Sometimes, potential levers for change simply lead to surface change or quick fixes that fail to move towards a universal caregiver model. For example, labour market inequalities between men and women are often addressed by initiatives to increase the sheer numbers of women in senior positions in the workplace without recognising that workplaces and men have to change too – an approach that reflects a universal breadwinner rather than a universal caregiver model.

Below we discuss briefly some of the more significant aspects of evolving national and workplace policies and practices and implications for gender equity in paid and unpaid work in the three countries (for more details see Gambles, Lewis & Rapoport, 2006). Gender differences and inequities in working and caring exist in all three countries, although there are differences. For example, although many women in Norway work part-time, they are more likely to be in full-time employment than in the UK and the Netherlands (Fagnani, 2003; OECD, 2001). Also, men spend more time participating in care and other unpaid activities in Norway than in the other two countries, with men in the UK spending slightly more time on care and unpaid activities than those in the Netherlands (Fagnani, 2003; OECD, 2001).

The UK

Legislative and policy developments

Although legislation for equal pay, outlawing of sex discrimination, and entitlements to paid maternity leave were introduced in the 1970s, there was minimal social policy support for men and women to combine paid work and care responsibilities prior to the election of New Labour in 1997[3] (Lister, 2003; Williams, 2004; Stanley, 2005). Dramatic shifts in government approaches in recent years – driven in part by EU Directives, economic concerns and a pledge to eradicate child poverty – included steady streams of initiatives to support lone mothers and mothers in low income households into paid work, alongside enhancements of maternity leave and attempts to stimulate affordable child care within the private sector. There is now growing rhetoric about the importance of father care along with measures such as the introduction of two weeks paternity leave immediately after the birth of the child and 'gender neutral' unpaid parental leave and rights for parents with children under six to ask for flexible working arrangements (see Stanley, 2005). There are also plans to extend current six months maternity leave with a further six months unpaid parental leave that can be taken by either parent (DTI, 2005). However, this second six months essentially remains the mother's to give to the father if she so wishes, which reflects strong assumptions about maternal needs and responsibilities and contrasts with Scandinavian approaches of encouraging men to take leaves.

There is also a high profile government 'work–life balance' campaign, supposedly aimed at changing workplaces. Parents with children under six have new rights to ask for flexible working, although this can be refused on 'business grounds', and Working Time legislation for a maximum of a 48-hour week currently comes with an opt-out clause, to which employees are often expected to sign up. The Government has published a wealth of 'best practice' case studies to support a business case for workplace change and has also allocated funding for organisational consultants to help bring about changes in working practices to support 'work–life balance' (the Challenge Fund). While this has the potential to move employers beyond policy to practice, funding has generally been short term and requires a quick reporting of results (Dex, 2003), while systemic change, necessary for supporting a universal caregiver model, or gender equity takes time to achieve (Rapoport et al., 2002).

Workplaces

In the context of a recent history of minimal state support, some employers, particularly larger organisations relying substantially on women's labour, began to adapt working practices in the 1980s and have continued to do so when needing to recruit and retain women employees for business reasons (Lewis & Cooper, 1999). The focus has been largely on developing policies and benefits, and, as elsewhere the impact has been limited, bringing about some change for women at the margins, but not affecting mainstream structures, culture and practices to enable both men and women to work and care (Lewis, 1997, 2001). Although there has been much recent hype about employer 'work–life balance' initiatives, with a few exceptions (Lewis & Cooper, 2005) these tend to be short termist and individualistic and to be undermined by a prevailing long hours culture (Lewis, 1997, 2001; Lister, 2003).

Public and workplace policy approaches thus focus most on enabling women to make adaptations to their paid work arrangements, and while rhetoric emphasises the needs of fathers as well as mothers, in practice it is much more difficult for men to adapt their working practices for family reasons. Thus, reciprocal change between men and women towards a universal caregiver model of gender equity is very constrained.

The Netherlands

Legislative and policy developments

Until recently, Dutch public policy actively supported a single breadwinner model although a series of Government initiated female emancipation programmes have been in place since 1974. Since the 1990s, there has been more emphasis on enhancing women's paid work participation, linked to concerns about economic development. This has included a number of initiatives to stimulate public–private partnerships for developing childcare.[4]

Here, too, there has been a shift in rhetoric towards an adult worker model, with growing attention to fathers – with a 'combination scenario' designed to encourage and enable fathers to reduce paid work commitments at the same time as women increase theirs (Den Dulk et al., 2004). For example, parental leave, first introduced in 1991, can be taken on a part- or full-time basis, and is paid in the public sector and in some private sector organisations where it is included in collective agreements. However part-time work remains associated with fewer opportunities for advancement and take-up of part-time parental leave by fathers is limited (Den Dulk et al., 2003).

Currently the Dutch Government recognises the need for changes in workplaces, families and communities to reflect any increase in women's employment rates (Den Dulk et al., 2003) and has funded projects to break down 'traditional' images of masculinity and femininity to try and encourage a shared care approach. It has also set up a Commission to promote and explore other innovative changes in adapting from a single breadwinner to a dual-earner model (Schaapman, 1995). However, the growth in women's employment has been mostly in terms of part-time work (OECD, 2001). Women remain the primary caregivers and their increase in paid work has occurred faster than men's participation in unpaid care (Den Dulk et al., 2003).

Workplaces

As in the UK, the tendency has been to encourage, rather than legislate for, workplace change. There is much discussion of flexible work arrangements, but policies are most likely to be developed in large organisations, especially in the public sector or where women's labour is needed, and are also more likely to be taken up by women, leaving workplace cultures and structures unchanged (Den Dulk, 2001). The approach to combining paid work with other parts of life is not entirely individualistic, as flexible working arrangements are increasingly part of collective agreements (Den Dulk, 2001), and some workplaces are now developing more innovative approaches, encouraged by the Government's support for bottom up experiments (see Lewis & Cooper, 2005). Nevertheless, systemic workplace change – that is, change in structures, cultures and practices – remains slow in the context of the high levels of part-time work among women and full-time work among men.

While public policy approaches are beginning to place more emphasis on a shared care, or universal caregiver, approach, as indicated by flexible parental leave rights and initiatives to break down 'traditional' images of masculinity and femininity, reciprocal changes between men and women in the Netherlands, as in the UK, remains limited, particularly because of a lack of systemic workplace level change.

Norway

Legislative and policy developments

Although Norway has a history of supporting women in their caring roles (Sainsbury, 2001), it now has one of the highest rates of female labour market participation in the world, with a growing rate of full-time employment among women (Fagnani, 2003; Gornick & Meyers, 2003). Over time, a substantial increase in the level of education among women, together with smaller families and government subsidised child care places, reflect a shift towards Fraser's universal breadwinner model, but there are also shifts that suggest a more concrete move towards a universal caregiver model, in comparison with the UK and the Netherlands. For example, paid parental leave with a 'daddy month' on a 'use it or lose it' basis, reflects government policies to actively encourage men's greater involvement in family life, with some success: fathers' take up of at least part of their parental leave in 2003 was 80 per cent (Fagnani, 2003).

Recent policy initiatives have also extended flexibility and choice for parents via a 'time-account' scheme, which gives men and women the opportunity to work shorter hours without a reduction in income until the child is two or three years old, again indicative of a universal caregiver approach. However, this has been less successful than the 'daddy month' in changing men's behaviour because it depends on negotiations between fathers and their managers (Brandth & Kvande, 2002). A recent 'cash for home care' policy as an alternative to day care is controversial, as some believe it encourages mothers to stay at home, reflecting a caregiver parity approach (although Ellingsaeter's 2003 research suggests that resources are used to pay for private care arrangements, and women's employment levels have not been affected).

Workplaces

In the context of strong legislation and regulations for employee protection, there has been less need for workplace policies, although the need to accommodate parental leaves has encouraged employers to develop flexible working practices. While pockets of awareness about the potential benefits of flexible working are emerging, there are currently many gaps between policy and practice (Brandth & Kvande, 2002) in Norway as elsewhere. Many organisations, particularly in the private sector, continue to define commitment in terms of time spent in the workplace (Brandth & Kvande, 2002) and as workplaces become more exposed to global economic competition, even taking the full one month leave by fathers may be frowned upon. Consequently, while our participants indicate that more and more fathers say they want to work less so as to be more involved with the care of their children (personal communication with research participants) – a sign of male support for a universal caregiver approach – it remains unusual for fathers to ask if they can work shorter hours.

Public policy approaches are moving towards a shared care, or universal caregiver approach, as exemplified by the 'daddy month', which engages with reciprocal change between men and women. However, while men in Norway are more involved in family life activities in comparison with the UK and the Netherlands, further reciprocal changes between men and women and evolutionary moves towards a universal caregiver model of gender equity are again limited by workplace cultures and practices.

Gender equity in the different contexts

There are thus some moves towards a gender equitable universal caregiver model at the policy level in each country, but this is evolving in diverse ways. The Norwegian context comes closest to supporting a universal caregiver model, although workplace constraints, especially in the context of global competition, limit such an approach in practice. Dutch policy makers appear to be experimenting with innovative strategies that reflect potential seeds of a universal caregiver model, but changes in men's behaviour remain somewhat elusive in practice. Recent policy approaches and suggestions in the UK could be viewed as attempts to move towards a universal caregiver approach. However, in the context of long working hours and a reluctance to address workplace cultures and practices, again this remains illusive. In each context, progress towards gender equitable models of combining paid and unpaid work is limited by lack of change at other levels, beyond public policy. Policy alone is not sufficient to overcome the many structural barriers and interlocking mindset barriers – connected with current gender orders and ways of 'doing' gender at multiple levels of society (Connell, 1987; Crompton, 1999; West & Zimmerman, 1987). We now explore some of these barriers, emerging from our study.

Some current barriers to gender equity and reciprocal change between men and women

Our interviews and country meetings with work–personal life 'experts' highlighted some perceptions of current barriers to the reciprocal changes between men and women, which we have argued are necessary for gender equity, and some thoughts about how to move beyond these, in the three national contexts. We focus on three major interconnected themes, relating to changes needed at individual, relational, societal and workplace levels in the wider global context.

Moving beyond 'women's issues' to reciprocal change between men and women: resistances at societal, relational and individual identity levels

A major theme in all three countries was the need to move beyond constructing challenges of combining paid work with care as women's issues, to include and engage men in discussions and strategies. However, there were some noticeable differences in approach across national contexts, reflecting different phases in evolutions towards gender equity.

In Britain, participants tended to focus on bringing men into the debate. This reflects current debates that are taking place at the policy level, although currently having only minimal impact in workplaces.

'Women have run God knows how many laps of the equality race . . . if men aren't engaged it will just go round and round in circles.' (British man, journalist)

'As long as we talk in terms of women and child care it remains a woman's issue. So I firmly believe that this is something we have to broaden to include men. And this is beginning to change.' (British woman, trade union)

In the Netherlands, the focus of such discussions was more practical, often focusing on an ideal of mothers and fathers working less, potentially reflective of a universal caregiver approach.

'In Holland, men are more included I think in the issue of work–family than in some of the surrounding countries so it's not so much that we have to bring a man in on the issue . . . but there is resentment just the same.' (Dutch woman, government official)

'Women tend to immediately take up on care when children are born. But both parents should work part-time and divide child care tasks as well . . . women should lay back some more, so men are forced to make the next move.' (The Netherlands, female participant, country meeting)

In Norway, where policy reflects and encourages an ideology of shared parental care, we found some evidence that debates were evolving beyond the need to include men in discussions about paid work and family, as in the UK, or the need for practical changes discussed in the Netherlands, towards recognition of issues of reciprocal change. This focuses attention on resistances and tension at individual and couple levels. As men become more involved with and attached to their children, challenging ideal worker and ideal carer assumptions, new conflicts can emerge. Participants discussed the difficulties women can feel in making further reciprocal change about sharing care with men, and that men can experience as they make further changes.

'Women use the children as a power institution. They say the child is more connected to them . . . they build a kind of fortress around the child and the men often stay scratching on the outside, wanting to come in. The woman only opens the door when it suits her and that is unfair on the men.' (Norwegian woman, scientist)

'We are talking about a transition not just for men, but for many women. A lot of women are unprepared in practice to take the full implications of it, which means actually giving up some control over how things are done in the home and relationships with children. This is a division that has to be reworked . . .' (Norwegian man, IT consultant)

'There is a conflict between men and women when men are more caring for the home and their children. There is often more fighting and there can be more divorce. The fighting increases because men are more attached to the children and in divorces their role is no longer simply to provide income, there are more feelings involved.' (Norwegian woman, manager)

'Male friends say now it is a hell of a rat race; they have to have a good career, be nice lovers, nice fathers, nice friends, nice intellectual talking partners and they say the pressure is coming at them from more fields.' (Norwegian woman, scientist)

In thinking about possible future reciprocal change, to move beyond these barriers, there was some discussion about the need to move away from competition between men and women towards providing both with a wider range of opportunities for equitable relationships. For example:

'Women have been so assertive about the need for them to be in high positions . . . and doing that makes men afraid, because it becomes competitive. We have to work around this and talk with men about how we can work better together instead of compete and respect the differences.' (Norway, female government official)

Although there was much less discussion about this sort of reciprocal change among the British and Dutch participants, one British man vividly articulated the need to conceptualise and examine issues of reciprocal men–women relationships as a means towards gender equity. He recognised the power dynamics involved as men and women may fear giving up things that are important to them without receiving anything in return.

'I almost visualise it now as men and women are sitting across the table from each other each has a gift for the other, neither, neither is quite prepared to hand over the gift because they aren't sure if they're going to get the other one back, and in many cases we might not know what we're going to get from it . . . but what's the incentive for men to change? That's the kind of big question that doesn't have a satisfactory answer . . . to do so, would mean losing power, and this is seen as a crap deal . . . A man wanting to be more involved in children and the home is a huge challenge for women, because they have to give up control of these issues and accept that men won't do things in the same way . . . this is an enormous challenge for women who are steeped in a culture of their own superiority in this area.' (British man, researcher)

Resistance to change in men and women's roles and relationships occurs at the level of individual identities, as well as within families, in workplaces and wider societies. When people try to change the ways in which they behave or think about these issues, this can challenge personal identity and beliefs stemming from social representations of what it means to be a 'man' or a 'woman' (West & Zimmerman, 1987; Woodward, 2000). The feminist movements, together with practical pressures women have faced in combining work with family life, have created clear challenges to 'traditional' assumptions about male and female roles. More recently, discussions of the ways in which notions of masculinity also limit opportunities and well-being for men have emerged (Burgess & Russell,

2003; Hawkins & Dollahite, 1997; Popay et al., 1999). Yet assumptions about what it means to be a man or a woman, like assumptions about ideal workers, which we discuss below, are deeply ingrained and resistant to change and come into play in different ways at different phases of social evolutions. Nevertheless, these issues, resistances and mindsets, relating to reciprocal change between men and women, are crucial to debates about gender equity and progress towards a universal caregiver model of the reconciliation of employment and family life.

Resistances in workplaces: implementation gaps and persisting 'ideal worker' assumptions

For progress to be made in the evolution of reciprocal changes between men and women, changes are needed in workplace structures, cultures and practices and the assumptions on which they are based, particularly assumptions that ideal workers do not have unpaid work responsibilities (Fletcher, 1999; Lewis, 1997; Rapoport et al., 2002). Despite attention to work and family issues in workplaces in all three countries, implementation gaps between policy and practice are widespread. Many employers are willing to adopt policies in a 'quick fix' approach to work and personal life challenges but are reluctant to accept the need for more systemic changes (Rapoport et al., 2002; Lewis & Cooper, 2005).

In all three countries, men and women discussed the interpersonal and workplace tensions, conflicts and practical difficulties they faced in combining multiple parts of their lives. Yet most of the men were reluctant to raise these issues with their managers because they felt it may be interpreted as a lack of commitment. Although there are some signs of change in more progressive organisations, men still risk being penalised if they try to adapt work for family. This is illustrated by the experiences of a Norwegian man. He worked in a company renowned for its innovative and flexible working, although the dominant culture makes it difficult for men, especially in relatively senior positions, to change their working practices beyond taking parental leaves.

In relating his experiences at this company, he described how he requested and reluctantly was allowed alternative working arrangements, only to be told, after six months, that he must return to 'normal' working patterns or move to a lower status position.

> 'I got the message that I didn't have a job there anymore, although I had the most knowledge of all of them ... because I asked for 80 per cent work.' (Norwegian man, formerly working for a large company)

Thus, ideal worker assumptions continue to undermine policy, constrain men's participation in unpaid work, and create barriers to women's full integration and advancement in the workplace. Moreover, this is exacerbated by contemporary changes in the nature of work.

Global trends and the invasiveness of paid work

'If you work in a company you have to spend your life more or less at work. You work and work and work.' (Norwegian man, formerly working for a large company)

'. . . why is work so dominant? It gives me pleasure, status and meaning. But why do other things not give so much meaning? Why is it so difficult to articulate the value of other things?' (British woman, in an NGO)

A theme emerging in all three countries was that ideal worker assumptions, far from receding to reflect a universal caregiver model, seem to be stronger than ever, often internalised and reflected in feelings of a growing invasiveness of paid work in people's crowding out other activities and values. This is linked to transformations in the nature of paid work, including technological developments, workplace reorganisation or restructuring, growing intensification of work and new management practices that aim to increase efficiency, productivity and competitiveness in the global economy. Many trends are double edged, facilitating flexibility to combine paid and unpaid work, but also permitting a blurring of boundaries that often result in people working more rather than less (Holt & Thaulow, 1996; Lewis, 2001, 2003; Brandth & Kvande, 2001; Perrons, 2003).

Transformations in and speeding up of paid work in the global economy can exacerbate challenges to reciprocal change between men and women, as many of our participants noted. For example:

'Women's aspirations and wanting to work coincided at a time when economic trends of work intensification really began to let rip. And you got this awful crunch where our aspirations went smack up against an accelerating economic trend.' (British woman, journalist)

In the Netherlands, pressures of work sustain the tradition of one and half earner couples.

'I think lots of women in the Netherlands do experience a sort of balance, and the men as well because they have profited from their partner being at home for half of the week.' (Dutch woman, researcher)

The Norwegian participants especially articulated the view that intense workloads often lead couples to retreat to more traditional gender patterns, and were aware of how this can jeopardise the fragile progress that has been made in evolving relationships between men and women and of the pernicious implications for gender equity.

'I have friends in the Oslo area . . . they have big jobs, big salaries, everything in order but they are stressed and their life is not so good. They want equality in the family but they can't keep it up. There are so many pressures at work . . . downsizing to keep up with world competition, you know . . . their wives decide to stop working for a while to care for the children and this is a good idea . . . but it should also be the husband of course.' (Norwegian man, entrepreneur)

When paid work is very demanding, it is often impossible for more than one household member to conform to 'ideal' worker expectations. This creates obvious problems for lone parents, and in dual-earner households it is usually women who reduce their involvement in paid work or take on a double burden of paid and unpaid work. Contemporary workplace demands and expectations, underpinned by prevailing models of global competitive capitalism, lead to time pressures and feelings of constant 'busyness', which makes it even more difficult for women and men to work through conflicts and tensions about gender identities and the ways this relates with current patterns of harmonising paid work with other parts of life.

'When you are very busy in an office you can't think about the fundamental things in life.' (Norwegian male, manager)

Some concluding reflections

This small qualitative study cannot indicate trends as such, but does illustrate the ways in which discussions are taking place among some of those involved in contemporary work and family issues in these three countries, at this phase in their social evolutions towards a universal caregiver model of gender equity. It points to the need to look beyond traditional policy areas and to focus on the need for interrelated changes at individual, family, workplace and wider societal levels. As social policy and other factors contribute to evolutions in women's behaviours, reciprocal and ongoing changes are needed by men, and again by women and men. Currently, these changes are held back by interconnected barriers at different levels, from the level of individual identity to societal norms, as we have begun to illustrate in this paper. In particular, persistent workplace assumptions about work and ideal workers reinforce and reproduce gender inequities and prevent reciprocal changes between men and women. The intensification and invasiveness of work in the contemporary global context exacerbates these processes. For this reason, solutions to issues of gender inequity in reconciling paid work and family will not be achieved by attention to the situation in Europe alone. The same tensions and barriers are increasingly experienced elsewhere and ways of working that squeeze out time and energy for family, communities and care of the self are being 'exported' to many 'developing' countries (Gambles et al., 2006).

Evolutionary progress towards gender equity within a universal caregiver model requires effective policies, but also has to address implementation gaps between policy and behaviour at multiple levels that block reciprocal change between men and women. Inherent in this is the biggest challenge: that of changing mindsets within and across multiple levels of society. Questioning many of the deeper assumptions connected with combining paid and unpaid work – such as assumptions about men and women's roles, or current conventional wisdoms about how to value particular skills and organise paid work, and more fundamentally, the value of economic and social developments underpinning contemporary ways of working – are very complex and often considered taboo. Nevertheless, in the words of Zygmunt Bauman in his discussion of the human consequences of globalisation, which we feel has particular relevance for the challenges raised in this chapter, 'questioning the ostensibly unquestionable premises of our way of life is arguably the most urgent service we owe to our fellow humans and our selves' (1998: 5).

Notes

1. This implies that within households, arrangements for 'sharing' caregiving and paid work do not necessarily mean taking equal parts. Instead, it implies that a framework of opportunities and constraints are available to *both* men and women who can then negotiate arrangements in ways that are perceived as just and fair. How men and women negotiate the sharing of paid work and care activities may vary, for example, across the life course and can be beset with tensions: hence our focus on an evolutionary and multi-level approach.

GARDNER HARVEY LIBRARY
Miami University-Middletown
Middletown, Ohio

2. This study was funded by the Ford Foundation with a grant to Rhona Rapoport at the Institute of Family and Environmental Research.
3. Low levels of benefits for those not in paid work have always been in place. But New Labour has attempted to make the transition from welfare-to-work more economically attractive and easier for marginalised groups. Welfare-to-work initiatives include the New Deal for lone mothers, the Working Families Tax and Child Care tax credits for low earning families.
4. See the Childcare Act, which came into force in January 2005. The Act encourages financial support away from providers towards parents to increase parental choice in terms of provision.

3
Social Policy in Europe: its Impact on Families and Work

Laura den Dulk and Anneke van Doorne-Huiskes[1]

Introduction

Whether or not Europeans are able to achieve a healthy work/life balance is due, at least in part, to the effects of social policies in the different nations. In the comparative literature on European social policy, the differences between various welfare regimes is an important and recurring theme. Europe is made up of a diverse collection of nations and there are wide variations in social policy across the European Union. The Esping-Andersen typology of welfare regimes still provides a convenient starting point for analysing the implications of social policy for the everyday lives of people. In this well-known typology, a distinction is made between the liberal, the corporatist and the social-democratic regime.

This typology of welfare regimes has received considerable criticism and comment in the past fifteen years. To begin with, it applies in particular to North-west Europe. A strong case has been made for a separate Mediterranean model (for example, Anttonen & Sipilä, 1996), and a fifth type of welfare regime has been introduced since the enlargement of the European Union: the post-communist regime (Blossfeld & Drobnič, 2001; see also Chapter 5). Secondly, and most important, the original Esping-Andersen typology devotes little attention to the role of the family, gender and non-paid activities in welfare states (Plantenga & van Doorne-Huiskes, 1992; Lewis, 1992; Orloff, 1993; Sainsbury, 1996). In response to this critique, Esping-Andersen (1999) introduced the concept of de-familialisation, which refers to the degree to which welfare state or market provisions ease the burden of care for families. According to Esping-Andersen, a de-familialised welfare state regime typically has public work/family policies, such as childcare and statutory leave arrangements. In contrast, in a 'familialistic' welfare state regime, care is primarily seen as the responsibility of private households. Esping-Andersen argues that markets only rarely substitute for public services or family self-service. Only when market services are cheap (because labour is cheap, as in the US) does it become worthwhile for a majority of families to outsource care tasks. In Europe, however, market services are expensive because of the high tax on labour and a relatively egalitarian wage structure (although, as we shall see in Chapter 7, Portugal may be a partial exception here). Market services, such as private day care, are therefore expensive and inaccessible for a majority of families. The effect of social policies on the work/life balance should not be overestimated, however; the cultural dimension of welfare states is also of importance. Attention should be paid to the way cultural ideals concerning motherhood and fatherhood are incorporated into existing social policies (Kremer, 2005; Sainsbury, 1996).

The first question raised in this chapter is: how do different types of welfare state regimes affect families and work, that is, the division of paid work and domestic work between men and women? Is it true that countries with social policies that explicitly enable people to combine work and family life, and that seek to promote the full participation of men and women in all fields of society (including care at home), show more gender equality in the division of paid and domestic work than welfare state regimes with more familial traditions and/or less explicit policies that support the work/care combination?

The second question is whether a more equal division of paid and domestic work between men and women results in less gender inequality in society, that is, a smaller pay gap between men and women and a larger percentage of women in senior managerial positions. In other words, is there more labour market gender equality in countries where paid and domestic work is more equally divided between women and men?

The next section describes social policies that support the reconciliation of work and family life in various types of European welfare states. The following section outlines the division of paid and domestic work between men and women across European welfare states and discusses whether some types of welfare state regimes generate more gender equality in the division of tasks. In section four, we focus mainly on the existing gender gaps in various European countries, in terms of earnings and the percentage of women in managerial positions. In addition, this section also considers whether an equal division of paid and domestic tasks between men and women is indeed a precondition for more gender equality in the labour market. The final section elaborates on possible consequences of this analysis for the social policy agenda of the European Union.

Various types of European welfare regimes

Policy instruments and their impact on work/life balance

A number of policy instruments are considered relevant for the way families combine work and family life. Generally, the literature in this area considers taxation policies, childcare facilities, leave arrangements, the availability of part-time work opportunities and other flexible working arrangements (OECD, 2001b; Den Dulk, van Doorne-Huiskes & Peper, 2005; Jaumotte, 2004; Plantenga & Remery, 2005).

Taxation systems vary in the degree to which they encourage men and women to share paid employment. Nowadays, most countries in Europe have separate, rather than joint, taxation systems, which tend to support the single-earner model. Nevertheless, the degree to which tax systems stimulate dual-earner families varies from one country to the next. An indicator for the degree to which a tax system encourages both partners to be active in the labour market is the relative tax burden for second earners, compared to those of single individuals. Within Europe, only Finland, Sweden, Greece and Hungary tax second earners and single individuals equally. On the other hand, countries like the Czech Republic, Iceland and Ireland have a very high relative tax burden for second earners (Jaumotte, 2004), which makes it less attractive for a second earner to remain in employment.

In addition to disincentives or incentives in the tax system, childcare policies are important determinants when it comes to deciding whether both partners will stay in part-time or full-time employment. In fact, there is a lot of empirical evidence that good quality and affordable childcare stimulates female employment, although the causal relationship is not clear. The European Union tried to encourage the development of childcare facilities in its member states in 1992 with its childcare recommendation, and again in 2002 at the Barcelona summit, by formulating childcare targets for 2010. By 2010, member states should provide childcare to at least 90 per cent of children between three and the mandatory school age, and to at least 33 per cent of children under three years of age (Plantenga & Remery, 2005). The focus here is on parents with young children and no targets have been set for after school care. Plantenga and Remery (2005) calculate that in 2003, only six countries had reached the target for the under threes: Belgium, Denmark, Iceland, France, Sweden and the Netherlands. Ten countries had reached, or were close to, the Barcelona target for children between three and the mandatory school age: Sweden, Denmark, Norway, southern European countries like Spain and Italy, and France, Belgium, Iceland and the Netherlands. However, it is not only the availability of formal childcare facilities that plays a role, but also the quality and price of childcare facilities, the presence of alternative informal care arrangements, and preferences or cultural norms regarding motherhood and the proper way to care for young children. In some countries, formal childcare is considered good for the well-being of children and their development, whereas in other countries parental care is seen as the ideal (Kremer, 2005).

Leave arrangements may also help to ease the combination of paid work and caring for children. All European countries have introduced maternity and parental leave for working parents. In some countries, this is supplemented by paternity leave and/or a special 'daddy quota' in the parental leave scheme. Paternity leave aims to encourage fathers to involve themselves more in raising their children, although in some countries this type of leave is restricted to two or three days. Parental leave is more substantial for both fathers and mothers with young children, allowing them to absent themselves from work temporarily, either full-time or part-time, in order to care for their children without loss of job security. For women, parental leave may be an encouragement to stay in employment, whereas without such an entitlement, they may decide to leave work. For men, parental leave may encourage them to become involved, caring fathers rather than focusing solely on the breadwinner role. In its Parental Leave Directive (1996), the European Union set a minimum of three months parental leave for each parent with a child under eight years of age. Today, parents with young children are entitled to this type of leave in all the European member states, although the scope and quality of the parental leave arrangement varies greatly from country to country in terms of income compensation rates and the duration of parental leave. Some countries, such as the UK, the Netherlands and Spain, offer the minimum stipulated by the European Union. Scandinavian countries offer much longer and generous parental leave schemes, however. Although countries like Germany and France also have long leaves, the income compensation is much lower than in the Nordic countries.

Welfare state regimes

Despite the growing number of European Directives and recommendations concerning work/family policies, large differences between EU countries remain in the scope and nature of work/family policies. In order to discuss the various institutional constraints that affect the gender division of work across Europe, we will distinguish between different welfare state regimes. Welfare state regimes offer a general framework and a starting point for analysing the differences and similarities in institutional contexts that affect the work/family strategies of working parents. The term 'regime' refers to the typical ways in which the provision of welfare is allocated between the state, the market and the family (Esping-Andersen, 1990; 1999). It acknowledges that one should consider the broader country-specific packages of work/family policies rather than the impact of one specific policy (Blossfeld & Drobnič, 2001). In addition, a broader framework takes into account the importance of not only policy measures, but also the dominant political ideology, preferences and labour market conditions. Based on the typology proposed by Esping-Andersen (1990, 1999), and following Blossfeld and Drobnič (2001), we distinguish between five welfare state regimes: the social democratic welfare state regime, the liberal regime, the conservative corporatist regime, the Mediterranean regime and the post-communist regime.

The social democratic welfare state regime

The social democratic regime is characterised by an elaborate system of public work/family policies that makes the combination of work and family life less difficult to manage. Universal services, for example a substantial public day care system, support the employment of working parents. The tax system is also individualised. The state is the main provider of welfare, with private welfare provision almost non-existent. In this type of welfare state regime, the state also plays an important role as an employer, especially within the service sector, where many women in particular tend to work. Within Europe, Sweden, Denmark, Norway and Finland come closest to this particular welfare state regime, and all have a high level of publicly funded childcare services, with professional care seen as beneficial for children (Kremer, 2005). Parents pay relatively little for childcare in these countries (see Table 3.1). These substantial public childcare provisions are combined with relatively long paid leaves. In fact, Sweden was the first country in Europe to introduce parental leave for both mothers and fathers. Nowadays, Swedish parents may take 18 months of leave per child; for the first 360 days, they receive 80 per cent of their normal earnings (up to a ceiling) and a flat rate for the remaining period. In Norway, parents are similarly entitled to one year of paid leave at 80 per cent of their normal earnings. In Denmark and Finland, parents are entitled to 32 and 26 weeks of parental leave, respectively. In the social democratic regime, gender equality is an important goal, as well as the well-being of children. To encourage fathers to take up leave, thereby promoting the equal division of care responsibilities between

Table 3.1: Leave arrangements and public childcare in the social democratic regime

	Denmark	Finland	Norway	Sweden
Maternity leave	18 weeks, partly paid (55% APW[1])	17.5 weeks, paid at 43%–82% of earnings	6 weeks of parental leave	14 weeks, paid at 80% of earnings
Paternity leave	2 weeks, partly paid (56% APW)	18 to 30 days,[2] partly paid	2 weeks unpaid leave	10 days, paid at 80% of earnings
Parental leave	32 weeks (55/56% APW)	26 weeks, until child is 3 care leave	42 or 52 weeks paid at 80% or 100% of earnings	18 months, paid, at 80% of earnings for 360 days; flat rate for the remaining period
Father's quota parental leave	None	None	4 weeks, paid at 80% of earnings	2 months, paid at 80% of earnings
Childcare cost as % of family net income*	10%	7%	12%	7%
Percentage of children 0–2 years in formal childcare	64% (1999)	25% (2003)	40% (1997)	65% (2003)

[1] % APW = payment as a percentage of the wage of an average production worker (Rostgaard, 2002).

[2] 12 days are conditional, granted only if fathers also take the final two weeks of parental leave (Plantenga & Remery, 2005).

* overall childcare cost (including benefits and tax concessions) as a percentage of family income for two full-time earners of 167 (100 + 67) per cent of APW (Immervoll & Barber, 2005).

Notes: for childcare, Immervoll & Barber, 2005; for leaves, Anxo and Boulin, 2005; Plantenga & Remery, 2005.

men and women, 'daddy quotas' have been introduced in Sweden and Norway, in addition to paternity leave. In Denmark, in contrast, special leave for fathers is restricted to two weeks paternity leave, and since 2002 there has been no specific father's quota for parental leave. Although Finland also has no specific father's quota for parental leave, since 2003, Finnish fathers can extend their paternity leave by an additional two weeks if they take at least two weeks of parental leave. Despite the emphasis on involved fatherhood and equal sharing of care responsibilities between men and women, fathers are taking less parental leave than mothers in all four countries. In Sweden, 42 per cent of eligible fathers took up parental leave in 2002, but on average they took only 28 days of leave, which equals 15.5 per cent of the total number of days of parental leave allowance. In Finland, 96 per cent of all parental leave days are taken by women. In Norway, the majority of women (79 per cent) take one year of parental leave and 85 per cent of fathers take the father's quota of four weeks leave (Plantenga & Remery, 2005). Nevertheless, compared to other welfare state regimes, incentives for fathers are well-developed and the take-up by fathers and mothers is relatively high.

The conservative corporatist welfare state regime

Compulsory social insurance and fragmented occupational schemes are important features of the conservative welfare state regime. Those without an employment relationship have access to only modest social security schemes. In addition, more importance is attached to the family, and in contrast to the social democratic regime, social policy is less individualised. Germany, Austria, the Netherlands, France and Belgium represent this type of welfare state regime. The leave arrangements offered differ in length but income compensation is generally less generous than in the social democratic regime (see Table 3.2). In addition, childcare costs as a proportion of family income are often much higher than in the social democratic regime. Incentives for fathers to take leave are also less substantial.

France and Belgium are ambiguous cases in this cluster of conservative welfare states. Both countries have extensive childcare and pre-school facilities. Other conservative countries like Germany and the Netherlands place much more emphasis on the role of parental care (Anttonen & Sipilä, 1996; Kremer, 2005), and large numbers of women work part-time in order to combine work and childcare. In Germany, 85 per cent of all eligible households take their parental leave, although it is usually the women who take it (only 5 per cent of fathers take parental leave). In the Netherlands, take-up of parental leave is much lower at 27 per cent of

Table 3.2: Leave arrangements and public childcare in the conservative regime

	Belgium	Austria	France	Netherlands	Germany
Maternity leave	15 weeks, paid at 75%–82% of earnings	16 weeks, fully paid	16 weeks, fully paid	16 weeks, fully paid	14 weeks, fully paid
Paternity leave	10 days, partly paid	None	2 weeks, of which 3 days fully paid, remaining days flat rate	2 days, fully paid	None
Parental leave	3 months	24 months, flat rate payment for 18 months**	36 months, unpaid or flat rate payment in case of 2 or more children	13 weeks, unpaid	36 months, paid at a flat rate on a means tested basis
Childcare cost as % of family net income*	14%	18%	17%	25%	6%
Percentage of children 0–2 years in formal childcare	30% (2000)	13% (2001)	30% (2001)	17% (1997)	9% (2001)

* Overall childcare cost (including benefits and tax concessions) as a percentage of family income for two full-time earners of 167 (100 + 67) percent of APW (Immervoll & Barber, 2005).

** If fathers take part of the leave, payment can be extended to 24 months (flat rate payment of 436 euro per month) (Plantenga & Remery, 2005).

Notes: for childcare, Immervoll & Barber, 2005; for leaves, Anxo and Boulin, 2005; Plantenga & Remery, 2005.

parents (42 per cent of mothers and 16 per cent of fathers) (Plantenga & Remery, 2005).

The Mediterranean regime

Southern European countries have fewer public provisions, but they also do not support the breadwinner family model with tax disincentives to women's paid employment, as in conservative countries like Austria, Germany and the Netherlands (in the latter case until 2001) (Esping-Andersen, 1999). Table 3.3 provides an overview of leave arrangements and childcare provisions in this cluster. Italy is the only country in this regime cluster that offers fathers an incentive to take up parental leave: if fathers take at least three months of leave, parents receive one extra month of parental leave.

The liberal welfare state regime

Compared to the social democratic and post-communist regimes, both liberal and conservative regimes take a minimalist approach to public work/family policies, but for different reasons: 'Liberals view servicing as a market activity, as an individual responsibility; conservatives insist that it be the prerogative of families' (Esping-Andersen, 1999: 76). In a liberal

Table 3.3: Leave arrangements and public childcare in the Mediterranean regime

	Portugal	Spain	Italy	Greece
Maternity leave	120 days, fully paid	16 weeks, fully paid	5 months, paid at 80% of earnings	17 weeks, fully paid
Paternity leave	5 days, fully paid	2 days, fully paid	None	2–5 days
Parental leave	6 months, unpaid	36 months, unpaid	10–11 months, paid at 30% of earnings	3.5 months, unpaid
Childcare cost as % of family net income*	25%	n.a.	n.a.	6%
Percentage of children 0–2 years in formal childcare	22% (2002)	5% (2000)	6% (1998)	3% (2000)

* Overall childcare cost (including benefits and tax concessions) as a percentage of family income for two full-time earners of 167 (100 + 67) percent of APW, (Immervoll & Barber, 2005).
Notes: for childcare, Immervoll & Barber, 2005, for leaves, Anxo and Boulin, 2005; Plantenga & Remery, 2005.

Table 3.4:   Leave arrangements and public childcare in the liberal regime

	Ireland	UK
Maternity leave	18 weeks, 14 weeks paid at 70% of earnings, 4 weeks unpaid	26 weeks for all women, 52 weeks for employed women with at least 6 months of service; 6 weeks paid at 90% of earnings; 20 weeks flat rate
Paternity leave	none	2 weeks, flat rate
Parental leave	14 weeks, unpaid	13 weeks, take up in blocks of 4 weeks maximum per year
Childcare cost as % of family net income*	34%	27%
Percentage of children 0–2 years in formal childcare	12% (1997)	26% (2003)

* Overall childcare cost (including benefits and tax concessions) in percentage of family income for two full-time earners of 167 (100 + 67) percent of APW, (Immervoll & Barber, 2005).
Notes: for childcare, Immervoll & Barber, 2005; for leaves, Anxo and Boulin, 2005; Plantenga & Remery, 2005.

welfare state regime, government involvement and national regulations are limited and the development of work/family arrangements is left to market forces. The UK was the last member state, in 1999, to introduce statutory parental leave. The British government remained ambivalent about introducing leave: the entitlement represented the minimum required by the EU Parental Leave Directive (13 weeks, unpaid) and could only be taken in blocks of a maximum of four weeks. The latter is considered an incorrect interpretation of the EU Directive (Deven, 2005). In addition, formal childcare is relatively expensive in the UK and Ireland.

Post-communist welfare state regime

Like the social democratic regime, the post-communist regime is typified by a broad range of public policies that support the combination of paid work and care for children. Under state socialism, women's labour market participation rate was high and the common employment pattern was based on a family model of two full-time earners (Blossfeld & Drobnič, 2001; see also Chapter 5). However, the issue of gender equality at home – that is, the equal division of housework and care tasks – was not acknowledged or debated as in the social democratic regime (Kocourková, 2002). Diefenbach (2003) analysed gender role orientation

Table 3.5:   Leave arrangements and public childcare in the post-communist regime

	Czech Republic	Hungary	Poland	Bulgaria
Maternity leave	28 weeks, paid paid at 69% of earnings	24 weeks, fully paid	16–18 weeks, fully paid	19.3 weeks, paid at 90% of earnings
Paternity leave	none	5 days paid leave	none	none
Parental leave	156 weeks, flat rate payment	24 months, paid at 70% of earnings	36 months, paid at 60% of earnings low-income families only	24 months, partly paid (minimum wage)
Childcare cost as % of family net income*	n.a.	9%	n.a.	n.a.
Percentage of children 0–2 years in formal childcare	1% (2000)	6–8% (2003)	2% (2003)	7% (2003)**

* Overall childcare cost (including benefits and tax concessions) as a percentage of family income for two full-time earners of 167 (100 + 67) percent of APW, (Immervoll & Barber, 2005). ** 0–3 years (Plantenga & Remery, 2005).
Notes: for childcare, Immervoll & Barber, 2005; for leaves, Anxo and Boulin, 2005; Plantenga & Remery, 2005.

in various OECD countries (using ISSP, 1994 data) based on the respondents' agreement or disagreement with the statement 'a man's job is to earn money; a woman's job is to look after the home and family'. An egalitarian gender role orientation (in other words, strong disagreement with the statement) was found in countries such as Sweden, Norway, East Germany and the Netherlands. In Eastern Europe, in contrast, the response was highly traditional.

After the transition to the market economy, state provisions declined but are still substantial compared, for instance, to liberal or conservative regimes. Generally, post-communist countries such as Poland, Slovenia, the Czech Republic, Bulgaria and Hungary witnessed a decline in childcare services and wage compensation (for leave arrangements). However, parental leave provisions are still considerable and vary from one year in Slovenia to three years in, for example, Hungary and the Czech Republic.

Working time options

Working time options, such as part-time work opportunities, flexible start-ing and finishing times or working time accounts, are also important deter-minants of the way women and men divide paid and unpaid work. Within Europe, flexible working practices are more widespread among the Northern European countries such as Sweden, Denmark, the Nether-lands, Germany and the UK. In Southern and Eastern European countries, in contrast, part-time work and flexible working hours are less common (for example, Anxo and Boulin, 2005; den Dulk, 2001; Peters & den Dulk, 2003). These types of practices are often introduced by organisa-tions or are included in collective agreements, but in some countries national governments have tried to encourage flexible work opportun-ities. Existing legislation focuses either on all employees or on working parents. Germany, Denmark, the Netherlands and Poland have national legislation to reduce the number of working hours that applies to all employees (Plantenga & Remery, 2005). The Dutch government, for instance, has introduced an Act that gives employees the right to reduce or extend their working hours. Employers can refuse employee requests if they can show that reducing or extending working hours would ser-iously damage their business interests. The Part-time and Fixed-Term Employment Act (2001) in Germany is similar and offers employees greater control over working hours (OECD, 2003). Sweden, Finland, Norway, Austria, Portugal, Greece, the Czech Republic, Slovenia and the UK all have national legislation that gives working parents the right to reduce work-ing hours in order to combine work and care duties more easily (Plantenga & Remery, 2005). In Sweden, for instance, working parents with young children are entitled to reduce their working hours by 25 per cent while retaining the right to return to work full-time if they wish, or when their child reaches the age of eight. Other examples of flexible work arrange-ments are the career break scheme in Belgium, which allows every employee to stop working or reduce his/her working hours for a certain period of time, or the Dutch life course scheme, in which employees can save hours to take up a period of paid leave later in life. Compared to leave or child-care schemes, employers are much more involved in developing flexible work arrangements. They may, for instance, offer flexible starting and fin-ishing times, a compressed working week or the option to work from home. Research generally shows that employers are more closely involved in these types of arrangements in the social democratic and conservative welfare state regimes than in the Mediterranean and former socialist regimes (den Dulk, Peters & Poutsma, 2005; Plantenga & Remery, 2005).

Paid and domestic work in Europe: a gendered division

Paid work

The first question raised in this chapter is how different types of welfare state regimes affect families and work, that is, the division of paid and domestic work between women and men. To give us some idea of this division, we will begin by looking at paid work and survey the employment activity rates of men and women in the different European countries (see Table 3.6).

If we look at the labour market participation rates of men and women across Europe, we find the highest employment activity rates among

Table 3.6: Employment activity rates (% of population aged 15–64) by gender, 2004

	Men	Women	Total
Social democratic regime			
Denmark	79.7	71.6	75.7
Finland	69.7	65.6	67.6
Sweden	73.6	70.5	72.1
Corporatist regime			
Austria	74.9	60.7	67.8
Belgium	67.9	52.6	60.3
France	68.9	57.4	63.1
Germany	70.8	59.2	65.0
Ireland	75.9	56.5	66.3
Luxembourg	72.4	50.6	61.6
The Netherlands	80.2	65.8	73.1
United Kingdom	77.8	65.6	71.6
Mediterranean regime			
Greece	73.7	45.2	59.4
Italy	70.1	45.2	57.6
Portugal	74.2	61.7	67.8
Spain	73.8	48.3	61.1
Post-communist regime			
Bulgaria	57.9	50.6	54.2
Czech Republic	72.3	56.0	64.2
Hungary	63.1	50.7	56.8
Poland	57.2	46.2	51.7
Slovenia	70.0	60.5	65.3
Slovakia	63.2	50.9	57
EU 25	**70.9**	**55.7**	**63.3**

Source: Employment in Europe, 2004.

women in the Scandinavian countries (see Table 3.6). In Sweden and Denmark, more than 70 per cent of the female population between the ages of 15 and 64 are active in the labour market. The lowest female activity rates are found in Italy and Greece (45 per cent). Female activity rates in Eastern Europe vary between 46 per cent in Poland and 60.5 per cent in Slovenia. All over Europe, the activity rates of women are still lower than those of men, including the Nordic countries, but the gender differences are small in the Scandinavian countries.

When analysing the activity rates from the perspective of welfare state regimes, as elaborated in section 2 ('Various types of European welfare regimes'), we see that the social democratic welfare state regime generates the highest level of gender equality in labour market participation. Apparently, social policies that explicitly enable people to combine work and family life and that seek to promote full participation of both sexes in paid labour, as is the case in the social democratic model, are successful – at least as far as paid work is concerned. Except for the Mediterranean model, all other countries showed more or less similar differences between male and female activity rates, although – as mentioned in section 2 – the various welfare state models differ rather significantly with respect to their traditions and the scope of the provisions they offer in terms of childcare, leave and part-time options. In the Mediterranean welfare state regime, the activity rates show relatively large gender gaps. This is in line with the rather restricted childcare, parental leave and part-time arrangements in the formal economy. It seems plausible that only explicit social policies, aimed and designed to enable the full participation of both sexes in the labour market, could lead to a situation that comes close to gender equality, at least in terms of paid employment.

An interesting question is to what extent gender differences in activity rates increase when part-time work is taken into account. Table 3.7 shows the percentages of men and women in the European countries who work part-time and the effects of part-time employment on the percentages of male and female full-time equivalents.

Table 3.7 shows that in most countries, gender inequality in terms of labour market participation increases when part-time workers are taken into account. If we first look at the Nordic countries, for instance Denmark, we see that the difference between the activity rates of men and women increases from 8 per cent to 13 per cent when the number of people working part-time is included in the statistics. In Finland, gender inequality in labour market participation increases from 4 per cent to 7 per cent, and in Sweden from 1.5 per cent to 9 per cent. The increase in gender inequality is even more significant in the countries belonging to the

Table 3.7: Part-time employment (% of total employment) by gender and FTE employment rates (% population aged 15–64), 2004

	Men	Women	Total	FTE (male)	FTE (female)
Social democratic regime					
Denmark	12.1	33.8	22.2	75.7	61.9
Finland	9.0	18.4	13.5	68.3	61.3
Sweden	12.0	36.3	23.6	70.9	61.6
Corporatist regime					
Austria	5.1	38.7	20.2	74.7	49.0
Belgium	6.8	40.5	21.4	67.6	44.3
France	5.3	30.1	16.7	67.6	50.5
Germany	6.5	41.6	22.3	67.8	45.5
Ireland	6.1	31.5	16.8	74.9	47.1
Luxembourg	2.4	40.2	17.8	72.5	41.1
The Netherlands	22.3	74.7	45.5	72.0	41.5
United Kingdom	10.3	43.9	25.8	73.6	50.8
Mediterranean regime					
Greece	2.2	8.5	4.6	74.1	43.8
Italy	4.8	25.0	12.7	68.9	40.2
Portugal	7.1	16.3	11.3	74.4	58.5
Spain	2.8	17.9	8.7	73.0	43.5
Post-communist regime					
Bulgaria	2.1	2.7	2.4	58.3	50.8
Czech Republic	2.3	8.3	4.9	72.1	54.6
Hungary	3.2	6.3	4.7	63.7	49.5
Poland	8.2	14.0	10.8	56.4	44.2
Romania	10.2	11.2	10.6	64.3	52.4
Slovenia	7.9	11.0	9.3	68.3	58.1
Slovakia	1.4	4.2	2.7	62.9	49.4
EU 25	**7.0**	**31.4**	**177**	**68.9**	**47.2**

Source: Employment in Europe, 2004.
FTE = full-time equivalent

conservative welfare state model. This is specifically true of the Netherlands, where the employment activity rates of women are relatively high (65.8 per cent). However, when Dutch female participation in the labour market is expressed in full-time equivalents, the activity rate falls to 41.5 per cent and the gender differences increase to 30 per cent. The United Kingdom and Ireland also show a substantial increase in gender inequality in paid labour when part-time work is specified. In the Southern European countries, the increase in inequality is fairly small; here, it is still less common for women to work part-time than it is in the Western and Northern European countries, at least in the formal economy. The same holds for the former socialist countries; the share of women who work part-time is still fairly low in Eastern Europe (see Chapter 5, Figure 5.3).

To conclude this section, the Nordic countries show the least inequality between women and men. Generally speaking, if we disregard gender differences within labour organisations, the social democratic welfare state regime offers the best conditions for gender equality in the labour market. What is more striking, however, is that everywhere in Europe, despite decades of equal opportunity policies initiated and encouraged by the European Union, gender is still a relevant factor in terms of labour force participation. This holds true even in countries where social policies aim to maximise women's opportunities to participate in paid labour.

Domestic work

The lower employment activity rates of women in all European countries correlate with female involvement in domestic work. It still is a more or less universal fact that on average, women spend more hours on domestic work than men: Eurostat data collected between 1998 and 2002 in ten European countries (no Mediterranean countries were involved) showed that women perform an average of between 60 per cent and 66 per cent of all domestic work, which includes childcare. However, women in Finland, Norway and Sweden spend less time on domestic work than women in other countries, and the relative share of domestic work performed by men is largest in Sweden (40 per cent), Norway (38 per cent), Finland (37 per cent) and Belgium (37 per cent). In the Nordic countries as a whole, women spend about 3.45 hours per day on domestic work, whereas women in all the other countries in this dataset spent more time on domestic work, ranging from 4.30 to five hours in the corporatist and liberal welfare states, to about five hours on average in the post-communist model. The differences between the Nordic countries and the rest are important, as they indicate that part of the domestic work has been taken over by facilities offered by the state and/or by local governments – specifically, childcare and after-school facilities.

To add some general figures from the Mediterranean countries, Peters et al. (2005)[2] have shown that employed men spend little time on domestic work and family care. On average, their share is nine hours per week, compared to 12.5 hours in the liberal model, 13.3 hours in the corporatist model, 16 hours in the social democratic model and 13.9 hours in the post-communist model. The average contribution to household work by employed women is far higher than employed men: 27 hours in the liberal welfare states, 31 hours in the corporatist model, 28 hours in the social democratic model and 35 hours in the post-communist welfare states.

Share of paid and domestic work performed by women and men

If we consider the relationship between paid and domestic work and the shares of these two forms of work accounted for by women and men, based on the same Eurostat data collected between 1998 and 2002, we can say the following: of all the countries surveyed, women in Finland, Norway and Sweden spend the largest share of the total time involved in paid and domestic work on gainful work, compared with the other European countries. Nordic women spend about 40 per cent of their time on paid work and – by implication – about 60 per cent on domestic work. These percentages are less evenly balanced in all other European countries: on average 65 per cent to 70 per cent of women's time is spent on domestic work and about 35 per cent to 30 per cent on paid work.

As it is a well-known fact that gender differences in the division of paid and domestic work increase when people have children, it is worth having a closer look at data on paid and domestic work by parents of young children. The presence of small children in families seems to intensify the traditional division of labour (see Table 3.8).

Table 3.8: Gainful and domestic work of parents living as a couple with youngest child aged up to 6, in hours and minutes per day and in percentages of total time (1998–2002)

	Women		Men	
	Gainful work	Domestic Work	Gainful work	Domestic Work
Social democratic regime				
Finland	2.14 (27)	6.05 (73)	5.15 (65)	2.48 (35)
Norway	2.15 (29)	5.26 (71)	4.47 (60)	3.12 (40)
Sweden	2.17 (29)	5.29 (71)	4.53 (59)	3.21 (41)
Conservative regime				
France	2.13 (28)	5.49 (72)	4.55 (66)	2.30 (34)
Belgium	2.38 (33)	5.27 (67)	4.47 (62)	2.57 (38)
Germany	1.12 (16)	6.11 (84)	4.32 (60)	3.00 (40)
Liberal regime				
UK	2.00 (25)	6.09 (75)	5.33 (67)	2.46 (33)
Post-communist regime				
Hungary	1.31 (17)	7.33 (83)	4.47 (60)	3.11 (40)
Estonia	2.03 (23)	6.51 (77)	3.32 (63)	2.41 (37)
Slovenia	3.01 (33)	6.15 (67)	5.38 (66)	2.54 (34)

Source: European Commission. Eurostat (2004), *How Europeans spend their time. Everyday life of women and men*. Data 1998–2002.

Parents with small children work longer hours. Their total working time per day is between one and two hours longer than the average for people aged 20 to 74. The fact that mothers with small children spend between 70 to 85 per cent of their total working hours on domestic work is particularly relevant. Young mothers see an increase in their total working time, but their share in paid work decreases significantly compared with women in general, and compared with men. There is no similar correlation between gainful and domestic work for the fathers. Men maintain their share of paid work, even when they have young children. In terms of economics, therefore, gender inequality increases significantly when children are born. This is true for all the welfare state regimes, although less so in the social democratic model, where women manage to spend almost 30 per cent of their total time on gainful work. The lowest percentages of gainful work for women are in Germany (16 per cent), Hungary (17 per cent) and Estonia (23 per cent).

In summary

Returning to the first question of this chapter: how do different types of welfare state regimes affect the division of paid and domestic work between women and men, we can conclude by saying that the social democratic welfare state model offers the best conditions for equality between women and men in terms of labour force participation. Even in the Nordic countries, however, gender is still a relevant category when considering employment activity rates. This is particularly true when part-time work is taken into account and participation rates for women and men are expressed in 'full-time equivalents' (see Table 3.7). In comparing different regimes, however, gender inequality in paid work appears to be most prevalent in the corporatist and Mediterranean welfare state models, where there is relatively little state support for the combination of work and family life. Institutional frameworks matter when it comes to women's opportunities to earn a living and participate in the labour force.

Interestingly, the figures suggest that domestic work is influenced less by the nature of the welfare state regime than by patterns of paid work. It is true that there is less gender inequality in domestic work in the Nordic countries than in the other European countries, although women still perform a significantly larger share of housework than men in all the countries. This is particularly clear when we consider couples with young children. Childcare and domestic work are apparently still considered by most people to be a woman's responsibility, at least when it comes to actual behaviour. Compared with mothers from other European countries, mothers in the social democratic welfare states still manage to spend the largest share of their total time on paid work, but even in the Nordic countries, men's and women's patterns of time use start to diverge significantly once children are born. This 'logic' seems to be deeply ingrained in European countries, even in countries where institutional arrangements offer women relatively good opportunities to participate fully in the labour market. The cultural dimension of welfare states is also of importance, as we stated in the introduction to this chapter.

Gender gaps

The second question raised in this chapter is whether more gender equality in paid and domestic work would result in less gender inequality in society. Perhaps this question needs to be rephrased, as the countries do not differ all that much in terms of the gender divisions of tasks, as shown in section 3 ('Paid and domestic work in Europe: a gendered division'). Is there a more direct relationship between welfare state regimes and gender (in)equality? To identify gender (in)equality in the European countries, we use two indicators: the gender pay gap, that is, women's average hourly earnings as a percentage of that of men, and the percentage of women in managerial positions.

Table 3.9 offers an interesting view of the extent to which social equality between men and women has been achieved in Europe. The gender pay gap has been diminishing in the past few decades, but the gross hourly earnings of women are still lower than those of men in all the European countries. Social policies supporting the work/care combination do not appear to make much difference in this respect: the social democratic model does not guarantee more gender equality in wages than the other types of welfare state regimes. Indeed, the gender pay gap appears to be the smallest in the Mediterranean model, which is characterised by low-level public provisions. This could be because women who work in the formal economy are mostly employed in full-time jobs. It should be noted, however, that this full-time work pattern is also common among women in post-communist regimes, where the gender pay gap is relatively large. The general conclusion must be that there are more similarities between countries than differences when it comes to the gender pay gap. All over Europe, women's hourly earnings are about 15 to 20 per cent lower than those of men.

When we consider the share of women in managerial positions, as represented by the ISCO indicators, we find that Ireland, the UK, France, Portugal and several Eastern European countries have relatively high percentages

Table 3.9: Wage gap: women's wages as a percentage of men's average gross hourly earnings and women in managerial positions in the EUR countries

Country	Gender pay gap – women's wages as % of men's[a] (* = 2003)			Women in managerial positions[b]
	1992	1999	2004	2004
Social democratic regime				
Denmark	82.6	86	82*	27
Finland	77.0	81	80*	29
Norway	—	83	84	30[c]
Sweden	89.0	83	83	30
Conservative regime				
Austria	78.0	79	83*	28
Belgium	74.5	89	—	29
France	81.0	88	88	35
Germany	75.8	81	77	28
Luxembourg	65.2	82	86	27
The Netherlands	76.7	79	81	26[c]
Liberal regime				
Ireland	69.0	78	89	39
UK	69.7	78	78	32
Mediterranean regime				
Greece	78.0	87	90	27
Italy	80.0	91	—	20
Portugal	76.0	95	91*	32
Spain	70.0	86	85	30[c]
Post-communist regime				
Bulgaria	—	—	82	30[c]
Czech Republic	—	78	81	28
Hungary	—	79	89	34
Romania	—	83	86	33
Slovenia	—	86	—	33[c]
Slovakia	—	77	76	34

Sources: [a] The wage gap figures are unadjusted, and reflect the average gross hourly earnings of all paid employees aged 16–64 who worked 15+ hours per week in 1999: http://www.infoplease.com/ipa/A0908883.html
[b] Eurostat, Labour Force Survey (LFS), 2004 (*note*: Managers are persons classified as Directors and chief executives, Production and operating managers, Other specialist managers and Managers of small enterprises (International Standard Classification of Occupations ISCO category 12 and 13).
[c] UNDP, Human Development Report 2005: Female Legislation Senior Officials, and Managers; % of total.

of female managers. It is plausible, however, that where more sophisticated criteria were used to measure gender differences in managerial
positions, for example salaries or level of authority, the differences
increased substantially. However, bearing in mind the key perspective of
this chapter, it is probable that such an increase would occur in all the
European countries, irrespective of the specific welfare state regime.
Nevertheless, when we restrict ourselves to senior management positions
within the private sector, larger gender differences become visible. In
June 2004, the European Professional Women's Network presented the
EPWN European BoardWomen Monitor 2004, a survey of women on the
corporate boards of the 200 most important European firms in the relevant sectors of industry and business services. On average, women
account for 8 per cent of corporate board members (in the Fortune 500
companies in the US, the share of women on corporate boards was 14
per cent in 2003; 10 per cent of the American companies surveyed have
no women on their corporate boards, compared with 38 per cent for the
European companies covered by the Monitor). Thirteen countries took
part in the EPWN Monitor (Norway, Sweden, Finland, Germany, United
Kingdom, Switzerland, the Netherlands, Austria, France, Denmark,
Spain, Belgium and Italy) and some striking differences were revealed.
Women are best represented on corporate boards in Norway (22 per
cent) and in Sweden (20 per cent). The share of female board members
is 10 per cent in the UK and Germany, while the lowest percentage of
women on corporate boards can be found in Spain (3 per cent), Belgium
(3 per cent) and Italy (2 per cent) (European PWN, 2004). In other
words, the institutional context appears to be an important factor for
women when it comes to corporate senior managerial positions. The case
of the United States suggests, however, that beyond social policy, affirmative action measures also play a significant role in this respect
(Fuchshuber et al., 2004).

Possible consequences for the social policy agenda of the European Union

Based on this analysis, and with rather rough indicators for gender
(in)equalities in the different welfare state regimes, it becomes clear that
variations in the scope and nature of work/family policies across Europe
are more striking than variations in gender (in)equality. What can be said,
however, is that institutional arrangements that support the work/care
combination lead to less gender inequality in the labour market, at least in
terms of numbers of participating women and men. The Nordic countries,

with their well-developed childcare facilities for young children, have the highest number of working women in Europe, even when patterns of part-time work are taken into account. If the aim is therefore to ensure gender equality in the public domain, and if we assume that welfare states need a high female (and male) labour force participation rate in order to survive, it makes sense to invest in childcare. Interestingly, the division of domestic work between women and men is very persistent, and seems to be affected less by the presence of social policies than patterns of paid work. Incentives for fathers to take up more parental leave and to become more involved in domestic work and childcare are fairly recent and have been introduced predominantly in the Nordic countries. It may be that in the long run, sharing leave more equally will result in an equal division of tasks, once mothers and fathers return to work.

Fuwa (2004) suggests that couples' decision-making regarding the division of domestic work is embedded in the macro social context and that women in more egalitarian countries are more able to negotiate an equal division of housework on the basis of their own resources, such as earning potential, than in less egalitarian countries. This too offers a strong rationale for developing affordable and high-quality childcare all over Europe. It is not unlikely that a more equal gender division of domestic work is more a consequence of the power and resources that women obtain through paid work, rather than a prerequisite for it.

There is a rather complex relationship between social policies and the female labour force participation rate on the one hand and gender (in)equality in terms of earnings and managerial positions on the other hand. Countries are more similar when it comes to gender pay gaps and gender inequality in managerial positions than they are in terms of their institutional arrangements. Apparently, these indicators of gender inequality refer to mechanisms that are deeply embedded in the cultural and structural arrangements of European societies. It should be noted that the policy measures themselves can be somewhat ambivalent. For instance, the presence of parental leave may strengthen the labour market commitment of women, but on the other hand, long leaves also have a negative impact on women's career opportunities. The same applies to working part-time as a strategy for combining work and family life. As long as it is mainly women who take up parental leave and who cut down on their working hours, senior level, well-paying jobs will remain beyond the reach of many.

More needs to be done to combat gender inequalities in the economy, as Social Affairs and Employment Commissioner Vladimir Spidla recently said. It should be noted that, although institutional arrangements supporting the work/family combination are vital to achieving more gender equality in economic life, they are not sufficient in and of themselves. Gender inequality is a multi-layered phenomenon (Lewis & Smithson, 2006) and social policy needs to be supplemented by negotiations between employers and employees in the workplace and between couples at home. In the end, gender equality is the collective effect of choices and decisions made by numerous women and men at home and at work, although as this chapter has demonstrated, they make these 'choices' in very different national contexts.

Notes

1. This chapter would not have been possible without the help and support of Marijke Veldhoen.
2. A study by Ecorys and ICS/Universiteit Utrecht for the European Commission.

4
Fertility Rates and Mothers' Employment Behaviour in Comparative Perspective: Similarities and Differences in Six European Countries[1]

Jeanne Fagnani

Introduction

Throughout Europe since 1965, no country has been able to resist the twin phenomena of a declining birthrate and a corresponding increase in women's participation in the labour force. Yet, while the overall trend is similar, there are significant differences between countries, whether it be in the levels of women's participation in the workforce or the extent to which fertility levels have declined. By making a cross-national analysis of six countries (Norway, Sweden, UK, Netherlands, France and Portugal), the complex array of factors explaining these differences will be investigated. Our aim will be to demonstrate that the various interactions between the levels of support provided by public policies to working parents, the employment patterns of women, and the cultural norms that govern childcare policy have to be considered together if we are to adequately explain the differences in birth rates across various countries.

The first section of the chapter will provide a description of the variations in fertility rates between the six countries. In the second part, similarities and differences in policies aimed at helping parents to combine paid work and unpaid work in these countries will be outlined. The ways in which these policies are inter-related with the employment patterns of mothers will also be explored. Finally, I will explore some of the interpretations we can make from the analysis of the existing differences between countries in terms of fecundity.

Theoretical background

The majority of women born after World War II, who as a whole have become progressively more educated, have demonstrated a desire for economic independence, with employment seen as a central component of their social identity. Moreover, in all European countries, thanks to widespread access to contraception, women can now exercise an overriding power of decision in family planning matters, by regulating their reproduction and planning, in consultation with their partners, as to when they will have children (Castles, 2003; McDonald, 2002). However, couples do not always have the number of children that they hope for, even if they often end up 'making a virtue of necessity'. Additionally, as a result of the enduring asymmetry between the sexes in family involvement, women, in particular, are often faced with difficult trade-offs between their maternal desires and professional ambitions. By having children, they also have to cope with the conflicting demands of paid work and family responsibilities (Fine-Davis et al., 2004; Pfau-Effinger & Geissler, 2005). This dilemma is intensified by the fact that mothers are confronted with these difficult choices at the precise moment when they need to be investing in their professional lives in order to establish themselves in a job or progress in their career. Indeed, in light of the increase in the mean age of motherhood since the 1960s, we can observe that this decision-making period neatly coincides with the time of childbearing and child-rearing.

In this context, the issue of work/life balance and support for working parents has come to the forefront of the social and policy agenda. Dealing with 'social care' (Daly & Lewis, 2000) has become imperative and boundaries between the state, the market and the family have been called into question in most European countries (Morgan, 2002; Pfau-Effinger & Geissler, 2005). Nevertheless, welfare state policies regarding the integration of mothers into waged work still differ considerably across Europe (Gornick & Meyers, 2003). Against this institutional and policy background, it has been observed that countries which have a high participation of mothers in the workforce and a relatively high fertility rate, are those whose policies advocate and support maternal employment (Castles, 2003; Sleebos, 2003; Fine-Davis et al., 2004). On the other hand, countries which have low birth rates and a low level of mothers participating in the workforce, Spain and Italy in particular, are those in which women have traditionally faced the greatest obstacles to full-time participation in professional life (Castles, 2003).

Several reasons can be given to justify the choice of the Netherlands, UK, France, Norway, Sweden and Portugal for our study. Firstly, in each of these countries, the policy objective of reconciliation between employment and family life has gradually moved – although at a different pace in the six countries – onto the political agenda. Despite considerable variations in the political impact of this issue, and in the public provision of services provided to families, a range of measures has been progressively implemented to reduce the conflicts between paid and unpaid work.

Second, each country has a different welfare regime (Pierson, 2001), which has strong implications as to how far each country places the onus for reconciling employment and family life on public policy and how much on individuals, families and employers. France and the Netherlands are part of the cluster of countries whose welfare regimes are categorised as 'conservative' (sometimes termed 'Christian democratic' or 'Bismarckian'). Among others, they include the following features: high levels of spending, high levels of payroll tax financing and explicit or implicit family policies. However, France differs from the other conservative welfare states (especially Germany) when social care is taken into account (Fagnani, 2007). The UK is classified in the liberal cluster and Sweden and Norway as social democratic. Among these six countries there are significant variations in the proportions of their social protection system devoted to 'family policy'.[2] On the one hand, Sweden, Norway and France have a well-established and long-standing early childcare system, while on the other, in the Netherlands and the UK, public provision of childcare generally lags behind. In Portugal, public provision for childcare varies according to the region, but is generally scarce.

Third, labour force participation rates and employment patterns of mothers still vary according to country and yet there are also numerous similarities. All are currently grappling with similar issues, due to the convergence of economic and social conditions in the European Community, and their welfare states are undergoing quite significant changes (Pierson, 2001). Decision-makers are attempting to tackle a number of issues – including reform of pension systems, reducing unemployment, fighting poverty and social exclusion, and limiting public deficits – and are confronted with a number of dilemmas. Against this background of cost containment and 'recalibration of welfare states' (Pierson, 2001), they have to make trade-offs and find compromises.

Fertility rates and fertility patterns: differences and similarities

Total and completed fertility rates: Norway and France at the top of the fertility table

The two main fertility indicators are the total period fertility rate (TFR) and the completed fertility rate (CFR). TFR in a specific year is the average number of children who would be born to a hypothetical cohort of women whose age-specific birth rates were the same as those actually observed in the year in question. The CFR is the average number of children born to women of a given generation at the end of their child-bearing years.[3] TFR may differ for long periods when fertility timing changes. For example, a delay in timing leads to a drop in TFR, even if the completed fertility rate of the generations is not modified.

In each European country, trends in the TFR have undergone profound changes over the last 30 years with a significant decline occurring between 1970 and 1985. Nevertheless, there remain marked variations in fertility levels between the different countries. France, Norway and Sweden all demonstrate fertility rates reaching, or approaching, replacement level while the three countries where the CFR is lower are no longer capable of replacing their populations. It is clear that we will need to look deeper into the various events and trends of the past decades in order to shed light on why we are experiencing such diversity at the dawn of the new millennium (Sardon, 2004).

Common ground: dramatic changes in the timing of births

Across Europe there have been increases in both the level of education and professional activity in the female population. Additionally, modern birth control measures have given couples greater power to make family planning decisions. The inescapable consequence of this convergence is a global increase in the age at which couples decide to have children, with the vast majority choosing to delay maternity until they are well established in their professional lives (Sleebos, 2005). With the sole exception of Portugal, this trend can be traced back to about 25 years ago, with the southern European countries lagging somewhat behind. It was not until well into the 1980s that the timing of births in Portugal fell into line with patterns observed elsewhere across the continent (Figure 4.1).

The Dutch: the mothers who delay childbirth the longest

Dutch mothers are distinguished by the fact that they delay childbirth the longest. Whereas mothers in Scandinavia, France and Britain tend to

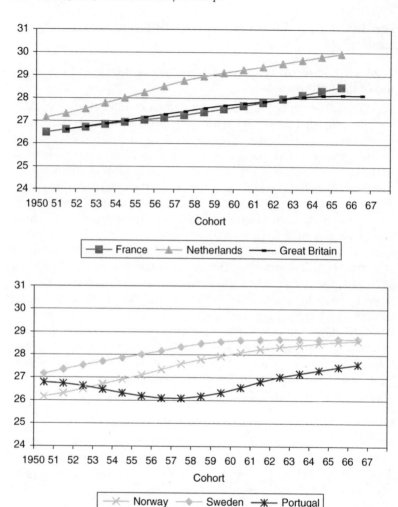

Figure 4.1:   Mean age of women at childbirth by year and by cohort
Source: Recent demographic developments in Europe 2001, Council of Europe.

become mothers between the ages of 28 and 29, in the Netherlands this figure is closer to 30 if we look at the figures for women's mean age of childbirth (for women born in 1965). In Portugal, it was not until the 1960s that any increase in the delay before childbirth was apparent, and even in more recent generations the tendency for women to become mothers at a younger age than in other countries has remained (27.5 for women born in 1965). Indeed, we can observe a steady rise in the age at

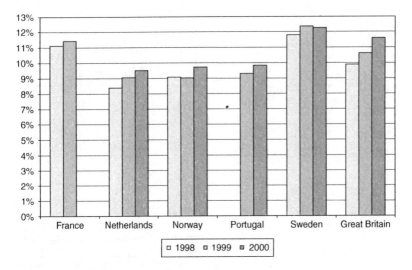

Figure 4.2:   Percentage of births among women from 40 to 44 years old in the total of live births
Source: Recent demographic developments in Europe 2001, Council of Europe.

which women choose to become mothers across all the countries which has only just begun to stabilise in the youngest generations in the UK and Sweden (28.1 and 28.7, respectively).

Around one child in ten is born to a mother aged 40 or more

Taking into account the fact that more and more mothers are choosing to delay childbirth, it should come as no surprise that we are observing a dramatic rise in first-time mothers over the age of 30. Focusing on the period that marks the end of women's reproductive lives, we find that more women in Sweden are likely to give birth between the ages of 40 and 44 (approximately 12 per cent), with France and the UK not far behind (Figure 4.2). Further down the list are Norway, the Netherlands and Portugal, where we can observe a rate of approximately 10 per cent. The repercussions of the decision to delay childbirth certainly merit our further consideration if we accept the fact that a lack of children in the early stages of a woman's reproductive life may not be adequately compensated for at a later stage.

Fewer and fewer children in Portugal

The evolution of the two principal measures of fecundity, the Total Fertility Rate (TFR) and the Completed Fertility Rate (CFR), will enable us to shed further light on our discussion (Figure 4.3). Portugal had an

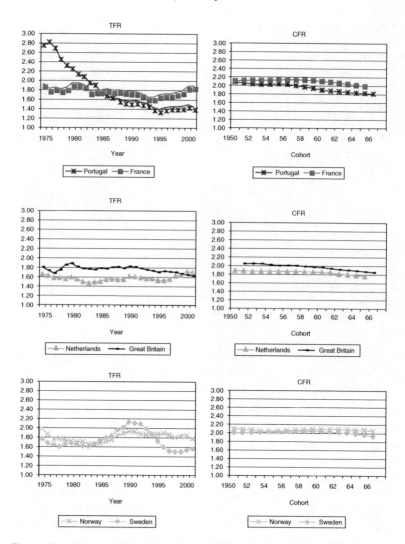

Figure 4.3:   Completed fertility rates and total period fertility rates
Sources: Recent demographic developments in Europe 2001, Council of Europe/ODE.

extremely elevated TFR in 1975 of 2.75 children for every female but, as with its Mediterranean neighbours (Sleebos, 2005), the country witnessed a sharp decline in the following years to the point where it has become the second country from the bottom in levels of fertility at 1.42 children for every female in 2004. France, Norway and the UK have been

Table 4.1: Total period fertility rates and completed fertility rates

	Total fertility rate (2004)	Completed fertility rate (women born in 1961)
France	1.90	2.10
Netherlands	1.73	1.84
UK	1.74	1.95
Norway	1.81	2.10
Portugal	1.42	1.87
Sweden	1.75	2.03

Source: Eurostat, 2006, http://epp.eurostat.cec.eu.int/portal.

spared such dramatic decreases and have maintained a TFR of between 1.7 and two during the past 25 years. Similarly, there has been little variation in the Netherlands, where the rate has oscillated between 1.5 and 1.7. Sweden on the other hand, due to a rather unique set of circumstances, saw its TFR rise rapidly between the beginning of the 1980s and 1985 when, against the backdrop of a booming economy, government policy favoured the economic emancipation of women. This was followed by a sharp decrease at the beginning of the 1990s when the country fell into an economic recession that necessitated a reduction in public spending and produced a sharp rise in unemployment with a disproportionate effect on women. This comes as no surprise, as the majority of active women in Sweden occupied, and still occupy, positions in the public sector (Fagnani et al., 2004).

As a measure, the CFR presents many advantages over the Total Fertility rate, not least in its ability to present a complete picture which remains unaffected by the variations in timing of births during childbearing years. The only disadvantage is that this measure can be taken only when a cohort of women has reached the end of their reproductive years. France and Norway remain the sole countries in Europe to have resisted the trend toward a lower CFR, reporting rates greater than two, despite modifications in the timing of births (Table 4.1). As for the rest of the countries studied, a clear decline in CFR would seem to indicate that the choice of mothers to delay childbirth is not being adequately compensated for by a corresponding increase in births during the final years of their reproductive lives (Figure 4.3).

A sharp increase in childlessness in Great Britain and the Netherlands

Not only are we witnessing decreased rates of reproduction but also an increase in the number of women who choose to remain childless. This trend can be observed in all countries but is most pronounced in those generations of women born in Scandinavia and Western Europe since the 1950s. Whereas this trend has been fairly moderate in France, Norway and Sweden, it has become quite marked in the Netherlands, as well as in the England–Wales portions of the UK (the only regions for which data are available), where the rate of childlessness for women born in 1960 has climbed to 17.7 per cent and 20.4 per cent, respectively. This trend began to appear in Portugal only with those generations of women born after 1960. Although little studied, this phenomenon suggests that in addition to the problems women encounter when they choose to delay childbirth, and the resulting effects on fecundity, we must also take into account a rising segment of the female population who no longer wish to have children at all.

Perhaps some of these differences in levels of fecundity can be partially explained by variations in public policy, taking into account that all six countries have different systems of tax benefits, cash benefits, exemptions from charges, subsidies and services in kind which assist parents with the costs of raising children (Bradshaw & Finch, 2002). In the following sections, therefore, we will examine these variations.

The impact of public policy on the lives of working parents: which measures are having an effect on fertility and employment patterns for women?

The increase in the employment of women, in particular mothers, has continued over the last two decades in the six countries studied, as in the rest of the European Union. Therefore, the difficulties they have to cope with in combining paid and unpaid work, and the support that the State and its institutions could (or should) provide them with, have come to the forefront of the social and political agenda. However, despite some evidence of convergence between the six European countries, in respect of changes in institutional arrangements and formal childcare provision, differences remain striking.

Norway, Sweden and France: robust and extensive support in early childhood

In comparative and cross-national research, Sweden, Norway and France are always part of the cluster of countries whose policies provide extensive support for maternal employment (Gornick & Meyers, 2003). In Norway, since the early 1990s, important reforms have taken place which have enabled both parents to better combine employment and parental responsibilities. The number of places available in day care institutions rose steadily in the 1990s and the percentage of children aged between one and five attending a day care centre increased from 19 per cent in 1980 to 61 per cent in 1999. This trend has continued over the last few years and in 2002, the coverage rate for children in the same age group was 66 per cent (Fagnani et al., 2004). Sweden, although experiencing a decline in the quality of its public services since the economic difficulties of the 1980s, remains an extremely attractive model for early childcare provision. All children from the age of one are welcomed full-time into community supported childcare facilities (OECD, 2005).

In France, the number of childcare places in crèches has increased regularly since the early 1980s – by on average 6400 places per year between 1981 and 1996 – to reach a total of 254,000 in 2004. Eleven per cent of children aged under three are cared for in crèches, compared with 4 per cent in 1982 (Chastenet, 2005). The Family branch of the Social Security Department, CNAF (National Family Allowance Fund), through the *Caisses d'Allocations Familiales* (Family Allowance Funds), participates in the development and running costs of crèches through the *contrats-enfances* (childhood contracts) which are designed both to assist and to encourage communities to construct and to bear some of the running costs of these facilities. However, as we shall see in Chapter 12, since 1994, the increase in funds allocated by the CNAF towards crèches has been modest in comparison with the much higher funding allocated to childcare carried out by individuals, whether registered child minders or nannies at home, or to the *Allocation Parentale d'Education* (APE, child rearing benefit) (Fagnani, 2006). Nevertheless, against a background of urgent demands for increased childcare arrangements and growing pressure from the women's movement and some family associations, the Ministry of Family Affairs decided to substantially increase the number of places in crèches in 2000, and once again in 2001. Two hundred and twenty-eight million euros have been channelled into public childcare facilities such as crèches and halte-garderies and 40,000 places are due to be created over the next three years.

Another essential component of France's family policy is a strong commitment to the near-universal enrolment of children under the age of six[4] in *écoles maternelles* (nursery schools), which are free and run by the Ministry of National Education. Open for 35 hours per week between the hours of eight a.m. and five p.m., this service is well suited to the needs of working mothers who are employed during these hours. All of these schools are equipped with canteen facilities – fees are income-related – and although many are closed on Wednesday, this is compensated for by a half-day Saturday session. By the age of three, almost 98 per cent of all children have begun to attend these *écoles maternelles*.

Great Britain, the Netherlands and Portugal: enduring scarcity of early childcare arrangements

The United Kingdom and the Netherlands, on the other hand, have less supportive political and social attitudes which are demonstrated in policies affecting pre-school age children. Historically, there has been little public commitment to the provision of childcare in either of these countries and both have traditionally supported the 'male-breadwinner' family model (Evers et al., 2005; Gornick & Meyers, 2004; OECD, 2002b; OECD, 2005). Nevertheless, since the late 1990s, the UK government has made efforts to increase the availability of childcare outside the family. The National Childcare Strategy, introduced by the new Labour Government in 1997, focused on provisions for three to four year olds and on the promotion of childcare in disadvantaged areas. By 2001, 95 per cent of three and four year olds were attending some form of early education, usually part-time (Evers et al., 2005). However, for children under three, childcare provision has remained somewhat patchy. Enterprises seeking to retain staff are often obliged to institute 'family-friendly' working practices in an effort to fill the gaps, with particular emphasis placed on flexible working hours. Some businesses may also provide subsidies to parents in order to offset the costs of private childcare services. What is noticeable, however, is that the employment of nannies, which is an option amongst the more well-off members of society, remains out of reach for the large majority further down the social ladder. The majority of women, therefore, are forced to limit the time they devote to paid work if they want to combine their job with family responsibilities.

We find a similar situation in Holland where, in the year 2000, only 21 per cent of children under the age of four were enrolled in early childcare facilities. After this age, children can attend nursery schools, although the effectiveness of these measures is minimised by the fact that both types of institution are open for a limited number of hours. In Portugal, the gaps in care are widespread but there has been a general increase in the numbers of children aged between three and five years being accepted into state supported preschools, moving from 64 to 76 per cent between 1997 and 2002 (OECD, 2004).

Maternity leave and parental leave: large disparities between countries

The policies of the Scandinavian countries provide the most attractive model for working parents in the provision of maternity and parental leave, with Sweden clearly leading the way (Moss & Deven, 2000, Math &

Meilland, 2004). Here, parents have the ability to vary their working hours and are able to benefit from a generous parental leave of 15 months which includes 12 months at 80 per cent of salary, with two months being non-transferable between parents in order to encourage the minority parent (usually the father) to get involved in childcare (Anxo et al., 2002, 2005). In addition, parents have the right to take leave for up to 60 days per year at 80 per cent of their salaries, in the event that their child falls ill. In Norway, since 1993, parents have benefited from a parental leave policy, with one month non-transferable, which provides for either 42 weeks at full salary or 52 weeks at 80 per cent. Lying in sharp contrast are the policies of Holland, the UK and Portugal, where parental leave remains short and unpaid. With maternity leave, the differences are no less marked: in the UK it is limited to six weeks at 90 per cent of salary and a fixed sum of 100 pounds for the 20 weeks that follow, which stands in stark contrast to France, where mothers benefit from 18 weeks at full salary.

Women with children: an essential component in the labour markets of Portugal, France and Scandinavia

In all the countries discussed in this chapter, claims by women have progressively gained acceptance, whether they are motivated by a desire for greater financial independence or the freedom to follow their chosen career paths. The rate of women's participation in the labour market has increased significantly since the 1980s, while the 'male-breadwinner' model has been gradually declining. Nevertheless, the rate and patterns of women's participation in the labour market in these countries is by no means uniform, and we find that it is in the Scandinavian countries, as well as in Portugal, that the female employment rate is highest, irrespective of the number of children in the family (Figure 4.4). However, this rate of activity can be somewhat misleading if we do not take into account the differences that exist in the actual number of hours being worked by women in the different countries. Sweden, France, and especially Portugal, stand out as the countries where the dominant model is full-time employment for both partners, whereas the UK and the Netherlands have tended to move towards a model where the male partner works full-time and the female part-time (Figure 4.5).

Great Britain and the Netherlands: part-time work providing a solution for mothers

In the UK and the Netherlands, the apparent consensus between governments and the majority of parents is that part-time work provides the

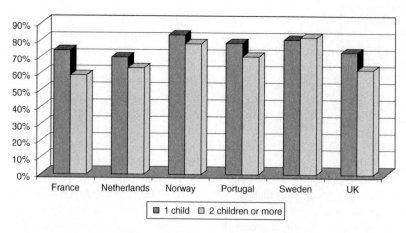

Figure 4.4:   Employment rates of women (aged 25–54 years) according to the number of children (2000)
Source: OECD, 2002a.

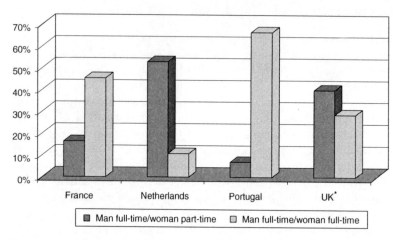

Figure 4.5:   Distribution of paid work between men and women: dual-earner couples with children (2000)
Source: Eurostat, 2002.
*1999

most effective solution to the problem of reconciling family life and professional life (Cousins & Tang, 2004). Indeed, in the Netherlands, this type of work for women has become the norm and unlike Sweden, Norway and France, where mothers tend to work longer hours, the trend for mothers in the Netherlands has been towards shorter hours of work.

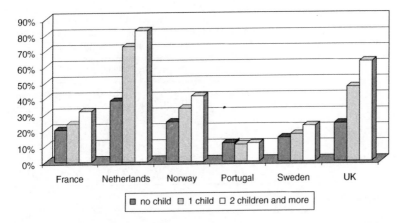

Figure 4.6: Percentage of women (aged 25–54 years) working part-time according to the number of children (2000)
Source: OECD, Employment Outlook, 2002a.

All countries, with the exception of Portugal (Figure 4.6) where part-time jobs remain scarce, have demonstrated that the frequency of part-time work increases along with the number of children being born into each household. Portugal's unique situation can be explained by the reluctance of government to put measures in place which would favour this type of employment, combined with low wages for most women which forces them to work longer hours. In addition, as we shall see in Chapter 7, low wages for Portuguese men serve to 'enforce' a dual-earner model as a consequence of family need.

In every European country, having children has a dampening effect on the employment rate of women, but level of educational attainment is also a discriminating factor. For example, in France, the employment rate of highly educated mothers living with a partner and at least one child aged under six is 72.2 per cent compared with 29.0 per cent for mothers with a low level of education (OECD, 2002a). Table 4.2 illustrates that the impact of motherhood on female employment patterns has both an employment rate and a working-time effect. However, there are still important differences across countries. In the UK and the Netherlands, even among women with a high level of educational attainment, being a mother has a more powerful effect on employment patterns than in Sweden, France or Portugal. In the UK and the Netherlands, full-time employment is much less frequent among highly educated women with children than among highly educated childless women – the percentage point difference is 43 per cent and 32 per cent, respectively – and the

Table 4.2:   The effect of the presence of children on the employment status of women*: percentage point difference in the frequency of a specific status between women with children (under 15 years of age) and women without children

	University/Tertiary		
	Non-employed	*Part-time*	*Full-time*
France	4.4	7.6	−12.1
Netherlands	7.5	35.5	−43
Portugal	−2	1	1
Sweden	−2.2	5.1	−2.9
UK	10.5	21.2	−31.7

Source: OECD, Employment Outlook, 2002a.
* Computed for the case of women aged 25–54.

frequency of part-time work among highly educated mothers is much greater than in the three other countries. In addition, among the poorly educated in both the UK and France, having children has a much larger impact on whether or not a woman will participate in the labour market. In France, for women with low levels of educational attainment, the difference between the percentage of non-employed among women with children and the percentage of non-employed among childless women is 13.6 points. This stands in stark contrast to Sweden and Portugal, where the presence of children has a relatively minor effect on levels of participation by women in the labour market, regardless of educational attainment.

The case of Portugal remains unique, in that the level of full-time participation by mothers in the labour market is very pronounced. This phenomenon can be partly explained by the high number of females engaged as independent labourers (27.5 per cent compared with 5.5 per cent in France in 1999); laws which discourage part-time employment; the high level of participation by women in the agricultural sector (12.2 per cent compared with 3 per cent in France in 1999); and the poor salaries received by women. All this would seem to suggest that for mothers living in Portugal, the decision to continue in employment or develop their careers can only be made if they are willing to accept limitations on the number of children they will have.

Conclusion

Through a comparative analysis of the six countries included in our study, we have been able to illustrate clearly what has already been hinted at in previously published research (Castles, 2003; Fagnani, 2006; McDonald, 2002; Sleebos, 2003). Where family-friendly public policy has had a positive impact on fertility levels, the common denominator has been the availability of affordable, high quality childcare, along with legal provisions regulating work leave and work schedules related to children. By drawing on a theoretical account derived from the current bodies of literature and using cross-country regressions as a method of analysis, a clear link has been identified between fertility and formal childcare provision, whether delivered by public or private means (Castles, 2003). Therefore, the examples of the six countries confirm that family-friendly public policies play a significant role in shaping both present day fertility behaviour and female employment patterns.

In fact, fertility acts as a variable of adjustment: couples make decisions about the number of children they will have based on the woman's professional plans and aspirations. If maternity threatens these plans because societal supports for combining work and family responsibilities are few or non-existent, women are likely to postpone childbirth and reduce the number of children they have. Moreover, aspirations in regard to paid work, and the norms and values that govern childcare policy, also have to fit together in such a way as to form a family-friendly environment where it is legitimate and socially acceptable to have a pre-school aged child being cared for outside of the home. Family-related policies do not only serve to encourage or, conversely, to thwart the employment of mothers through the taxation system, benefits, and childcare provision: these policies are in themselves the very expression of the dominant value systems. They are a reflection of the cultural context which contributes to a more or less guilt-inducing climate for mothers who wish to work.

We can observe that the countries where the presence of mothers in the labour market is pronounced and the fertility rate elevated – Norway, Sweden and France – are those which have opted for policies which encourage the 'working mother' model. The majority of women in these countries no longer feel forced to make the decision between an active professional life and raising a family. In France, the progressive introduction since the 1970s of measures and schemes to assist working mothers, and a concomitant modernisation of childrearing norms, have combined to justify the decisions of couples, and more particularly women, to have children as well as being in paid employment.

By comparing France, the Netherlands, the UK, Norway, Sweden and Portugal, I have suggested that to gain a better understanding of fertility behaviour, it is useful to focus on the complex set of interactions between cultural norms with respect to childcare outside of the home, attitudes towards working mothers and family policies. In particular, it is important to investigate whether the premises of each country's respective family policies are in tune with the normative attitudes of women and men towards maternal employment and childcare arrangements outside of the home. As has already been demonstrated by several studies on fertility behaviour and preferences, those societies where changes in women's economic roles and aspirations are not matched by similar changes in institutions and the division of labour within the family are likely to continue to witness a decline in levels of fertility (Esping-Andersen, 1999; McDonald, 2002; Sleebos, 2003).

The increase in female labour market participation rates appears to be irreversible. The European Union has taken a hands-on approach, most notably through the measures employed through the Employment Policy Guidelines drawn up at the 1997 European Summit on Employment in Luxembourg and reaffirmed in later years. Within this framework it was stated that the goal for Europe of higher rates of employment will not be met without a substantial increase in the number of women participating in the labour market. Governments are assisting with this process by adopting appropriate measures, particularly those which favour a more fluid relationship between professional and family life. This more pronounced participation of women will no doubt need to be accompanied by a redistribution of childrearing responsibilities between the family, the state, the business community and civil society. This higher rate of participation will also necessitate a renegotiation in the distribution of labour between men and women in the home and by implication, the gender contract between the sexes. Without these ameliorations and substantial changes, there is a danger that countries which already suffer from low fertility rates will struggle to stem even further losses in the years to come.

Notes

1. This chapter is based partly on information and data drawn from the report 'Context Mapping', which evolved from European Commission funded research projects which took place through the European network 'Transitions' (2003–2005). The objective of this network was to produce a comparative analysis of the possible trajectories for persons aged between 25–39 in their professional and family life through a thorough analysis of public policy with a particular focus on the family policies of the EU member states (including Bulgaria and Slovenia).

2. See Fagnani et al. (2004.) *Context mapping for the EU framework 5 funded study*.
3. This is calculated by adding the fertility rates by age of the mother observed for successive years, when the cohort has reached the age in question (in general only ages between 15 and 49 years are considered). In practice, CFR can be estimated using the rates observed for previous generations, without waiting for the cohort to reach the end of the reproductive period.
4. In France, compulsory school attendance begins at the age of six.

5
Fertility Decline, the Postponement of Childbearing and the Increase in Childlessness in Central and Eastern Europe: a Gender Equity Approach

Hana Hašková

Introduction

There has been a marked trend towards the postponement of childbearing and increased childlessness in Central and Eastern Europe (CEE) since the 1990s. In this chapter, current scientific debates and theories of fertility decline in CEE are briefly reviewed, with a particular focus on the case of the Czech Republic. The potential contribution of a gender equity focused approach for explaining current demographic trends in CEE is then discussed, drawing on evidence from the 1994 and 2002 International Social Survey Programme (ISSP) surveys.

Demographic background

The decline of the birth rate to below population replacement level, as well as the postponement of childbearing and an increase in childlessness, have become important research and political topics in CEE. Elsewhere in Europe, these trends began in the 1960s–1980s, but in the former Eastern European bloc, fertility decline far below replacement level did not begin until the 1990s (see Figure 5.1), after which time it became the region with one of the lowest total fertility rates in the world.

In the Czech Republic, for example, the mean age at first childbirth has risen from under 24 years to 26 in the post-communist era, and the mean age of first marriage from 21 to 26. By the age of thirty, a third of university educated women, and a smaller proportion of women with lower education, are still childless. Between the 1950s and the early 1990s,

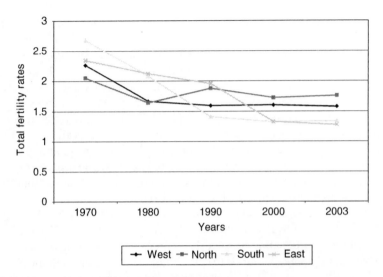

Figure 5.1:   Total fertility rates in selected European countries
Average total fertility rates (TFRs) are recorded for each group of countries by
summing TFRs of different representative countries in each and then dividing
by total number of countries.
Western Europe = the Netherlands, France, UK, Switzerland, Luxembourg,
Liechtenstein, Germany (former FRG before unification) and Austria.
Northern Europe = Norway, Sweden, Finland and Denmark.
Southern Europe = Italy, Spain, Portugal and Greece.
Central and Eastern Europe = Czech Republic, Slovakia, Poland, Hungary,
Slovenia, Romania, Bulgaria, Latvia, Lithuania, Estonia, Ukraine, Russian
Federation, Germany (former GDR), Croatia, the former Republic of Macedonia,
Serbia and Montenegro, Bosnia and Herzegovina, Moldova, Georgia and
Armenia.
Source: Recent Demographic Developments in Europe 2004. Council of Europe
on http://www.coe.int/t/e/social_cohesion/population/Demo2004EN.pdf

Czech fertility rates fluctuated between 2.8 and 1.8, but since 1996, Czech
total fertility rates have been fluctuating between 1.2 and 1.1.

Current theories of the postponement of childbearing and increase in childlessness in CEE: ideational shifts, individualism, and socio-economic uncertainty

The fact that fertility changes took place much later and more rapidly in
CEE than elsewhere in Europe is related to the different social, political,
and economic conditions in the former East and West European blocs and
the limited contacts between them. A number of interrelated factors,

specific to the 'state socialist' era have been identified, including: a) a shortage of high-quality contraception and a reliance on abortion; b) insufficient motivation to achieve higher education because of wage-levelling, and limited chances of self-fulfilment, within the labour market; c) limited leisure-time opportunities, in particular, travel; d) a small proportion of university educated people within the population as a whole; e) the necessity and practice of intensive inter-generational family support (and thus also control), due to a lack of services and goods for families; f) the perception of the family as a private haven; and g) pro-population measures applied in many Central and Eastern European countries (CEECs) that gave advantageous treatment to young married couples with children born early after the marriage (Frejka, 1983; Popov & David, 1999; van de Kaa, 1996; Macek et al., 1998; Macura et al., 2000; Možný, 2002; Rabušic, 2001a; Sobotka, 2004; Večerník, 1999).

In the Czech Republic (previously a part of Czechoslovakia), changes occurred from pre-communist to communist times, and again in the post-communist era. Age at first marriage and first birth dropped and remained low during the period of the communist regime. Early marriages and childbearing were supported by interest-free loans and supportive housing policy for young married couples with children born shortly after the marriage that were applied in the 1970s. Marriage and parenthood usually preceded the establishment of a career at a time of communist wage-levelling and virtually guaranteed jobs.

Many scholars interpret current demographic changes in post-communist countries, including the postponement of childbearing and increased childlessness, with reference to the theory of a 'second demographic transition' and a focus on the role of value changes (van de Kaa 1997, 1998). Others, however, regard fertility changes in CEE as a consequence of socio-economic constraints and uncertainty associated with social and economic transformations. The two approaches are not mutually exclusive, however, because the constraining crisis factors and broad ideational shifts may indeed operate together (Philipov, 2003; Lesthaeghe & Surkyn, 2002).

The ideational shifts are characterised as long-term transitions in values and life orientations towards individualism and self-expression. It is argued that ideational shifts in the region were speeded up by contacts between the 'East' and the 'West' after the fall of the former Eastern European bloc, as socio-economic and political transformation in CEE brought about a wider range of possibilities for individual self-fulfilment (Rabušic, 2001).[1] The main driving force behind these changes is regarded as a long-term shift in attitudes that started before 1989 in the region and, according to Možný (2002) and Rabušic (2001), found its expression in political changes in 1989. However, Čermáková et al. (2002) emphasise that people from different socio-demographic groups have varying (and unequal) chances to make use of the new opportunities connected to consumption, leisure and investments in education and labour market position. This differentiation is also stressed within the other explanatory framework relating to fertility patterns in CEE, which focuses on the influence of external socio-economic constraints. These constraints include: unemployment and fear of unemployment and thus greater socio-economic uncertainty; the cutting back of social security systems, including the abolition of pro-population policies, leading to higher direct costs of childbearing; and an increase in income differentiation resulting in greater poverty and self-identification with the poor within some groups. All of these constraints stem from the socio-economic and political transformations in CEE after 1989 (Večerník, 1999; Kuchařová & Tuček, 1999; Rychtaříková, 2003; Čermáková et al., 2002).

Kohler, Billari and Ortega (2002: 656) use the term 'strategic postponement' when referring to the situation in CEE, where long-term commitments are deferred 'in the expectation that the uncertainty about future prospects will be reduced over time'. However, Huinink and Kreyenfeld (2004: 24) found evidence in East Germany that unemployment might in fact accelerate childbearing. Using Czech data, Kantorová (2004: 265) found that educated women, for whom the opportunity costs of childbearing have increased considerably, seem to postpone family formation until after the consolidation of employment. Less educated women, however, are more at risk of job loss in the current labour market, and have few career opportunities. For these women, the difference between earned income and welfare benefits may be relatively unimportant, in which case motherhood may be perceived to reduce uncertainty.

The explanations of current fertility changes in CEE that emphasise the effects of ideational changes are embedded in theories of individualisation and cultural change. Such theories point to growing individualism and autonomy, increasing emphasis on postmodern values, democratisation within heterosexual partnerships, and a weakening of traditional means of social control within developed and prosperous societies (Giddens, 1992; De Singly, 1999; Lesthaeghe, 1995). According to Inglehart (1995, 1997), the current change in values and lifestyle orientations should be understood as the consequence of a 'silent revolution' which started in developed, prosperous, western countries after World War II, but emerged later in CEE. An ideational change towards individualism may, however, be contrary to investments such as raising children.

Other explanations of current fertility changes in CEE that emphasise the effect of external socio-economic barriers have links with rational choice models of fertility (Becker, 1991). The proponents of this view stress that the desire for children is constrained by the costs of childbearing, and call for family policies to reduce the costs of childbearing. Yet further explanations of current fertility changes, focusing on the effect of external socio-economic barriers, draw on social anomie theory, in which authors emphasise the effects of overall crisis, uncertainty, discontinuity and stress during the socio-economic and political transformations within the region. The theory of social anomie differs from gradual ideational changes, as it focuses on the effects of sudden change and discontinuity (Philipov, Spéder & Billari, 2005).

Gender equity in fertility theory and research on postponed childbearing and increased childlessness in CEE

In recent years, an alternative theory has been developed by McDonald (2000a; 2000b; 2002), who argues that modern-era capitalism and its associated institutions bring about very low fertility. Like Beck (1992) and Blossfeld and Mills (2003), he perceives the increasingly competitive nature of labour in the market economies as interfering with childbearing plans and family life, with risk-averse individuals avoiding life-long commitments and therefore remaining childless.

Beck (1992) argues that life in market societies supports a value framework which is suitable for the principle of rationality, preferring mobile, free and childless individuals with no commitments who are able to readily react to changing market requirements, rather than established family life. Current socio-demographic changes are therefore caused by the tension between the market and the family. While the family (an altruistic domain) pursues a long-term aim of reproduction, the market is oriented to short-term goals, in which individualism, competitiveness and mobility are of the greatest importance. As a result, the rationality of market economies does not provide enough space for raising children. In other words 'the labour market demands mobility without regard to personal circumstances . . . The market subject is ultimately the single individual, "unhindered" by a relationship, marriage or family. . . . the ultimate market society is a childless society' (Beck, 1992: 116).

Similarly, McDonald (2000a; 2000b; 2002) argues that in increasingly liberalised markets, people are simultaneously expected to be 'competitive, individualistic and risk averse' at work, yet in the family be 'self-sacrificing, altruistic and risk accepting'. Macura and MacDonald (2003: 62) summarise the argument as follows: 'Switching from one mode to another within a 24-hour cycle simply does not work and the "competitive, individualistic and risk averse" triad gets the upper hand, driving, inter alia, their partnership and reproductive behaviour, resulting in low fertility.'

According to McDonald (2000a; 2000b; 2002), low fertility results from the contrast between a relatively high level of gender equity in modern institutions, oriented towards individuals (such as educational systems or labour markets), and the persistence of a low degree of gender equality in the institutions and spheres that deal with individuals as members of groups or families (such as industrial relations in terms and conditions of employment, family services, the tax system, social security and the family itself). Specifically, 'if women are provided with opportunities near to equivalent to those of men in education and market employment, but these opportunities are severely curtailed by having children, then, on average, women restrict the number of children to an extent which leaves fertility at a precariously low, long-term level' (McDonald, 1997).

International comparisons show that at present, fertility rates are higher in European countries (especially northern European countries) with the most liberal attitudes towards gender roles and relatively good opportunities for the harmonisation of paid work and parenthood, than in other European countries (especially southern European countries), in which rather conservative (traditional) attitudes towards gender roles and a lack of opportunities for the harmonisation of paid work and parenthood persist (McDonald, 2005). For example, in the former West Germany, the pressures of the social security system, the lack of public childcare institutions and, in particular, a persisting normative standard of stay-at-home mothers for pre-school and young school-age children, have led to a situation where almost 30 per cent of women aged 35–39 are now childless, and 17 per cent of childless women aged 20–39 would prefer to remain childless. Among women graduates, these percentages are even higher.

Even though a 'gender equity approach' has not been systematically used to explain fertility changes in CEE to date, the socio-economic transformations in CEE have created:

a) a shift from a centrally managed economy and full employment to a competitive market economy
b) a country-specific drop in the number of childcare facilities (e.g. Macura & McDonald, 2003)
c) a shift from paternalist social security systems to more 'safety-net' social security systems (Čermáková et al., 2002)

d) an increase in the importance of education and vertical labour market mobility (Večerník, 1999)
e) an increase in opportunities for work, free-time and study, but also demands in terms of time and mobility, and a decrease in labour market security (Čermáková et al., 2002).

There also remain:

f) the most traditional opinions on gender roles and gender division of household tasks in Europe (ISSP, 2002)
g) the lowest part-time job opportunities in Europe (Council of Europe, 2003)
h) a relatively high level of full-time labour market participation of women (Council of Europe, 2003), as well as a high desire for women to participate in the labour market (ISSP, 2002).

Thus, it might be argued that the 'gender equity' theoretical approach provides good understanding of current fertility changes within CEE. It seems a reasonable assumption to make that interactions among the factors listed above contribute to conflict between women's roles, a postponement of childbearing and an increase in childlessness in the region.

Given the long-term and extensive participation of women in the labour markets of CEE and their perception that they are (co)-breadwinners, the dual-income model is prevalent overall. More than 80 per cent of ISSP 2002 respondents in CEECs agreed with the statement: 'Both women and men should contribute to household income'. Nevertheless, traditional opinions relating to gender roles (with the man as the main breadwinner and the woman as secondary breadwinner, as well as the main carer of children and household) are more prevalent in CEECs than in other European countries (see Figure 5.2).

A high level of women's labour market participation, together with conservative attitudes towards gender roles, has led to an extensive 'double-burden' for women in the former Eastern European bloc. Since the 1990s, due to changes in labour markets and social security systems in the region (reducing the number of childcare facilities[2] and increasing the retirement age[3] included), the conflict between conservative gender roles, women's willingness to have a paid job and the prevailing need for two incomes in a family, has increased. Minimal opportunities to work part-time in CEE (see Figure 5.3) have also contributed to reduced confidence in the possibilities of combining paid work and motherhood in CEE than in other European countries (see Figure 5.4).

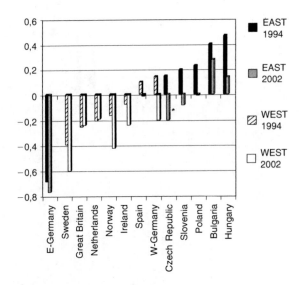

Figure 5.2: Agreement with the statement 'A man's job is to earn money; a woman's job is to look after the home and family' (% in 1994 and 2002 in European countries, ISSP data)

Source: ISSP 1994 and 2002.

Note: Similar results were obtained through the comparison of the percentages of agreement with other gender-conservative questionnaire questions tested in the ISSP research: 'A job is all right, but what most women really want is a home and children' and 'It is not good if the man stays at home and cares for the children and the woman goes out to work.'

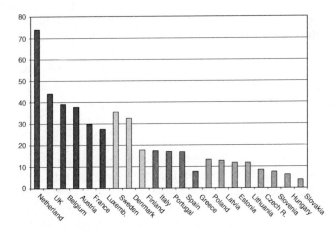

Figure 5.3: Percentage of part-time working women among the total numbers of employed women in European countries in 2003

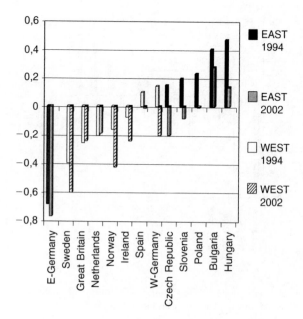

Figure 5.4: Confidence in the possibilities of combining paid work with motherhood in 1994 and 2002 in Europe
Source: ISSP 1994 and 2002.

The values in Figure 5.4 were calculated on the basis of coded responses from respondents according to the degree to which they agreed or disagreed with the following three statements: 'All in all, family life suffers when the woman has a full-time job'; 'A pre-school child is likely to suffer if his or her mother works' and 'A working mother can establish just as warm and secure a relationship with her children as a mother who does not work'. Values over 0 indicate a lack of confidence in the possibilities of combining paid work with motherhood and values below 0 signal positive evaluations of such opportunities.

Conclusion

In this chapter, I have outlined current debates relating to fertility decline, postponement of childbearing and the increase in childlessness in CEE, and explored some of the explanatory frameworks that have been adopted, as well as the theoretical approaches on which they are based. I then highlighted a gender equity theoretical approach to studies of fertility decline in CEE, which has not previously been systematically applied. By identifying several dimensions that could be analysed in future country (and possibly also class-specific) comparative studies on fertility changes in CEECs, I have attempted to demonstrate its potential contribution to this area of study. These include (amongst others) the most traditional attitudes towards gender roles amongst the European countries, the most limited opportunity for part-time work amongst European countries, and the country-specific decline in childcare facilities and changes in social security systems within CEE (e.g. social policies resulting, through interactions with conditions in the labour market, in an increase in women's day-long childcare for children up to the age of four in the Czech Republic – see Hašková, 2005). These factors contribute to people living within Central and Eastern Europe having the lowest level of confidence, amongst the European countries, in the possibilities of combining childcare with work responsibilities.

Data sources

Census of people, houses and flats. 2001. Prague: Czech Statistical Office.

Council of Europe 2003 on www.czso.cz.

ISSP 1994 – an international representative longitudinal questionnaire survey on work and family life (33,590 respondents from 24 regions in the world; 1024 respondents from the Czech Republic). The survey lasted from 1993 till 1995. It followed the ISSP 1988 survey.

ISSP 2002 – an international representative longitudinal questionnaire survey on work and family life (42,793 respondents from 33 regions in the world; 1289 respondents from the Czech Republic). It followed the ISSP 1994 survey.

Recent Demographic Development in Europe 2002. Council of Europe on http://www.coe.int/t/e/social_cohesion/population/demographic_year_book/2002_Edition.

Notes

1. Ideational shifts are usually measured by shifts in opinions and attitudes of populations in longitudinal surveys even though there is much critique on measuring values and life orientations (ideational shifts) by measuring opinions and attitudes.
2. In the Czech republic, as the result of the drop in the availability of childcare facilities for children under three years of age, today's capacities can only accommodate 3 per cent of the total number of children who would have been easily placed in such facilities in 1989 in the CR. Childcare facilities for pre-school children from three years of age have been reduced by about one-quarter which roughly corresponds to the birth rate decline in the CR.
3. This fact problematises the previously extensive use of grandmothers for childcare.

6

Main Patterns in Attitudes to the Articulation Between Work and Family Life: a Cross-National Analysis

Karin Wall

Introduction

This chapter examines one of the most important social changes that has taken place over the last few decades in the articulation between work and family life – the changes in the attitudes, expectations and practices related to women's work, particularly women with families and children. In the European Union (15 member states) female employment rates have been rising since the 1950s and stood at 54 per cent in 2001 (Eurostat, 2003).

Changes in both the attitudes to and the economic behaviour of women has led social analysts to underline the erosion of the 'male breadwinner model' of work/family life, where men were assumed to provide for the family ('breadwinning') whilst women took the major responsibility for childcare, housework and family life ('unpaid homemaking and care-giving'). Along with the continuing decline of the 'male provider/female carer' model is the anticipation of an increase both in women's work and in new attitudes to specific forms of articulation between work and family life, such as the dual earner/dual carer model and mothers' work outside the home (Lewis, 1993; Beck et al., 1995; Crompton, 1999).

However, although the gap between men and women's labour force participation has narrowed, gender differences are still substantial: men have a much higher employment rate (73 per cent), occupational segregation limits the choice of women entering or re-entering the labour market, female unemployment rates are higher, and part-time work is highly femininised (33 per cent of women in employment are working part-time, compared with only 6 per cent of men) (Eurostat, 2003). Research has also shown that men's employment patterns over the life-course are predominantly 'full-time, always-working' trajectories, whereas women still have a variety of patterns: 'stay-at-home' trajectories, 'in and out of full-time work' trajectories, 'full-time, always-working' trajectories, 'full-time alternating with part-time work' or simply 'part-time earner' trajectories (Wall & Guerreiro, 2005). As a result, the paid division of labour, in families of couples with children, is rarely a full-time, dual-earner division of labour. In fact, in several European countries – West Germany, Ireland, Spain, Italy, Luxembourg – the male breadwinner/full-time housewife pattern is still a predominant, even if not the only, pattern (Franco & Winqvist, 2002).

Attitudes and norms, on the other hand, have been shown to be more favourable to women's and mother's work in some countries than in others. In general, attitudes are classified along a conservative–liberal continuum (or a traditional–modern one) and roughly portrayed according to three patterns: a 'modern' (dual-earner/dual carer) pattern, where women are more work-orientated; a 'traditional' pattern (male earner/female carer); and an intermediate pattern ('one and a half earner', also labelled the 'adaptive' pattern (Hakim, 2003)), where women are said to prefer to adjust their working hours to fit in with their caring responsibilities. The persistence of diversity in attitudes towards work/family articulation has been attributed to different factors – social, cultural, labour market constraints, public policies (lack of childcare services, for example), family preferences, etc. – but there is an expectation, based on the past increase in women's work, that the societal movement toward gender equality and individuation will imply a development of the 'dual full-time earner/dual carer' model. Within this 'modern' cultural model of articulation between work, childcare and family life, both partners in two parent households have professional careers, both participate in childcare and household tasks, and reconciliation between work and family is not only negotiated within the couple but is also supported by family-friendly workplaces and by governmental measures, such as leave and childcare services. Sweden and the other Nordic countries are usually considered as the main advocates of this modern integration of work and family life.

Other studies in cross-national perspective have mapped slightly different attitudinal patterns to married/cohabiting[1] women's employment. Treas and Widmer (2000), on the basis of a cluster analysis of 23 countries, found three broad attitude clusters: a work-orientated pattern where respondents are more likely to endorse women's paid work overall and mothers' part-time paid work when there are pre-schoolers (represented by Sweden, Norway, Israel, the Netherlands, Canada, the US); a family-accommodating pattern that supports a traditional, gender-based family division of labour (Austria, West Germany, Australia, Great Britain, Italy,

Japan); and a motherhood-centred pattern, with very strong preferences for women with children to stay at home (Bulgaria, Czech Republic, Hungary, Ireland, Poland, Slovenia, Spain). The authors emphasise that there is a remarkably high country-to-country similarity in attitudes. Despite some minor differences (which reflect welfare regimes), they conclude that there is a high level of agreement that mothers with children should reduce their labour force involvement by staying at home or working part-time.

In this chapter, I explore the diversity in attitudinal patterns to work/family articulation and the factors which influence them. Although attitudes are not the only factor influencing work/family practices, they are important, and they do not seem to be converging in a simple fashion towards the so-called 'modern' model or even the 'one and a half earner' model. Methodologically, this means that we will be challenging the idea of a cultural attitudinal change moving in one direction and trying to examine in greater depth the new ways in which norms and attitudes are evolving.

To develop an analytical strategy that might help us to identify different attitudinal patterns, we draw on recent analysis of gender regimes and the family/work system. Theoretical discussions have shown that it is essential to take into account various dimensions underpinning the cultural construction of work/family integration. Two important dimensions concern the attitudes to the family division of paid work and the family division of unpaid work. Beliefs and expectations concerning who should work outside the home (full-time or part-time), who should care for young children and be responsible for housework, who should spend more time at work or at home, are fundamental in order to understand families' and individuals' attitudes toward managing work and family life. For example, strong agreement with the ideal of the husband as main provider and the wife as secondary provider (part-time work) will make it difficult for the mother not to assume her conventionally assigned role of main childcarer and homemaker.

Recent discussions regarding gender regimes have also shown that it is essential to take into account the social construction of motherhood (Leira, 1992; McMahon, 1995; Pfau-Effinger, 1999). Motherhood may be interpreted in different ways, as a long phase of life in which (i) the special tasks of caring totally absorb women's capacity for work, thereby excluding maternal employment altogether; (ii) only certain periods absorb women's capacity for work, an approach which advocates that maternal employment during certain periods of the life-course has a negative impact on family life and the mother's relationship with children, particularly young children or (iii) motherhood does not absorb women's capacity for work and maternal employment does not have a negative impact on children and should be managed alongside childcare and family responsibilities.

A further significant dimension is the cultural construction of the relationship between working parents and the Welfare State. In European societies, we have different ideological frameworks regarding the articulation between family and state. One point of view is that care for children may be regarded primarily as the task of the state. The underlying ideal, in this context, is that children are future citizens, and therefore the state is seen as more competent in fulfilling the task of care and education than private households. Caring for children, however, may alternatively be considered as a family task – the underlying attitude being that children need special care and support (usually by the mother) to become competent and balanced individuals. This alternative ideological framework is quite strong in Southern European countries but it is also present in other countries and seems to be part of an ongoing policy debate in most European countries.

The chapter will be divided into two main parts. First, the measures we derived using data from the International Social Survey Programme's Family and Gender Relations module, which was fielded in 2002, are briefly described. I then focus on attitudinal patterns to work/family articulation in seven different countries: Portugal, Spain, the Czech Republic, West Germany, Great Britain, France and Sweden. The main criterion for choosing these countries was to introduce diversity in different welfare regimes (Esping-Andersen, 1990), to include one example of an ex-state-socialist country, and to have countries with varying levels of female economic participation (see Appendix 6C). In the second part, I examine the impact of different factors in shaping these patterns: social factors (education, political positioning, religious attendance); work and work/life factors (the number of weekly working hours and the level of work/family stress); and demographic factors (age, sex, marital situation and household composition) (Appendix 6B).

Cross-national variations in attitudinal patterns to work/family articulation

For the seven countries under discussion, we derived three different measures which are related to the above-mentioned dimensions. A division-of-paid-work index was computed from the individual responses to the five following statements and one question (α: 0.68 for the seven countries):

- A job is all right but what most women want is a home and children
- Being a housewife is just as fulfilling as working for pay
- Having a job is the best way for a woman to be independent

- Both the man and the woman should contribute to household income and family
- Do you think women should work outside the home (part-time, full-time, not at all) when there is a child under school age?

A division-of-unpaid-work index was computed from the individual responses to the following statements (Pearsons' correlation = 0.70, $p < 0.001$ for the seven countries):

- Men ought to do a larger share of the household work than they do now
- Men ought to do a larger share of childcare than they do now.

Finally, a maternal-employment index was computed from the individual responses to the following three statements (α: 0.72 for the seven countries):

- A working mother can establish just as warm and secure a relationship with her children as a mother who does not work
- A pre-school child is likely to suffer if his or her mother works
- All in all, family life suffers when the woman has a full-time job.

Tables 6.1 and 6.2 show the main patterns in family/work attitudes in Portugal and Great Britain. Higher scores (close to five) are indicative of greater work/family conservatism, lower scores (close to one) of greater work/family liberalism. As can be seen from Table 6.1, five main patterns of attitudes to family/work articulation were identified in Portugal.[2] The *strong traditional* pattern is conservative on all three indexes, meaning that, overall, individuals strongly agree with the male breadwinner/mother stay-at-home carer model. On the contrary, the *strong traditional modified* pattern of articulation is very conservative in terms of the division of paid work and the maternal employment index but very liberal concerning the division of unpaid labour. This is an interesting pattern, indicating a model in which individuals support segregated roles in terms of paid work but also want some sharing inside the home. In other words, it reveals a pattern of work/family articulation in which individuals advocate a male breadwinner model with respect to paid work, but find it difficult to accept the norm of total gender separation in daily domestic life, as if the values of modern family life – emphasising companionship, sharing, communication – imply a certain refusal of gender differentiation at home even when the husband is the main provider.

The *modern strong motherhood* pattern is quite different from the previous patterns, being liberal in relation to the division of paid work and unpaid work, but extremely conservative in relation to *maternal employment*.

Underlying this pattern is therefore another type of ambiguity, based on the contradiction between strong support for egalitarian professional roles and carer/homemaker roles accompanied by strong support for mothers who do not work full-time, as this has a negative impact on young children and family life. In Portugal, advocates of this work/family attitudinal pattern are supportive of part-time work for women when children are young (71 per cent), as in most of the seven countries (Table 6A.1, Appendix 6A).

The fourth pattern – the *modern moderate* – has scores that are close to the average scores on all three indexes; compared to the *modern motherhood*, however, it does not endorse dual-earning as strongly and, when mothers have young children, respondents are divided between support for stay-at-home and part-time working mothers. Finally, the *strong modern* pattern has scores which are much higher on all three indexes, indicating strong endorsement of the dual earner and the dual carer models of

Table 6.1: Main attitudinal patterns to work/family articulation – Portugal (average scores for 3 indexes*) (n = 1004)

Main attitudinal patterns	%	3 indexes – average scores*		
		Division of Paid Work Index (Portugal: $\alpha = 0.55$; 7 countries: $\alpha = 0.68$)	Division of Unpaid Work Index (Portugal: 0.51, $p = 0.000$; 7 países: 0.70; $p = 0.000$)	Maternal Employment Index (Portugal: $\alpha = 0.60$; 7 countries: $\alpha = 0.72$)
Strong traditional	8.4	2.91	2.59	2.70
Strong traditional modified	25.6	2.54	4.16	1.82
Modern strong motherhood	28.1	3.56	4.37	2.25
Modern moderate	23.1	3.01	4.12	3.10
Strong modern	14.8	4.01	4.46	3.88
All individual responses	**100.0**	**3.18**	**4.12**	**2.61**
Variance analysis		$F(4,999) = 354.83$, $p < .000$, $Eta^2 = .59$	$F(4,999) = 205.43$, $p < .000$, $Eta^2 = .45$	$F(4,999) = 613.11$, $p < .000$, $Eta^2 = .71$

* Meaning of scale:

1 – Greater Attitudinal Conservatism 5 – Greater Attitudinal Liberalism
(male breadwinner, female homemaker   (dual-earner, dual homemaker and
and carer, negative impact of   carer, no negative impact of
maternal employment)   maternal employment)

work/family articulation, and disagreement with the fact that maternal employment, particularly full-time, has a negative impact on young children and family life.

Compared to Portugal, attitudinal patterns of work/life articulation in Great Britain are more varied. Within the more traditional patterns, there is a distinction between a *strong traditional*, a *strong traditional modified*, and also a *traditional* pattern which comes closer to average scores and is less negative in relation to maternal employment than the previous strong traditional patterns. The other patterns are quite similar to Portugal's, except for a new attitudinal pattern to work/family articulation which we labelled the *modern unequal caring* pattern. In the latter, individuals are quite liberal in relation to the division of paid work and the impact of mother's employment on family life, but very conservative regarding men's participation in the domestic sphere, even more conservative in fact than the individuals in the *strong traditional* pattern. In other words,

Table 6.2:　Main attitudinal patterns to work/family articulation – Great Britain (average scores for 3 indexes) (n = 1494)

Main attitudinal patterns	3 indexes – average scores		
	Division of Paid Work Index (GB: α = 0.38; 7 countries: α = 0.68)	Division of Unpaid Work Index (GB: 0.70; p = 0.000; 7 países: 0.70; p = 0.000)	Maternal Employment Index ((GB: α = 0.45; 7 countries: α = 0.72)
All individual responses	3.03	3.63	3.22
1. Strong traditional	2.45	2.70	1.98
2. Strong traditional modified	2.37	3.98	2.01
3. Traditional	2.79	2.99	3.08
4. Modern strong motherhood	3.11	4.11	2.61
5. Modern unequal caring	3.40	2.62	4.08
6. Modern moderate	2.98	3.99	3.73
7. Strong modern	3.83	4.19	4.29
Variance analysis	$F_{(6,1486)}$ = 320.42, $p < .000$, $Eta^2 = .56$	$F_{(6,1486)}$ = 534.75, $p < .000$, $Eta^2 = .68$	$F_{(6,1486)}$ = 1166.29, $p < .000$, $Eta^2 = .83$

these are individuals who advocate women's paid work and do not think this has a negative influence on family life, but do not agree with the dual carer/homemaker norm, in which men would be expected to do more household tasks and more childcare. In Table 6A.1 (Appendix 6A) we can see that in Great Britain and the other countries where this pattern emerges (Sweden, West Germany, France, the Czech Republic), respondents supporting this type of work/family articulation generally favour part-time work for women when children are pre-school age.

Figures 6.1 to 6.7 show the specific work/family attitudinal patterns and the relative proportions of each within the seven countries. Figures 6.1 and 6.2 highlight the same types of patterns in Portugal and Spain, with very similar proportions with regard to the traditional attitudes. In both countries, the *strong traditional* patterns represent just over one-third of the total (34 and 35 per cent). It is important to note, however, that the *strong traditional modified*, where agreement with a male breadwinner model also includes support for some sharing inside the home, is more popular in both countries than the old-fashioned male-breadwinner/female carer model. When we look at the other patterns, however, we see that the proportion of *modern strong motherhood* is very high in Portugal (28 per cent) whereas in Spain the proportion is lower (16.6 per cent) and the *modern moderate*, more supportive of stay-at-home as well as part-time working mothers, emerges as a more predominant pattern. Overall, however, three main patterns stand out in these two countries: the strong traditional modified, the modern strong motherhood, and the modern moderate.

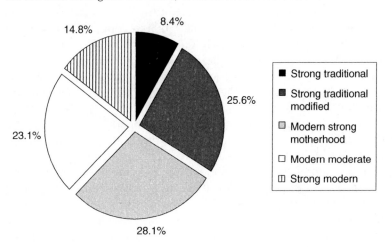

Figure 6.1:   Main attitudinal patterns to work/family articulation, Portugal (%) (n = 1004)

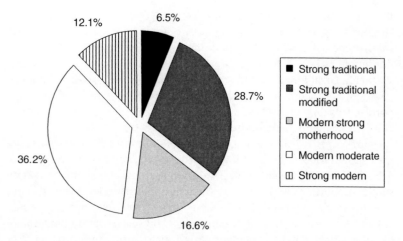

Figure 6.2:   Main attitudinal patterns to work/family articulation, Spain (%) (n = 1993)

The Czech Republic (Figure 6.3) reflects a very different picture, the most striking feature being the very high proportion of *strong traditional* patterns. Together they represent 45 per cent, almost half of all responses. The *modern strong motherhood* is also a predominant pattern, the modern *unequal caring* is very low, and the two more *modern* patterns together stand at 30 per cent, a percentage which is one of the lowest within the seven countries but is nevertheless quite significant if we consider the 16 per cent of the *strong modern*, the main attitudinal pattern in the seven countries which is more supportive of full-time work for mothers over the lifecourse.

West Germany also features very high values in the more traditional male-breadwinner patterns. The *strong traditional* patterns alone represent nearly one-third (31 per cent), and if we include the *traditional* pattern, 46 per cent of the German respondents support more conservative work/family arrangements. For example, in these three aforementioned attitudinal patterns, the majority of German respondents agree that the mother of a pre-school child should stay at home (90 per cent of the *strong traditional*, 83 per cent of the *strong traditional modified* and 62 per cent of the *traditional* respondents). With the other patterns, we can observe that the *modern strong motherhood* represents quite a high proportion (18 per cent), the *modern unequal caring* an average value (8 per cent) and the two *modern patterns*, if taken together, the lowest percentage (28 per cent) of all the seven countries.

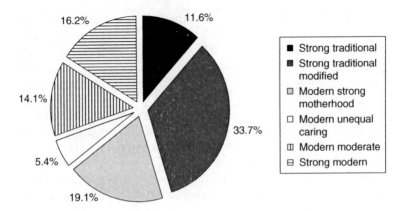

Figure 6.3: Main attitudinal patterns to work/family articulation, Czech Republic (%) (n = 1121)

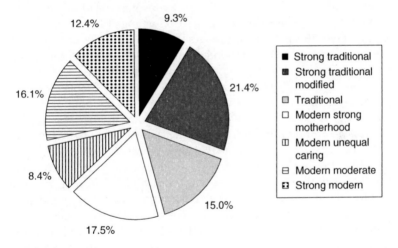

Figure 6.4: Main attitudinal patterns to work/family articulation, West Germany (%) (n = 646)

Great Britain initially appears to be rather similar to West Germany due to the diversity of its patterns. In fact, the differences are quite significant. First, support for the *traditional modified* is not as high as in the two previous countries, bringing supportive attitudes to the more traditional work/family patterns down to roughly one-third (36 per cent) of all respondents. Secondly, the *modern* patterns represent a high proportion (38 per cent in all, with 17 per cent for the *strong modern*; this last percentage is important, especially as this work/family pattern is the only one in Britain in which a majority of respondents advocate part-time employment (82 per cent) or full-time work (14 per cent) for mothers with young children. Finally, work/family attitudes in Great Britain are more evenly spread across the spectrum of patterns than in some other countries, in which two or three particular patterns predominate.

In France, one pattern of attitudes to work/family articulation stands out in relation to others (Figure 6.6). We labelled it the *modern moderate motherhood (mmm)* due to the fact that it behaves similarly on the three indexes as in the other countries, but is slightly less conservative on the *maternal employment* index than either Spain, Portugal, West Germany, Great Britain or the Czech Republic. In other words, the idea that maternal employment has a negative impact on young children and family life is, even in this pattern, less pronounced in France. Nevertheless, the *modern motherhood* French respondents mostly adhere, as in other countries, to the expectation that mothers with young children should work part-time (52 per cent) or stay at home (45.7 per cent) (Table 6A.1) (see Chapter 12). In contrast, in the *modern* pattern the majority of respondents (73.4 per cent) advocate part-time work for mothers, and in the *strong modern* either full-time (54.8 per cent) or part-time work (45.7 per cent). It is also important to note that although the *strong traditional* patterns have lower proportions than the countries above, they still represent 28 per cent. Again, however, it is the *modified* version of the male breadwinner model that is more popular (20 per cent of respondents). Compared to the other countries, the French respondents thus emerge as more supportive of egalitarian gender roles in paid and unpaid work, but also as strongly protective of the mother's role in the home when children are young. Nevertheless, together with Spain and Portugal, half of their strong modern respondents approve of full-time work for mothers with pre-schoolers.

The Swedish attitudinal patterns to work/life articulation (Figure 6.7) are fairly similar to the French in relation to the prominent position of

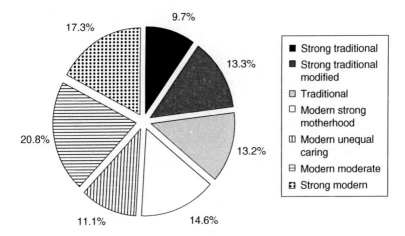

Figure 6.5: Main attitudinal patterns to work/family articulation, Great Britain (%) (n = 1494)

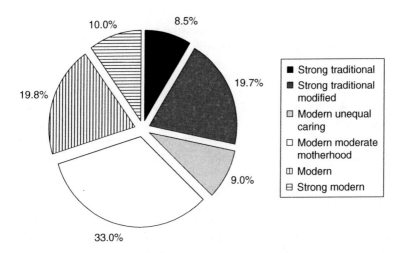

Figure 6.6: Main attitudinal patterns to work/family articulation, France (%) (n = 1546)

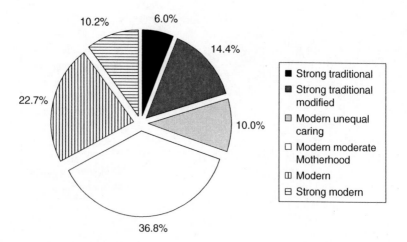

Figure 6.7:   Main attitudinal patterns to work/family articulation, Sweden (%)
(n = 772)

the *modern moderate motherhood* pattern and an average value for the *modern unequal caring* pattern (9 per cent). Nevertheless, compared to the French, who prefer either part-time or stay-at-home mothers, the majority of Swedish *mmm* respondents advocate a work/childcare balance based on mother's part-time work (83.5 per cent). Sweden also marks itself off from the other countries by the low proportions of the *strong traditional* patterns (14 per cent for the *strong traditional modified*, the lowest of all seven countries). Finally, we can see that the *modern patterns* represent, as in several other countries, one-third of the total. However, it is important to mention that, compared to some countries with a lower tradition of part-time work, such as France, Portugal and Spain, where the *strong modern* respondents are more supportive of mothers' full-time work even when the children are young, the majority of *strong modern* respondents in Sweden tend to support part-time work (63.3 per cent) for mothers with young children (Table 6A.1). In summary, Sweden is a country where attitudes have drawn away much more sharply from the male-breadwinner/female carer model (in comparison to all the other countries), but where the majority of respondents advocate a work/family balance with young children centred on mothers' part-time work within a dual earner/dual carer model.

Main factors having an impact on attitudinal patterns to work/family articulation

In order to assess the relative impact of social, demographic and work-related factors (see Appendix 6B), we carried out a logistic regression with some of the main attitudinal patterns as the dependent variable.

The logistic regression on the *strong modern* pattern for all seven countries together (Table 6.3) shows that four variables are associated with this attitudinal pattern to work/family articulation: not being married or cohabiting (i.e. single, divorced); full-time female employment; higher levels of education (more years in school); and lower levels of religious attendance. The influence of two main factors – women's employment situation and levels of education – stand out as the two most important determinants.

Country by country, however, the determining factors vary slightly (Table 6.4). A higher level of education, an important measure of social positioning, continues to be a significant determinant in all countries except Great Britain and the Czech Republic. In the latter, sex (female) is the main shaping factor of *strong modern* attitudes to work/family articulation, whereas in Great Britain, the number of hours women work (more hours) and households with more young children are the only two predictors. The model is also the least predictive of all, and Great Britain thus emerges as a country where strong modern attitudes toward work/family articulation are more likely to be transversal, cutting across social positioning, religious attendance, sex or age.

Table 6.3: Logistic regression on *strong modern* (7 countries) (n = 4037)

	B	Wald	Sig.
Marital situation	0.19	4.09	0.04
Women's employment situation	0.25	102.66	0.00
Education (years in school)	0.09	50.90	0.00
Religious attendance	0.13	25.26	0.00
$R^2 = 0.08$			

If we now look at the most popular of the traditional patterns – the *strong traditional modified* – findings show that, at the level of all seven countries, there is an interaction between several determinants (Table 6.5), some of which are more significant than others, namely: the number of hours

Table 6.4:   Logistic regression on *strong modern*, by country

		B	Wald	Sig.
West Germany	Education (years in school)	0.18	19.08	0.00
$R^2 = 0.17$	Women's employment situation	0.42	23.97	0.00
Great Britain	Number of persons in household	0.48	9.85	0.00
$R^2 = 0.06$	(children below age 5/6)			
	Womens' working hours	0.02	28.40	0.00
Sweden	Age	0.02	28.40	0.00
$R^2 = 0.09$	Sex	−0.03	6.17	0.01
	Education (years in school)	0.70	5.46	0.02
Czech Republic	Sex	0.15	11.80	0.00
$R^2 = 0.06$	Difficulty in fulfilling family	1.01	16.74	0.00
	responsibilities			
Spain	Education (years in school)	0.51	5.90	0.02
$R^2 = 0.11$	Religious attendance	0.06	6.05	0.01
	Number of persons in household	0.17	7.50	0.01
	(children below age 5/6)			
	Women's employment situation	0.01	3.89	0.05
France	Education (years in school)	0.33	26.60	0.00
$R^2 = 0.12$	Religious attendance	0.22	13.98	0.00
	Women's employment situation	0.30	5.25	0.02
Portugal	Education (years in school)	0.23	10.64	0.00
$R^2 = 0.14$	Religious attendance	0.16	24.37	0.00
	Political positioning	0.25	10.80	0.00
	Difficulty in fulfilling family	0.16	3.84	0.05
	responsibilities			
	Men's working hours	0.36	5.01	0.03

women work (less hours), age (older respondents), lower levels of education, a more right-wing political positioning, and the presence of children under five or six years of age in the household. The determining configurations again vary by country (Table 6.6). In the countries where traditional patterns have higher proportions, level of education is the most common factor exerting a major influence. However, Great Britain and the Czech Republic continue to be outliers: being a woman is the only determining factor in the Czech Republic, whilst fewer weekly hours of female work and higher religious attendance are the variables which have an impact in Great Britain (associated nevertheless with an extremely low level of prediction). In the countries where the traditional patterns have lower proportions (Sweden and France), most of the main predictive factors are those emphasised for all the seven countries: age, lower levels of education, higher religious attendance (France only) and a work/life stress factor – more difficulties in concentrating at work (Sweden only).

In summary, we may say that supportive attitudes of the *strong traditional modified* pattern of work/family articulation are quite consistently

Table 6.5: Logistic regression on *strong traditional modified* (7 countries) (n = 4663)

	B	Wald	Sig.
Men's employment situation	0.13	7.14	0.01
Women's employment situation	0.25	14.13	0.00
Women's working hours	−0.02	17.68	0.00
Age	0.02	27.46	0.00
Education (years in school)	−0.06	26.92	0.00
Political positioning	0.07	17.29	0.00
Difficulty in concentrating at work	−0.21	15.38	0.00
Number of persons in household (children below age 5/6)	0.01	24.28	0.00
$R^2 = 0.05$			

Table 6.6: Logistic regression on *strong traditional modified*, by country

		B	Wald	Sig.
West Germany	Education (years in school)	−0.09	4.33	0.04
$R^2 = 0.08$	Marital situation	−0.91	8.01	0.01
Great Britain	Women's working hours	−0.01	4.22	0.04
$R^2 = 0.02$	Religious attendance	−0.16	7.16	0.01
Sweden	Age	0.03	7.63	0.01
$R^2 = 0.11$	Education (years in school)	−0.11	8.78	0.00
	Difficulty in concentrating at work	−0.69	14.70	0.00
	Men's employment situation	0.13	3.79	0.05
Czech Republic	Sex	0.71	14.89	0.00
$R^2 = 0.04$				
Spain	Education (years in school)	−0.05	4.49	0.03
$R^2 = 0.03$	Age	0.02	4.97	0.03
France	Age	0.04	12.75	0.00
$R^2 = 0.11$	Education (years in school)	−0.10	6.56	0.01
	Religious attendance	−0.17	4.75	0.03
	Womens' working hours	0.01	6.15	0.01
Portugal				
$R^2 = 0.12$	Education (years in school)	0.18	19.35	0.00

associated with certain variables, such as lower levels of education (which usually imply lower levels of satisfaction with professional life) and age, often pointed out as important determinants of more conservative attitudes to family life. Nevertheless, it is important not to forget two points. First, other factors which have nothing to do with older and less educated individuals are present in the explanatory models (religious attendance or being married/cohabiting, for example). Secondly, age does not always exert a major influence. Provisionally, we may interpret this to mean that support for the *strong traditional modified* cuts across age groups in some countries and this attitudinal pattern is therefore not necessarily moving systematically in the direction of a decline.

Curiously, the logistic regression on *modern strong motherhood* gives us a very weak predictive model (Table 6.7). When we take into account the five countries within this pattern (Table 6.8), three variables appear to exert some influence: lower educational levels, higher religious attendance and more difficulties in fulfilling family responsibilities. Overall, however, it is the last variable which seems to have a major impact. Country by country, it is also this factor which exerts some influence in Great Britain and Portugal. On the other hand, when we look at the determinants of *modern moderate motherhood* in France and Sweden (Table 6.9), the latter country is also associated with age (older individuals) and a high number of people living in the household, while France is more associated with the above-mentioned variables: more difficulties in fulfilling family responsibilities, less hours of female and male work, lower levels of education and marital situation (unmarried/uncohabiting).

Table 6.7:   Logistic regression on *modern strong motherhood* (5 countries) (n = 2608)

	B	Wald	Sig.
Education (years in school)	−0.03	5.16	0.02
Religious attendance	−0.05	4.72	0.03
Difficulty in fulfilling family responsibilities	−0.21	19.26	0.00
$R^2 = 0.02$			

Finally, the regression carried out on *modern unequal caring* shows an explanatory profile centred on age (younger individuals), married/cohabiting persons, individuals living in households with a large number of members, women who tend not to work full-time and less difficulties in fulfilling family responsibilities (Table 6.10). Situational variables, particularly younger age, and women's part-time work, are therefore the factors that exert an influence, whereas social factors, such as levels of education and political positioning, do not. In summary, findings suggest that the idea of managing work and care through *unequal caring* (in which individuals disagree with men's increased participation in the home) is linked to younger couples where women do not work full-time and individuals experience less stress in carrying out household and caring tasks.

Country by country, it is interesting to examine two or three cases in detail. In France, where this attitudinal pattern has quite a high proportion (9 per cent), four variables are predictive. The factor which exerts a major influence is age (younger individuals), which interacts with three other

Table 6.8: Logistic regression on *modern strong motherhood*, by country

		B	Wald	Sig.
West Germany $R^2 = 0.02$	Marital Situation	0.67	6.05	0.01
Great Britain $R^2 = 0.01$	Difficulty in fulfilling family responsibilities	−0.25	5.82	0.02
Czech Republic $R^2 = 0.01$	Religious attendance	−0.13	4.46	0.04
Portugal $R^2 = 0.02$	Difficulty in fulfilling family responsibilities	−0.25	5.83	0.02
Spain	–	–	–	–

Table 6.9: Logistic regression on *modern moderate motherhood*, by country

		B	Wald	Sig.
Sweden $R^2 = 0.05$	Age	0.03	17.16	0.00
	Total number of people in household	0.25	13.15	0.00
France $R^2 = 0.06$	Education (years in school)	−0.08	5.97	0.02
	Men's working hours	−0.02	11.35	0.00
	Women's working hours	−0.02	6.87	0.01
	Marital situation	0.45	5.19	0.02
	Difficulty in fulfilling family responsibilities	−0.28	8.25	0.00

significant variables: individuals' marital situation (married/cohabiting), sex (men) and fewer difficulties in fulfilling family responsibilities. The fact that this attitudinal pattern of work/family balance is more associated with men is obviously of interest, particularly as individuals advocating this work/family articulation do not agree that men ought to do more household work and childcare. Nevertheless, in Great Britain, where this pattern has a high proportion of 11.1 per cent (Figure 6.5), predictors also

Table 6.10:   Logistic regression on *modern unequal caring* (5 countries) (n = 3546)

	B	Wald	Sig.
Women's employment situation	−0.19	5.07	0.02
Women's working hours	0.02	11.27	0.00
Marital situation	−0.37	7.05	0.01
Age	−0.02	12.57	0.00
Number of persons in household	0.30	8.41	0.00
Difficulty in fulfilling family responsibilities	0.33	22.79	0.00
$R^2 = 0.04$			

Table 6.11:   Logistic regression on *modern unequal caring*, by country

		B	Wald	Sig.
France	Marital situation	−0.94	9.77	0.00
$R^2 = 0.10$	Sex	−0.67	5.94	0.02
	Age	−0.59	21.09	0.00
	Difficulty in fulfilling family responsibilities	0.26	4.02	0.05
Great Britain	Age	−0.03	10.16	0.00
$R^2 = 0.04$	Difficulty in fulfilling family responsibilities	0.34	7.56	0.01
Sweden	Religious attendance	0.18	3.92	0.05
$R^2 = 0.03$	Number of people in household (children below age 5/6)	0.47	7.16	0.01
Czech Republic	Men's employment situation	0.60	11.96	0.00
$R^2 = 0.12$	Religious attendance	−0.29	6.88	0.01
West Germany	Number of people in household (children below age 5/6)	0.80	9.23	0.00
$R^2 = 0.05$	Difficulty in fulfilling family responsibilities	0.39	3.84	0.05

include age (younger individuals) and fewer difficulties in fulfilling fam-ily responsibilities, but sex does not emerge as a significant influence.

Conclusion

A substantial body of research has documented a decline in the male-breadwinner model of work/family articulation, and an increase in more favourable attitudes to married women's work and a dual earner/dual carer model. Nevertheless, research has also shown that, despite the changes in attitudes and practices over the last few decades, gender gaps in employ-ment and in unpaid work are still considerable. Some authors have even emphasised that the general move is in the direction of a model based on the acceptance of women's employment, coupled with the view that mothers with children should work fewer hours or not at all, rather than one based on the norm of full-time employment for married women across the life-course (Treas & Widmer, 2000).

The aim of this chapter has been to look at the diversity in attitudes to work/family articulation and to try to identify and compare current attitu-dinal patterns within each country (seven in all). By establishing a country analysis as well as a cross-national one, our objective was to understand the attitudinal diversities and contrasts which are developing in European society in relation to work/family articulation. Rather than the idea of a consensual move in the direction of a *dual earner/dual carer* model or in the direction of a *one and a half earner/mother carer* model, we sought to provide a methodological context allowing for the analysis of different patterns.

Our findings suggest that there are a variety of attitudinal patterns to work/family articulation within each country. Some correspond quite clearly to the work/family articulation endorsed by traditional gender and family ideologies. For example, the male breadwinner/female stay-at-home carer model (labelled *strong traditional*), albeit a minority pat-tern (varying between 6 and 12 per cent), is identifiable in all seven countries. The fact that it is a minority pattern does not necessarily mean it is disappearing; in fact, cross-tabulation by age and sex shows, in some countries, that it is not only the older generations but also a sig-nificant proportion of the 30–44 male age group that endorses this type of work/family articulation (Wall, 2006).

At the opposite end of the spectrum, we find a *strong modern* attitudinal pattern, with only low to medium proportions (between 10 and 17 per cent), but it is interesting to see that this is the only pattern in all countries which emerges as strongly supportive of the dual-earner/dual carer/employment for mothers with young children with no negative impacts. Even so, within this strong support for the dual earner/dual carer model, attitudes vary toward the type of employment for mothers with young children. In Sweden, the country with the lowest proportions of traditional patterns, we find that two-thirds of strong modern respondents advocate part-time work for mothers with pre-schoolers (in practice, more than two-thirds of mothers with pre-schoolers are at home or in part-time work (Table 6C.2, Appendix 6C). In 'conservative' West Germany, this proportion of strong modern individuals advocating part-time work rises to 81 per cent, in the Czech Republic to nearly 70 per cent and in 'liberal' Great Britain to 82 per cent (in all three countries, less than a quarter of mothers with pre-schoolers actually work full-time). A different situation occurs in France, where family policy until the late 1990s strongly supported childcare services for pre-schoolers rather than longer leaves, as in the Scandinavian countries. In France, more than half of all strong modern respondents advocate full-time work for mothers with pre-schoolers and 42 per cent of mothers effectively work full-time (Table 6C.2). In Portugal, where part-time work is rare and family policy has boosted childcare services since the late 1980s, a similar situation emerges: 42 per cent of the strong modern respondents advocate full-time work and 66 per cent of mothers with young children actually work full-time. Finally Spain, an outlier in this context, has *strong modern* respondents with similar attitudes to the French and Portuguese respondents (62 per cent think mothers with young children should work full-time) but only a quarter of women with children below school age actually work full-time. In contrast with Portugal, where political changes in 1974 led to strong support for women's employment and later on to the development of childcare services, public policies in Spain have lagged behind in terms of support for married women's employment: paid leaves are short, as in other Southern European countries, and childcare services have only been consistently developed over the last decade in some regions (Escobedo, 2005).

If some attitudes are clearly very traditional or modern in all countries, analysis also shows the development of other specific patterns. Two attitudinal patterns to work/family articulation stand out as particularly significant today. First, findings reveal a new traditional pattern (*strong traditional modified*: percentages between 15 and 36 per cent) which strongly supports the model of the male breadwinner/female carer/stay-at-home mother with young children, while advocating the increased participation of the male breadwinner in caring and household tasks. In other words, gender segregation is endorsed at the level of the family division of paid work as long as there is some sharing and involvement by the father/husband in the home and in childcare. Secondly, data point to a *modern motherhood* pattern (with high values in most countries, varying between 15 and 37 per cent) where individuals are strongly in favour of the dual earner/dual carer model, but believe maternal employment has a negative impact on young children. Contrary to the aforementioned *strong traditional modified*, this attitudinal pattern favours part-time working mothers rather than stay-at-home mothers. Curiously, while the first pattern is strongly associated with lower levels of education, older age groups and more pre-schoolers in the household, the second pattern is mainly associated with difficulties in fulfilling family responsibilities and hardly at all with social or demographic factors.

Apart from these two more significant patterns, a third pattern, *modern unequal caring*, which is endorsed by only 5 to 10 per cent of respondents in some countries, strongly supports women's work and maternal employment but does not endorse increased male participation in childcare and household tasks. Part-time work for mothers with young children is advocated, but attitudes also spill over in favour of full-time work. In summary, this makes for a dual earner/unequal caring model in which attitudes are not opposed to maternal employment but do not support equality inside the home. In France, for example, it is associated with young men, rather than women, who are married or cohabiting (and this may be associated with the relatively high levels of domestic traditionalism in France, see Chapters 7 and 12).

In identifying attitudinal patterns in these seven rather different countries, we have shown, as might have been anticipated, that countries which have been placed as more 'modern' in relation to work/family articulation (such as Sweden and France) are in fact made up of a diversity of attitudinal patterns. For example, 'modern' Sweden is characterised by its fairly low proportions of *traditional* male-breadwinner patterns, an average proportion of *modern unequal caring*, a high proportion of the *modern motherhood* pattern and quite high proportions of *strong modern* and *modern* patterns. Overall, we can say that, apart from a third of Swedish respondents who are *traditional* in relation to work/family articulation (20 per cent in favour of the male breadwinner model and 10 per cent advocating a dual earner/unequal caring model), the majority of respondents endorse a dual earner/dual carer model in which part-time work for women with young children is a fundamental element of attitudes to work/family articulation.

Cross-national comparisons at the level of the seven countries show some differences, even if some countries are more similar than others. The Czech Republic and West Germany, where nearly half of all respondents advocate traditional patterns, emerge as the countries that are currently highly supportive of the male breadwinner model (even if some respondents also associate it with some sharing in the private sphere). Great Britain presents itself with a wide variety of attitudinal patterns and, compared to West Germany, is less supportive of the male breadwinner models, modified or other, and with higher levels of the strong modern pattern. However, as discussed before, a majority of respondents in all three countries support part-time work for mothers with pre-schoolers (the Czech Republic, however, is more in favour of full-time work than the other two countries). In Portugal and Spain, on the other hand, respondents are on the whole very conservative concerning the impact of maternal employment on children (an attitude which may be partly explained by the fact that both countries emerge as very child-centred in terms of family values; Aboim, 2006) and divide themselves between four patterns: the *strong traditional modified* (but with values well below those of the Czech Republic and West Germany), the *strong motherhood* pattern and the *modern* and *strong modern* patterns. In the latter, however, a high proportion of respondents advocate full-time employment for women with pre-schoolers, a characteristic which draws them nearer to France. Finally, France and Sweden are similar on the low values of the male-breadwinner models and the presence of the modern unequal caring pattern, but differ in relation to their attitudes concerning mother's employment, with a high proportion of strong modern French respondents endorsing full-time rather than part-time employment for mothers with young children.

This chapter has also explored the shaping factors of some of the attitudinal patterns of work/family articulation. It is important to observe that not all the explanatory models are very predictive, and also that the major determining factors for specific patterns are not always the same for all countries. For example, social determinants, namely levels of education, are a major influencing factor of the *strong modern* attitudes to work/family articulation in all countries except for Great Britain, where women's longer working hours are the major influence, and in the Czech Republic, where sex (female) is the main determining factor. On the other hand, social and demographic variables do not always have an important effect on all patterns. The main example of this is the *strong motherhood* pattern, which is not only less predictive, but also seems to cut across social factors and to be mainly influenced by work/life situations, such as difficulties in fulfilling family responsibilities. Of course, the number of independent variables we used are limited and it would be interesting to see if this particular pattern is influenced by other factors such as specific family values (for example, the importance of mothering).

Our discussion so far suggests that we must be careful in interpreting the indicators related to gender roles and work/family articulation in European societies. Rather than subscribe to the idea of a movement in the direction of one or other attitudinal pattern, our data suggest that, within a general cultural context of a contested male-breadwinner model and of strong valorisation of motherhood and childhood, a plurality of attitudinal patterns to work/family articulation exists within and across the different countries. National cultures, political changes, recent and decade-old welfare policies, full-time or part-time working traditions for women and for mothers in particular, can all be detected as influences on current attitudinal patterns to work/life articulation in each country. Rather than leading toward two or three models, however, the restructuring of attitudes to work/family integration seems to have produced a more complex variety of work/family attitudinal patterns. In this short chapter, we have merely carried out an exploratory analysis. The existing variations suggest that further research on this topic should continue to explore not only the interaction between paid and unpaid work, but also how they relate in each country to the restructuring of gender and family ideologies, particularly motherhood, fatherhood, and the value of children.

Appendix 6A: Cross tabulation of attitudinal patterns to work/family articulation, by country, with responses to the statement 'Do you think women should work outside the home – part-time, full-time, not at all – when there is a child under school age' (%)

Table 6A.1

	Full-time	Part-time	Not working	Total
West Germany (n = 646)				
Strong traditional		10.0	90.0	100.0
Traditional	1.0	37.1	61.9	100.0
Strong traditional modified		16.7	83.3	100.0
Modern moderate	1.0	39.4	59.6	100.0
Modern strong motherhood	2.7	79.6	17.7	100.0
Modern unequal caring	5.6	59.3	35.2	100.0
Strong modern	12.5	81.3	6.3	100.0
Total	2.8	45.4	51.9	100.0

(Continued)

Table 6A.1   (Continued)

	Full-time	Part-time	Not working	Total
X^2 = 241.26, DF = 12, p < .000, cf = .52				
Great Britain (n = 1494)				
Strong traditional	0.7	9.7	89.6	100.0
Traditional		20.8	79.2	100.0
Strong traditional modified		2.0	98.0	100.0
Modern moderate		43.9	56.1	100.0
Modern strong motherhood	1.4	43.8	54.8	100.0
Modern unequal caring	11.4	60.5	28.1	100.0
Strong modern	14.3	81.8	3.9	100.0
Total	4.0	40.4	55.6	100.0
X^2 = 640.49, DF = 12, p < .000, cf = .55				
Spain (n = 1993)				
Strong traditional	2.3	16.2	81.5	100.0
Strong traditional modified	1.1	22.1	76.9	100.0
Modern strong motherhood	23.0	69.4	7.6	100.0
Modern moderate	19.4	60.3	20.2	100.0
Strong modern	61.4	38.6		100.0
Total	18.7	45.4	35.9	100.0
X^2 = 1076.58, DF = 12, p < .000, cf = .59				
France (n = 1545)				
Strong traditional		11.4	88.6	100.0
Strong traditional modified		22.4	77.6	100.0
Modern unequal caring	23.0	61.2	15.8	100.0
Modern moderate motherhood	2.4	52.0	45.7	100.0
Modern	7.5	73.4	19.0	100.0
Strong modern	54.8	44.5	0.6	100.0
Total	9.8	47.0	43.2	100.0
X^2 = 824.08, DF = 10, p < .000, cf = .59				
Portugal (n = 1005)				
Strong traditional	13.1	21.4	65.5	100.0
Strong traditional modified	0.4	13.6	86.0	100.0
Modern strong motherhood	16.0	71.5	12.5	100.0
Modern moderate	1.7	48.5	49.8	100.0
Strong modern	42.3	53.7	4.0	100.0
Total	12.3	44.5	43.5	100.0
X^2 = 514.08, DF = 8, p < .000, cf = .58				

Table 6A.1 (Continued)

	Full-time	Part-time	Not working	Total
Czech Republic (n = 1122)				
Strong traditional		21.5	78.5	100.0
Strong traditional modified	1.9	37.8	60.3	100.0
Modern unequal caring	54.1	29.5	16.4	100.0
Modern strong motherhood	15.4	63.1	21.5	100.0
Modern moderate	13.3	60.1	26.6	100.0
Strong modern	27.1	69.1	3.9	100.0
Total	12.7	48.5	38.8	100.0

$X^2 = 411.10$, DF = 10,
p < .000, *cf* = .52

	Full-time	Part-time	Not working	Total
Sweden (n = 772)				
Strong traditional		6.5	93.5	100.0
Strong traditional modified	0.9	43.2	55.9	100.0
Modern unequal caring	26.0	74.0		100.0
Modern moderate motherhood	2.8	83.5	13.7	100.0
Modern	29.7	68.0	2.3	100.0
Strong modern	36.7	63.3		100.0
Total	14.2	66.6	19.2	100.0

$X^2 = 428.10$, DF = 10,
p < .000, *cf* = .60

Appendix 6B: Description and coding of variables used in the regressions (7 countries)

Independent Variables	Coding
Demographic and Social Variables	
Sex	1 male...............2 female
Age	Minimum 18.............maximum 96
Marital situation	1 married/cohabiting ......2 not married/not cohabiting
Number of years in school	0 no schooling.........30 years (95 – still at school; 96 – still at university)
Political positioning: left–right	1 left.............10 right
Religious attendance	1 several times a week......8 never
No. of persons in household (children below age 5/6 years)	0...........................4 children
Total number of people in the household	1...........................14
Work and Work/Life Variables	
Men's employment situation	1 not working; 2 <part-time; 3 part-time; 4 full-time
Women's employment situation	1 not working; 2 <part-time; 3 part-time; 4 full-time
Men's weekly working hours	0...........................96
Women's weekly working hours	0...........................90
Difficulty in fulfilling family responsibilities	1 several times a week......4 never
Difficulty in concentrating at work	1 several times a week......4 never

Appendix 6C: Characteristics of respondents in the seven countries by employment situation and sex

Table 6C.1: Respondents' employment situation (18–65 years)

	7 Countries (n = 8876)	West Germany (n = 775)	Great Britain (n = 1648)	Sweden (n = 903)	Czech Republic (n = 1113)	Spain (n = 1965)	France (n = 1591)	Portugal (n = 882)
Men								
Full-time work	71.9	71.6	73.4	75.8	73.4	69.4	70.1	72.4
Part-time work	3.0	1.1	4.5	4.5	0.6	4.3	2.1	2.6
<part-time	0.8	0.0	0.7	2.1	0.4	1.3	0.3	0.2
Not working	24.3	27.3	21.4	17.5	25.7	24.9	27.5	24.8
Total	100.0	100.0	100.0	100.0	100.0	100.0	100.0	100.0
Women								
Full-time work	42.0	34.2	40.8	46.8	51.7	33.3	44.6	48.1
Part-time work	15.9	16.3	23.7	26.4	3.3	13.6	17.2	6.4
<part-time	2.2	1.3	3.4	2.1	0.5	2.3	2.9	1.3
Not working	39.9	48.2	32.1	24.7	44.4	50.8	35.3	44.1
Total	100.0	100.0	100.0	100.0	100.0	100.0	100.0	100.0
All respondents								
Full-time work	56.1	52.4	55.2	60.4	62.2	51.2	55.9	60.0
Part-time work	9.8	8.9	15.2	16.2	2.0	9.0	10.5	4.5
<part-time	1.5	0.6	2.2	2.1	0.4	1.8	1.8	0.8
Not working	32.6	38.1	27.4	21.4	35.4	38.0	31.8	34.7
Total	100.0	100.0	100.0	100.0	100.0	100.0	100.0	100.0
cf	0.31	0.38	0.33	0.32	0.23	0.34	0.30	0.24

Table 6C.2: Employment situation of respondents with children below age 5/6 (pre-school), by sex

	7 Countries (n = 3530)	West Germany (n = 118)	Great Britain (n = 267)	Sweden (n = 139)	Czech Republic (n = 143)	Spain (n = 306)	France (n = 288)	Portugal (n = 154)
Men								
Full-time work	65.7	86.0	82.7	85.5	84.6	88.7	91.5	82.2
Part-time work	3.1	2.0	0.0	5.8	0.0	4.0	2.1	2.7
<part-time	0.9	0.0	0.0	0.0	1.5	0.0	0.0	0.0
Not working	30.3	12.0	17.3	8.7	13.8	7.3	6.4	15.1
Total	100.0	100.0	100.0	100.0	100.0	100.0	100.0	100.0
Women								
Full-time work	28.3	13.2	24.5	25.7	23.1	26.4	42.3	53.1
Part-time work	14.9	23.5	31.9	32.9	2.6	14.3	25.3	11.1
<part-time	1.8	2.9	0.6	4.3	1.3	2.7	2.6	1.2
Not working	55.0	60.3	42.9	37.1	73.1	56.6	29.9	34.6
Total	100.0	100.0	100.0	100.0	100.0	100.0	100.0	100.0
All respondents								
Full-time work	45.5	44.1	47.2	55.4	51.0	51.6	58.3	66.9
Part-time work	9.5	14.4	19.5	19.4	1.4	10.1	17.7	7.1
<part-time	1.4	1.7	0.4	2.2	1.4	1.6	1.7	0.6
Not working	43.6	39.8	33.0	23.0	46.2	36.6	22.2	25.3
Total	100.0	100.0	100.0	100.0	100.0	100.0	100.0	100.0
cf	0.36	0.59	0.51	0.52	0.53	0.52	0.43	0.30

Notes

1. Hereafter married is used to denote married or cohabiting.
2. These patterns were obtained through a two-step cluster analysis of the three indexes. The first procedure was a hierarchical cluster analysis of the indexes using the Ward method. Having obtained six meaningful clusters, the next procedure was a 'quick cluster' classification, that allowed us to optimise, through cluster centres readjustment, the first hierarchical cluster classification.

7

Occupational Class, Country and the Domestic Division of Labour

Rosemary Crompton and Clare Lyonette

Introduction

The continuing increase in the level of paid employment amongst women raises important questions as to the allocation of domestic work. As the total of paid working hours within households continues to rise, who will carry out the domestic work traditionally undertaken (unpaid) by women? One solution is for men to undertake more caring and domestic work, and Fraser (1994) has argued that this outcome, that is, a move towards a 'universal caregiver' or 'dual earner/dual carer' (Crompton, 1999) society, is a necessary one if true gender equity is to be achieved. Another solution is the 'outsourcing' of childcare and other domestic tasks – that is, to pay someone else (usually another woman) to do them. Alternatively, women can continue to work a 'double shift' – in other words, retain the responsibility for household and domestic work whilst being in paid employment. What is the impact of these rather different solutions? Does it matter who does the housework as long as it gets done? In this paper, we will, in a preliminary fashion, begin to explore these questions.

It remains the case that, in all 'western' countries, despite the fact that women are increasingly in employment, they still take major responsibility for domestic tasks. Empirical evidence suggests that men increased their share of domestic work (following second-wave feminism) during the 1970s and 1980s, but this increase slowed during the 1990s. The recent 'convergence' in men's and women's contribution to domestic work, therefore, is largely a consequence of women doing less, rather than men doing more (Bianchi et al., 2000; Harkness, 2003). The empirical evidence suggests that time availability (whether the woman works full-time, part-time or not at all), as well as extent of the man's working hours (Gershuny et al., 1994; Bianchi et al., 2000; Coltrane, 2000), relative resources (which will of course be linked to time availability) and gender role ideology are all mechanisms that are common to all countries in having an impact on the gender division of household tasks. More 'liberal' gender role ideologies are themselves associated with individual educational levels and occupational class location.

The nature of the gendered division of household tasks also varies by country-specific factors that may be normative as well as structural. The dominance (past or present) of religions, or political regimes, that ascribe 'traditional' roles to women is likely to be associated with continuing domestic traditionalism (Korpi, 2000). State 'welfare regimes' (Esping-Andersen, 1999) also vary in the extent to which they provide alternatives to women's traditional caring responsibilities, and/or promote gender equality. Thus, Geist (2005) for example, has demonstrated that the gender division of household tasks is more traditional in conservative welfare regimes, even when individual-level mechanisms are controlled for.

Our empirical analysis, therefore, will draw upon a number of individual country data sets gathered within the International Social Survey Programme's (ISSP) Family 2002 module (Britain, Finland, France, Norway, and Portugal). In 2002, interviews were carried out with a stratified random sample of 1475 respondents in Norway, 2312 in Britain, 1353 in Finland, 1903 in France, and 1092 in Portugal. The same questions are asked in all countries. The common language of the ISSP is English, and questions are agreed and back-translated in order to ensure cross-national comparability of meaning.

The five countries under investigation in this chapter represent a range of contrasting cases as far as the investigation of the domestic division of labour is concerned. Both Norway and Finland may be described as universal or social democratic welfare states. Universal welfare benefits are associated with a high level of employment for women, and 'state feminist' policies (particularly in relation to childcare) have specifically targeted gender equality in relation to caring work (for example, Brandth & Kvande, 2001). Britain would be considered a 'liberal' welfare state. The individualistic tenor of political and economic liberalism has promoted the idea of equality of men and women, but the separation of the state from civil society means that the nature of the gendered division of labour in the domestic sphere has not been addressed. Although France and Portugal are very different, in the broadest terms they would both be described as 'corporatist' (or conservative) welfare states. Portugal might additionally be described as 'familialist', as the family has generally been regarded as the major provider of welfare.

However, as far as the study of gender, and gender equality, is concerned, France represents an interesting, if rather contradictory, case. There is a history of state support for employed mothers, and indeed, Lewis (1992) has suggested that France represents a 'modified male-breadwinner' welfare state. However, French women were not given the vote until after the Second World War, and did not acquire a number of other formal civil rights until the 1960s (for example, husbands could formally bar their wives from taking up paid employment until 1965). Moreover, the French approach to the question of equality rejects the possibility of 'special' treatment for particular groups as being inherently unequal.[1] Thus 'women' have rarely been identified as a category deserving of particular support or special treatment (for example, support for working mothers is perceived as support for families, rather than for women as such; see Jenson, 1986). The French state has never sought to exclude women from employment, and (in part because of pro-natalist policies), supports for working mothers have been relatively generous. For example, state nursery care (écoles maternelles) has long been available in France. Previous research has demonstrated a high level of support for working women (particularly mothers), but rather more traditionalism in respect of gender stereotyping, as well as in the domestic division of labour (Crompton & Le Feuvre, 2000). Qualitative research has also demonstrated a higher level of domestic traditionalism in France than in Britain (Gregory & Windebank, 2000).

The gendered division of domestic work

Domestic work is not all of a piece, and even when men do undertake household work, they are more likely to carry out some tasks than others. Recent evidence suggests that men are more likely to participate in childcare, shopping and cooking, and less likely to take on less creative and interesting domestic work – particularly cleaning and laundry (Duyvendak & Stavenuiter, 2004). We therefore devised a measure that focused on these most gender-stereotypical, least attractive, household tasks, reasoning that evidence of men's participation in these areas would be indicative of a significant shift away from gender traditionalism. From questions in the ISSP surveys asking who 'usually' carries out a range of household tasks, we constructed the following categorical measure of the domestic division of labour:

1) Traditional = both laundry and cleaning done always or usually by woman
2) Less traditional = woman always or usually does one task; other task shared with man

3) Shared = woman does one task and man does the other; both tasks are shared; one task shared and the other outsourced
4) Non-traditional = man always or usually does both tasks; man does one task and other task shared with woman; man does one task and other task outsourced
5) Outsourced = woman always or usually does one task and other task outsourced; both tasks outsourced.

Our measure includes 'outsourcing' – that is, when either cleaning or laundry is done by another person. It is perhaps a reflection of the low status of cleaning and washing that intuitively, it is widely assumed that it is a matter of indifference as to who carries them out: 'It matters little to most people . . . who vacuums their floors or cleans their toilets' (Folbre & Nelson, 2000: 129), although in practice, it will usually be another woman. Previous research using a categorical measure of the domestic division of labour (Geist, 2005: 28) has included 'outsourcing' within the 'shared' category. The Central Bureau of Statistics in the Netherlands has also produced figures on household tasks which do not differentiate between shared tasks and outsourcing (CBS, 2002). This makes the implicit assumption that 'outsourcing' has either a neutral impact and/or makes things better for the woman with access to it. However, is this a valid assumption to make? The evidence we present indicates that this may not necessarily be the case.

We suggest that it is important to focus on outsourcing given that, with the increase in women's employment, it is also likely to increase in volume. In Europe and the US, the numbers of domestic servants declined sharply during the twentieth century, and it was widely assumed that this occupational category would simply disappear. However, it has recently been suggested that the number of domestic helpers in Europe are now 'very similar to what they were a century ago' (Lutz, 2002: 91). Historically, in Europe and the US the presence of household domestic workers was a measure of the prestige of bourgeois families, whose women did not go 'out to work'. Although family status persists as a rationale for the employment of domestic servants (in some countries more than others), in these days, household domestic workers are more likely to be employed in order to facilitate women's employment. In circumstances in which dual earner households access marketised reproductive work, largely via the hiring of domestic servants, even full-time employment amongst women may easily co-exist with enduring traditionalism in gender relations, as we shall see in the case of Portugal.

A wide range of cross-national evidence (for example, OECD, 2002) has demonstrated that women with higher levels of education (professional

Table 7.1:   Domestic division of labour by country (women in employment only)

	Finland % in country	Norway	Britain	France	Portugal	Total
Traditional	164 (57.5%)	212 (61.6%)	240 (55.0%)	246 (57.9%)	118 (71.5%)	980 (59.2%)
Less traditional	75 (26.3%)	71 (20.6%)	90 (20.6%)	121 (28.5%)	18 (10.9%)	375 (22.7%)
Shared	33 (11.6%)	43 (12.5%)	67 (15.4%)	35 (8.2%)	9 (5.5%)	187 (11.3%)
Non-traditional	10 (3.5%)	8 (2.3%)	18 (4.1%)	4 (0.9%)	1 (0.6%)	41 (2.5%)
Outsourced	3 (1.1%)	10 (2.9%)	21 (4.8%)	19 (4.5%)	19 (11.5%)	72 (4.4%)
Total	285 (100%)	344 (100%)	436 (100%)	425 (100%)	165 (100%)	1655 (100%)

and managerial women) are more likely to remain in continuous employment, and these women are the most likely to have the resources to pay for outsourcing. We will therefore be looking at class, as well as national, variations in outsourcing and its impact. In this paper, our major focus will be on employed women. This is for a number of reasons: first, because the question of domestic work will be particularly acute for employed women, and second, because men consistently report a greater level of involvement in domestic work than women report as being carried out by their male partners. Unfortunately, even with relatively large country samples, this strategy means that our numbers are sometimes rather low. However, we suggest that the importance of the developing trends we investigate justifies this speculative work. Table 7.1 describes, using our categorical measure, the domestic division of labour in the five countries under investigation in this paper.

In all countries, women, even when they are in employment, report that they carry out most of the cleaning and laundry, and only a very small minority of men (in other words, the 'non-traditional' category) are largely responsible for these domestic tasks. If we examine the two 'least traditional' categories – shared and non-traditional – we can see that 15 per cent and more of working women in Finland, Norway and Britain report non-traditional arrangements, as compared to under 10 per cent in France and Portugal. Previous research (Geist, 2005; Gershuny & Sullivan, 2003) has suggested that the extent of non-traditionalism in the domestic division of labour is very similar as between liberal and social democratic welfare regimes, and our findings would support this argument.

Portugal stands out as having a relatively high proportion of outsourcing, which is not surprising as domestic work is one of the largest occupational categories for women in this country. International Labour Organisation (ILO) data for 2000 showed that a total of 518,000 women in Portugal were classified as 'domestic and related helpers, cleaners and launderers', representing a total of 12 per cent of all women in paid employment, as compared to well under 10 per cent in all of the other countries examined here.

Class and gendered domestic work

In all five countries, professional and managerial women were significantly less likely to report a 'traditional' division of domestic labour (ddl) than women in the other two occupational class groupings.[2] In all countries, under 50 per cent of professional and managerial women reported a traditional ddl. The percentage difference in domestic traditionalism between professionals and managerials and 'intermediate' occupational class groupings varied between 31 per cent (Portugal) and 17 per cent (France) – there being less variation between intermediate and routine and manual groupings in ddl traditionalism. As noted above, professional and managerial women are most likely to have access to outsourcing, and in Portugal, this accounted almost entirely for the reduced levels of ddl traditionalism reported by professional women in Portugal, suggesting that professional and managerial men in Portugal carry out very little domestic work (as noted in Chapter 3, men in the Mediterranean countries carry out only low levels of domestic work). Thirty four per cent of managerial and professional women in Portugal used outsourcing, and the extent of *shared* ddl reported by Portuguese working women, even in the 'managerial and professional' category, was very low. In the other countries, however, the lower level of traditionalism reported by professional and managerial women was a consequence of more help from their partners. In Britain, Finland and Norway, over 20 per cent of professional and managerial women reported a shared or non-traditional ddl, and in each of these countries, there was a 10 percentage point difference between professionals/managerials and intermediate/manuals in the extent of domestic traditionalism. However, in France only 13 per cent, and in Portugal 9 per cent, of professional/managerial women reported a shared ddl, and the proportions in the other class groupings were even lower.

In all countries, outsourcing was largely used by professional and managerial women. The precise nature of the 'other person' was not specified in the answer to the question as asked. However, it seems reasonable to assume that professional and managerial women were most likely to be paying – that is, using marketised domestic services – for laundry and cleaning. However, in the case of the women in the lower occupational categories, we suggest that this 'other person' is more likely to be another member of the household – such as an elder daughter, mother or mother-in-law.

In summary, although the distribution of domestic work varies by country, in all countries, professional and managerial women receive more assistance with domestic work than women in other occupational class groupings. This is not a particularly surprising finding, as occupational class will act as a proxy for both higher educational levels and more liberal gender role attitudes, both of which have been demonstrated to result in a lower level of traditionalism in domestic arrangements. Professional and managerial women will also be more likely to be able to afford paid domestic help. Nevertheless, a range of other factors might also be anticipated to have an impact on domestic traditionalism, including whether or not the woman works full-time, the extent of partners' working hours, and whether or not there is a child in the household.

We therefore carried out a multinomial regression on ddl arrangements (women in employment only, with traditional ddl as the reference category). This demonstrated that some, but not all, of these factors had a significant impact (Table 7.2). The extent of women's employment had a significant impact, as anticipated, as full-time employed women were more than twice as likely as those employed part-time to be in non-traditional ddl arrangements ($p < 0.001$). However, the extent of the *partner's* working hours did not have an impact on ddl and was therefore excluded. Having a child in the household significantly reduced the likelihood of having a non-traditional ddl ($p < 0.05$). However, occupational class, and country, continued to have a significant impact on ddl arrangements.

Managerial and professional women were more than three times as likely as manual women to be in non-traditional ddl arrangements ($p < 0.001$), but as our previous cross-tabulations had suggested, there were no significant differences in domestic traditionalism between intermediate and routine and manual working women. Country was important, as suggested by Table 7.1, and women living in Britain were significantly more likely than women in Portugal to have a non-traditional ddl ($p < 0.001$), as were women in Finland ($p < 0.01$) and in Norway ($p < 0.05$). However, for women, living in France was not significantly different from living in

Table 7.2: Regression on ddl arrangements

Ddl arrangements	Predictor variables	B (unstandardised)	Beta (standardised)
Less traditional	*Intercept*	*−2.342*	
	FT work	0.537	1.711***
	PT work	–	–
	Professional/ managerial	0.328	1.388
	Intermediate	−0.075	0.928
	Manual	–	–
	Child in household	−0.337	0.714**
	No child in household	–	–
	Living in Britain	1.098	2.999***
	Living in Finland	1.311	3.710***
	Living in France	1.323	3.755***
	Living in Norway	0.975	2.652**
	Living in Portugal	–	–
Non-traditional	*Intercept*	*−3.721*	
	FT	0.880	2.412***
	PT	–	–
	Professional/ managerial	1.120	3.066***
	Intermediate	0.256	1.292
	Manual	–	–
	Child in household	−0.402	0.669*
	No child in household	–	–
	Living in Britain	1.651	5.212***
	Living in Finland	1.244	3.468**
	Living in France	0.826	2.285
	Living in Norway	1.065	2.901*
	Living in Portugal	–	–
Outsourced	*Intercept*	*−5.201*	
	FT	0.306	1.358
	PT	–	–
	Professional/ managerial	4.510	90.903***
	Intermediate	2.689	14.721*
	Manual	–	–
	Child in household	0.416	1.516

(Continued)

Table 7.2:   (*Continued*)

Ddl arrangements	Predictor variables	B (unstandardised)	Beta (standardised)
	No child in household	–	–
	Living in Britain	−1.312	0.269***
	Living in Finland	−2.826	0.059***
	Living in France	−1.443	0.236***
	Living in Norway	−2.224	0.108***
	Living in Portugal	–	–

Note: The reference category is: traditional.
* p < 0.05; ** p < 0.01; *** p < 0.001.

Portugal in terms of having a non-traditional ddl arrangement. As anticipated, living in Portugal significantly increased the likelihood of using outsourcing in comparison with all the other countries. Britain was the next closest, followed by France, then Norway and Finland, two countries that both have very low numbers of women using outsourcing. Managerial and professional women were significantly more likely to use outsourcing than women in the two other occupational class categories, but there was no significant difference between women employed full and part-time in this respect.

Managerial and professional women, therefore, get significantly more help with the less attractive domestic chores described in our measure – although it should not be forgotten that the majority of managerial and professional women still take the main responsibility for them. Nevertheless, the question still remains as to *what* kind of domestic assistance working women find to be most helpful – does it really not matter who does the cleaning and laundry?

We had a number of questions available measuring life happiness and family stress, including 'If you were to consider your life in general, how happy or unhappy would you say you are, on the whole'; 'All things considered, how satisfied are you with your family life'; and 'My life at home is rarely stressful'. When we examined the impact of the domestic division of labour on the answers to these questions, there was a general tendency for those reporting a less traditional ddl to express greater satisfaction on all of these items. This was not particularly surprising, as, for example, Coltrane (2000) has demonstrated that women with a more 'balanced' domestic division of labour experience less depression, enjoy higher marital satisfaction, and so on.

Table 7.3: Regression on 'Life at home is rarely stressful' (women in employment only)

	Predictor variables	B (unstandardised)	Beta (standardised)
	Intercept	*0.579*	
Agree or strongly agree	FT work	−0.038	0.963
	PT work	−	−
	Professional/ managerial	0.056	1.058
	Intermediate	0.193	1.212
	Manual	−	−
	Child in household	−1.253	0.286***
	No child in household	−	−
	Living in Britain	−0.125	0.883
	Living in Finland	1.276	3.581***
	Living in France	0.518	1.679*
	Living in Norway	0.702	2.018**
	Living in Portugal	−	−
	Traditional ddl	−0.273	0.761
	Less traditional ddl	0.179	1.196
	Non-traditional ddl	0.706	2.026*
	Outsourced	−	−

Note: The reference category is: disagree/strongly.
*p < 0.05; **p < 0.01; ***p < 0.001.

Domestic help from a partner, therefore, would appear to reduce stress at home and contribute to greater happiness amongst women (Crompton & Lyonette, 2005). What, however, is the impact of paid domestic help as far as reducing stress amongst women is concerned? Here we focus on a single question 'life at home is rarely stressful'. The data for the 'neither agree nor disagree' category is not presented here.

The regression in Table 7.3 demonstrates no significant effects of class, or full-time versus part-time working. However, child in household, the domestic division of labour, and country are all highly significant. Those women with a child in the home are significantly less likely than those women without a child to agree that life at home is rarely stressful (p < 0.001). When compared with Portugal, Britain is not significantly different in the likelihood of agreeing that life is rarely stressful; France is slightly more likely to agree (p < 0.05), Finland is more than three times more likely to agree (p < 0.001); Norway is more than twice as likely to agree (p < 0.005). In other words, Portuguese women overall are the least likely to agree that life at home is rarely stressful, followed by British women, then France, then Norway and finally, Finland. In fact, cross-tabulations show that 46 per cent of all Portuguese working women dis-agreed that life at home is rarely stressful; as compared to 39 per cent of British women, and 30 per cent of French women, but only a small minority of Norwegian and Finnish women. These findings lend support to the argument that positive dual-earner policies in the Scandinavian countries contribute to a 'societal effect' resulting in lower levels of work–life conflict (Crompton & Lyonette, 2006b).

One of our major objectives in carrying out the regression, however, was to investigate the impact of varying types of help with domestic chores on stress at home. When compared with those using outsourcing, women in traditional and less traditional domestic arrangements are not significantly less likely to agree that life at home is rarely stressful. However, those women in non-traditional domestic arrangements are more than twice as likely to agree that life at home is rarely stressful than those women using outsourcing (p < 0.05). In other words, contribution from a partner is most likely to reduce stress at home, but outsourcing has no significant effect on stress at home for the pooled sample.

Outsourcing, therefore, does not seem to reduce levels of stress for working women – suggesting it *does* matter who vacuums the floor or cleans the toilet. Checking the results for individual countries, however, we found considerable variation by country and class. Having the cleaning and laundry done by another person is associated with less stress at home for the small numbers of intermediate and manual women who had access to help – perhaps reinforcing our suggestion that this 'other person' might be another family member. However, for managerial and professional women (who were more likely to use outsourcing), outsourcing is *not* associated with less stress at home in Britain and France, but it *is* associated with less stress at home in Portugal, and for the (very) small numbers of professional women using outsourcing in Finland and Norway.[3]

We are confident that a shared or non-traditional division of domestic labour makes for less stress at home for many women, and that managerial and professional women are more likely to have shared or non traditional ddl, but it would seem that, particularly for professional and managerial women, the impact of paid domestic help varies from country to country. Paid domestic help can be a contentious issue. The decline of domestic service during the twentieth century was associated with rising living standards and the emergence of better-paid jobs for young women, together with an increasing societal egalitarianism in which the notion of personal servitude was increasingly rejected by many (Nakano, 1992). However, the parallel development of the 'housewife' model for married women meant that domestic work and caring was recast as a 'labour of love' (Finch & Groves, 1983). One of the arguments of 'second-wave' feminism was that this perspective on caring and domestic work was misleading. Caring, it was argued, was essential to human reproduction and should, therefore, be regarded as 'work', even though unpaid (Sevenhuisjen, 2002b; Glucksmann, 1995). One consequence of these recent and complex economic and normative developments is that women with feminist or egalitarian leanings may feel uncomfortable with the thought of 'exploiting' other women by offloading more unpleasant domestic tasks (Ehrenreich & Hochschild, 2003). This discomfort may be exacerbated if the woman concerned has 'liberal' gender role attitudes, but lacks help from her partner. Paid help can also absolve men from the need to undertake domestic work and hold back change – a problem for women with 'liberal' attitudes (Lewis et al., 1992).

However, developments in respect of paid caring and domestic work have varied much between different countries. With considerable oversimplification, the proportion of household servants is likely to be greater in societies characterised by moderate to high inequality, where educational levels are relatively low and/or there is a relative scarcity of 'good' (in other words, well-paid) jobs for women. For example, in Brazil, 20 per cent of urban women are domestic servants (2001 figure), in Chile, 16 per cent (2000), and in Paraguay 21 per cent (2000).[4] There are considerable difficulties in gauging the real extent of paid domestic employment, as much of this employment will be a consequence of informal arrangements, and therefore not included in official statistics (Gregson & Lowe, 1994). Nevertheless, to the extent that paid household help is viewed as an ordinary 'fact of life' by those who can afford it, its use is unlikely to give rise to tension and conflict. Some indication of the extent of private household services is given by ILO (International Labor Organisation) data. The ISCO-88 (International Standard Classification of Occupations) classification includes category 913: 'domestic and related helpers, cleaners and launderers'.[5] Amongst the countries reviewed in this paper, in 2000, 6 per cent of female employees in Finland, 5 per cent in Britain, and 8 per cent in France, fell into this category. In Portugal, ISCO-88 913 was the largest single category of female employment, at 12 per cent[6] (detailed breakdowns were not available for Norway).

Our analysis so far has revealed considerable variation by country in the manner in which domestic tasks are accomplished. In all of the five countries, employed women undertake most of the cleaning and laundry, thus the 'double shift solution' to the 'problem' of household labour brought about by the increased employment of women would seem to be the most frequent occurrence. In all five countries, professional and managerial women are the most likely to report a less traditional division of domestic labour. However, employed women in France and Portugal report significantly less help from their partners with cleaning and laundry than in the other three countries, and as we have seen, not only does the extent of paid domestic help vary from country to country, but its impact would seem to be positive in some cases, but not in others. We therefore examine in more depth the case of Portugal, where the impact of paid domestic help *would* appear to reduce home stress for managerial and professional women (here we are conscious of the small numbers involved, and the speculative nature of our discussion).

Portugal

Portugal has seen the relatively recent collapse of the Salazar regime, which was in power from the 1930s until 1974, a series of colonial wars, and high levels of poverty within the population. Industrialisation was slow and relatively late in Portugal, and Salazar's early ideal of a rural society slowed any potential progress by 'maintaining a tiny internal market with low purchasing power, the absence of a large middle class, lack of human capital and technology, and industrial agents who sought omnipresent state protection' (Wall, 1997). Salazar's corporate state was intended to protect the traditional societal elites and to keep the masses under control, not by imposing any form of radicalism but by maintaining traditional conservatism (Lloyd-Jones, 1994). Salazar himself is quoted as saying 'I want to make Portugal live habitually . . . Men change little, and the Portuguese hardly at all.' Women were subordinate to their husbands and any work decisions were controlled by men. By law, they were also responsible for managing the home (Wall, 1997; see also Chapter 11). The Salazar regime, while emphasising the importance of women's domestic duties, did not exclude women from working. The dual-earner model of family life, based on the traditional rural system, combined with the rise of industrialisation and the depletion of the male workforce due to colonial wars meant that women's employment was always accepted, if underpaid.

Recent OECD data has shown that Portugal has the lowest per capita income in the euro area and, until the recent expansion, it also had the lowest overall in the EU. Thus, as a recent report has argued: 'In Portugal, many families need a full-time second earner to sustain family income, and dual full-time earnership among couples with children has been the norm since the late 1980s' (OECD, 2004: 17). However, attitudes to gender roles, and the family, remain highly traditional in Portugal (Crompton & Lyonette, forthcoming (a)). The majority of Portuguese women, therefore, remain responsible for domestic work, even when in full-time employment. As we have seen in Table 7.3 above, for the pooled sample, occupational class did not appear to have a significant impact on stress at home for employed women. However, when we examined the relationship between occupational class and stress at home separately by country, whereas we found that in Britain, France, Norway and Finland there was no significant relationship between occupational class and stress at home, in Portugal, 49 per cent of intermediate/manual women disagreed that 'life at home is rarely stressful', as compared to only 35 per cent of professional and managerial women – a significant difference. Indeed, in terms of expressed levels of stress at home, the level expressed by Portuguese intermediate/manual women was the highest of any of the country/occupational class groupings of employed women that we have been examining in this paper.

In Portugal, therefore, traditionalism in the domestic division of labour is reflected in high levels of family stress for women in the lower occupational categories (these women also demonstrated high levels of work–life conflict, see Lyonette et al., forthcoming 2007). Managerial and professional women in Portugal report a relatively high level of paid domestic help, and in the case of Portugal, this is associated with lower levels of stress at home. One interpretation of this finding might be that in Portugal, the presence of domestic servants is normatively acceptable (as it will be in other countries where domestic workers are cheap and widely available) and therefore not a source of stress or tension for the women who can afford it.

Discussion and conclusions

In this paper, we have begun to explore the rather complex issues shaping the domestic division of labour in different countries. Our major focus has been on women in paid employment, as being most likely to be directly affected by variations in the domestic division of labour. Our measure has also focused on the less attractive domestic tasks (cleaning and laundry as opposed to cooking and childcare), that are most likely to be carried out by women. In broad outline, our results serve to confirm Geist's (2005) argument as to the structural impact of conservative welfare regimes in that Portugal, and to a lesser extent France, demonstrated a more traditional division of domestic labour. However, Geists's analysis classified household tasks 'done by another person' as being split (or shared) between partners

(Geist, 2005: 28). Our analysis suggests that this might be a misleading strategy, particularly in countries in which better-off women have ready access to paid domestic help. For example, if 'outsourcing' had been classified as a split in household tasks between partners, then over 40 per cent of professional and managerial women in Portugal would have been classified as having a 'shared or non-traditional' division of domestic work, which would have been, obviously, misleading.

In France and Britain, just over 10 per cent of employed professional and managerial women reported that they relied on outsourcing for cleaning and laundry (under 5 per cent of professional and managerial women in Finland and Norway used outsourcing). However, in some contrast to Portuguese women, domestic outsourcing did not reduce stress at home for the women who used it (although sharing by partners did reduce home stress in both countries). French women report a significantly more traditional division of domestic labour than British women, a finding that confirms previous Franco-British comparative work (Gregory & Windebank, 2000). Indeed, in comparison to the other three countries discussed here, domestic traditionalism in France more closely resembles the Portuguese case. However, in comparison to Portugal, attitudes to gender roles and women's employment are much less traditional in France. For example, whereas only 22 per cent of ISSP respondents in France 'agreed' the 'a man's job is to earn money, a woman's job is to look after the home and family', 34 per cent of respondents in Portugal agreed with this statement.

Previous work has indicated that this contrast between relatively 'liberal' gender role attitudes and domestic traditionalism might be a particular source of conflict for French women. For example, we have previously demonstrated a significant relationship between domestic traditionalism and work–life conflict for women in France (Crompton & Lyonette, 2006; see also Chapter 12).[7] In respect of the analyses carried out in this paper, in France, it was noticeable that the contrast (in relation to life and family happiness) between employed women involved in a non-traditional or shared division of domestic work and other women in more traditional relationships was very striking. There was a marked difference in levels of satisfaction with family life between women in the different ddl categories in France. For example, whereas 68 per cent of working women in shared or non-traditional domestic relationships said they were 'completely or very' satisfied with family life, only 43 per cent of women in traditional domestic relationships in France held this view – a considerably greater contrast than in the other countries.

Nevertheless, despite the differences in domestic traditionalism between the two countries, Britain and France are similar in that domestic outsourcing does not appear to reduce stress at home for professional and managerial women. We can only speculate as to why this should be the case. It is likely that women will retain the overall responsibility for the organisation of domestic outsourcing, and this may itself be a source of stress. Given the relatively low level of gender role traditionalism in Britain and France, it might be the case that women using outsourcing might actually prefer to have assistance from their partners, and this might be a source of stress – but again, this can only be speculation.

What would seem to be clear, however, is that the sharing of domestic tasks between partners does contribute to less stress at home for women. In all countries, professional and managerial women are more likely to report domestic sharing (although the proportions are significantly lower in Portugal and France). As, in all countries, the proportion of women in professional and managerial occupations continues to rise, then in the long-term, we may anticipate a slow increase in the sharing of domestic work between men and women within households.

However, we cannot be confident of this outcome. Increases in the occupational status, and extent of employment, amongst women is also likely to be met by recourse to marketised domestic work and workers, and this kind of employment is also likely to increase. If women's labour in the home is simply replaced by paid domestic work, then this arrangement is quite compatible with a continuing traditionalism in the domestic division of labour between men and women within the household. Moreover, our evidence suggests that the availability of paid domestic work does not necessarily reduce stress at home for the women who have access to it. Neither should we forget that, even in those countries (Britain, Finland and Norway) in which professional and managerial women report the greatest level of assistance from their partners, over 40 per cent of professional and managerial women, even when they are employed, remain personally responsible for household cleaning, washing and ironing. Despite the very real changes in women's employment, therefore, our evidence suggests that the extent of change in the domestic division of labour remains glacial.

Notes

1. As was widely noted at the time of the recent urban racial conflict in France, data is not available on the distribution of different ethnic groups in France, as this would offend this principle.
2. The (admittedly rather crude) measure of occupational class used in this paper has been derived from the ISCO-88 occupational classification, which is available on all ISSP data sets.

3. As under 5% of managerial and professional women in Finland and Norway had access to outsourcing, and as the level of outsourcing in these countries is so very low (Table 7.1), we will not include specific reference to these countries in our subsequent discussion.
4. Thanks to Irma Arrigaudia for this information.
5. This data excludes agricultural workers. See www.laborsta.ilo.org; segregat data.
6. It should be noted that levels of education amongst women in Portugal are also relatively low.
7. This association was demonstrated using a domestic division of labour scale that did not include outsourcing, and included a wider range of domestic tasks. However, the patterns of domestic traditionalism by class and by country using the ddl scale were identical to the patterns revealed using the categorical measure we employ in this paper.

8
Gender, Social Class and Work–Life Balance in the New Economy

Diane Perrons, Linda McDowell, Colette Fagan,
Kath Ray and Kevin Ward

Introduction

Women in the European Union are increasingly expected to be in paid employment to meet the Lisbon Strategy targets for growth and competitiveness and to offset the rising costs of welfare, given increased ageing and declining fertility. Yet despite the passing of equalities legislation over 30 years ago, gender inequalities remain in the scale and character of paid employment and in the division of domestic labour.[1] The lack of any real change in the gender distribution of domestic work to match women's increased paid employment has led to debates about how to reconcile paid work and family life, now more usually expressed as work–life balance. Policy discussions revolve around the relative roles of the state and market in meeting the care deficit and how employment practices can be modified to enable both women and men to meet their caring obligations. In addition to these pragmatic issues, in some states, notably the UK, moral questions have also been raised about the desirability of mothers of young children undertaking paid work, especially on a full-time basis.

Underlying the change in social expectations regarding the role of women are a range of complex processes relating to the structure and composition of employment, associated in part with the transition to a service economy, and women's rising educational credentials, as well as changes in lifestyle preferences and aspirations regarding working, living and loving arrangements. The significance of these issues and the ways in which they are resolved varies with the different cultural and institutional contexts across Europe, as well as by social class, family and individual circumstances. Understanding outcomes is correspondingly complex. This chapter focuses on how these changes have been experienced in the materiality of everyday life in UK households with young children. Discussion is situated within debates about work–life balance, also referred to as work–life articulation,[2] work–life reconciliation[3] and work–life conflict,[4] and relatedly within the debate concerning the relative significance of choice and constraint in shaping outcomes regarding women's employment.[5]

The chapter begins by discussing the changing composition and character of employment in the UK, making reference to increasing polarisation, work intensity and uncertainty about job and partnership security. Next, we discuss the findings of a qualitative study of mothers with dependent children in London and Manchester that was undertaken to obtain a grounded understanding of the ways that differently situated households make decisions about employment and caring strategies.[6] We compare our findings with large scale aggregate and attitudinal data, in particular to the works of Rosemary Crompton and Clare Lyonette (2005) and Susan Himmelweit and Maria Sigala (2004) and provide some insights into the processes shaping decisions. Our findings suggest that decisions are shaped by the way that a range of contingent and contextual circumstances intersect with more structural characteristics at particular moments rather than demonstrating any fixed or long lasting preferences or orientations towards mothering or paid work.[7] While decisions are individual, outcomes from our study are mirrored in the aggregate statistics that indicate the continuing significance of qualifications and the age of the youngest child on employment probabilities in the UK. Overall, we also found a close correspondence between women's actual employment behaviour and their attitude towards paid employment, consistent with studies such as those by Himmelweit and Sigala (2004) and Crompton and Lyonette (2005). This latter study found, for example, that more highly qualified households were more likely to have liberal attitudes with respect to mothers' working, although many mothers in our survey expressed some ambivalence and regret that there were not more hours in the day to enable them to fulfil all of their aspirations.

Contemporary working patterns in the UK

In the UK, the feminisation of employment has taken place within a paradoxical policy framework that advocates expanding employment to raise competitiveness and economic growth in line with the Lisbon strategy, and in order to reduce child poverty, but where childcare costs are among the highest in Europe and state-provided care is limited. The UK is unique in having a high female employment rate, limited childcare facilities and long working hours, especially for fathers. This 'circle is squared' by many mothers working short part time hours fitted around their children's care (Himmelweit & Sigala, 2004: 455). Undeniably, 'flexible' working practices facilitate work–life balance to some degree but are also integral to the UK neo-liberal market agenda, a further feature of which is rising earnings and income inequality.

Increased female employment meets the objectives of the European Employment Strategy (EC, 2005) but also reflects the Third Way politics of rights and responsibilities. UK policy is encapsulated by the slogan 'work for those who can, security for those who cannot' (Hyde, Dixon & Joyner, 1999) and enacted through labour market activation policies, tax credits intended to 'make work pay', together with some financial support for childcare costs. These policies reflect a turnaround in social expectations (Lewis, 2001) as mothers are increasingly expected to be in paid employment, and lone parents (92 per cent of whom are mothers), whose youngest child is aged five or older, are specifically encouraged by the state to seek employment.[8] However, the policies have done little to counter low wages and low productivity in the UK economy. Even allowing for the new tax credits, low-paid jobs are not always viable, especially in London, because of high childcare and transport costs. A lone parent living outside London, for example, with two children and childcare costs, is better off returning to work at the minimum wage, but in London the same parent would need to earn almost 1.75 times the minimum wage in order to benefit financially (Bivand, Gordon & Simmonds, 2003).[9] More generally, tax credits have a negative impact on the second earner in dual person households everywhere.[10] These policies were being implemented and strengthened at the time when the qualitative research was being carried out.

As increasing proportions of women have entered the labour market, however, they have done so in a context of widening overall inequalities and continuing patterns of vertical and horizontal segregation. Since the 1970s, employment has become more polarised in the UK, with expansion at opposite ends of the earnings distribution (Green, 2006). Maarten Goos and Alan Manning (2003) demonstrate this phenomenon by defining 'good and bad jobs' based on occupational and industry/sectoral categories. 'Good' jobs, for example, accountancy in the finance sector, have earnings in the top two deciles and 'bad' jobs such as clerical work in retail, in the lowest decile. They demonstrate growth in both of these categories between 1979 and 1999, especially in the former, but a decline in employment in jobs in the middle of the distribution. There is also a gender dimension to this polarisation, as the fastest growing occupations in the 1990s were in the caring services such as nursery nurses, hairdressing and housekeeping, sectors in which women are over represented, as well as in sectors linked to the knowledge economy, such as professional and managerial jobs including software engineers and computer programmers, where men are more prevalent.[11] At the same time, the disappearance of relatively well paid and comparatively secure jobs in the middle of the distribution arising from the decline in manufacturing employment has undermined the capacity of men to be breadwinners in the traditional sense.[12] This changing employment composition takes different forms in different regions of the UK with earnings inequalities being most pronounced in London where the most highly paid jobs are found, in addition to jobs throughout the distribution.[13]

While the aggregate evidence on employment insecurity is inconclusive, it is clear that work intensity has been rising in the UK (Green, 2006), as has the number of hours committed to some form of paid or unpaid work, on days where some work is done, especially among highly qualified women (Gershuny, 2005). The UK is also characterised by a high level of divorce and separation, a high proportion of lone parents, as well as new, more individualised, living arrangements. These issues, including the processes leading to and sustaining these inequalities, are discussed further elsewhere (Perrons et al., 2006). This chapter focuses on how households make decisions with respect to paid work and caring within this divided and uncertain context.

While female employment has increased overall, the extent of participation continues to vary systematically among women. The female participation rate continues to be highest among the more highly qualified and children continue to represent a constraint on mothers' working patterns. The working hours of fathers also tend to be longer than those of men in general (Harkness, 2003). Statistical data on labour market trends and attitudinal data from large scale surveys do not, however, convey the rationale underlying the different outcomes or attitudes or the differential degrees of complexity which households and individuals experience in managing their work–life balance. To explore these complexities, we now discuss some findings from our qualitative study of 'Living and labouring in London and Manchester'.

Illustrations from London and Manchester

The qualitative research is based on 139 interviews, predominantly with mothers, the majority of whom live in households with one person in paid employment and at least one child under 10 years old. The interviews took place between 2002 and 2003 in three residential areas in Central London and three in Manchester, characterised by different socio-economic profiles. SPSS was used to assist the analysis of numerical variables and the discursive material was analysed following a grounded theory approach using Atlas Ti. From this analysis we differentiate households into a number of categories or 'types' defined on the basis of their current employment patterns which emerge from our data. Our analysis and interpretation differs, however, from the essentialist characterisations based on preferences or orientations linked to behaviour, as found for instance in the work of Hakim (2000, 2002, 2004).[14] Our empirical categories (see Table 8.1) are matched with a view to identifying similarities and differences that are critical in shaping outcomes with respect to paid employment, recognising that in many cases, these decisive factors are highly contingent. In particular, we identify how the ease with which paid work and childcare can be combined varies especially by social class and employment sector, in addition to more individual circumstances such as precise geographical location and the number and age range of children.[15] Should these circumstances change, it would almost certainly lead to a re-negotiation of working arrangements including the decision to be in paid employment or not.

Household categories

Our survey covered a wide range of household working patterns displayed in Table 8.1, including two couples who had consciously chosen role reversal with respect to paid work, and four more where role reversal had arisen through redundancy or other chance happening. We also

Table 8.1: Household partnership and working patterns

Household type	Number
Dual full-time earners	39
Dual earner male full-time/female part-time	40
Dual earner both part-time	4
Male sole earner dual household	22
Female sole earner dual household	5
Female full-time earner single household	13
Female part-time earner single household	6
Female no earner single household	4

Note: In addition we had one dual mother household where both worked long part-time hours, one single father working part-time and one male breadwinner working part-time.

Table 8.2a: Broad socio-economic groups and working patterns for married and co-habiting mothers

Socio-economic group	Location	Occupational sector	LFT (>40)	FT (31–40)	PT (1–30)	NSW
Professional/ managerial	London	Public	4	2	9 (Brenda)	16 (Zoe)
		Private	7 (Frances, Sandra, Nasrin)	2	6	
	Manchester	Public	2	1 (Dawn)	6	
		Private	2 (Amanda)	13 (Caitlyn)	2	
Non-professional	London	Public	—	3	1 (Melissa)	4
		Private	2	2	3	
	Manchester	Public	—	4	6	
		Private	—	1	7 (Janette, Sarah)	

Note: The classification is based on mothers' broad occupational categories. There were very few managers, though professionals working in organisations sometimes had managerial responsibilities. The model pattern for partners was full time work, some working long hours, especially in the private sector. There were a minority of instances where the traditional breadwinner model was reversed, with the father working part time or not being in employment. The majority of couples were, however, in the same broad occupational group. LFT = less than full-time (less than 40 hours per week)
FT = full-time
PT = part-time
NSW = not seeking work.

interviewed a same sex female couple where roles were more equitable. In devising the categories and in discussing the interviews, we differentiate further by professional and non-professional status, working hours and location (see Tables 8.2a and 8.2b).[16] The names in Tables 8.2a and 8.2b are pseudonyms and include those mothers who we refer to in the discussion.

The discussion is divided into three parts. We begin by identifying some commonalities across the data, then we focus on how coordination issues vary with partnership status and social class, and finally we discuss how the outcomes are experienced. In the process, we illuminate more generally some of the contextual circumstances that influence employment outcomes and attitudes towards employment found in more aggregate patterns.

Table 8.2b: Broad socio-economic groups and working patterns for single parents

Socio-economic group	Location	Occupational sector	LFT	FT	PT	NSW
Professional	London	Public		1		
		Private	2		2	
	Manchester	Public		1	1	
		Private		1		
Non-professional	London	Public			1	4
		Private			(Diana)	(Jenny)
	Manchester	Public	1	3		1
		Private			3	

Notes: (i) We have included the numbers in each category and placed by name (pseudonym) the respondents highlighted in the discussion.
(ii) Those currently not seeking work are categorised by their last job.
(iii) Some mothers' working hours and employment forms are variable and mixed such that they did not fit these categories. Katherine, for example, a single parent, worked 56 hours a week divided between her own small business in personal services and a part-time lecturing job.
LFT = less than full-time (less than 40 hours per week)
FT = full-time
PT = part-time
NSW = not seeking work.

Some common trends

Qualifications

Overall we found that our data reflected the national patterns with respect to the positive relationship between qualifications and the age of the youngest child and the likelihood of mothers' paid employment, irrespective of partnership status or geographical location. Graduates, for example, were more likely to be in full time employment and have longer hours of work than other groups. Of the four lone parent graduates, all of whom lived in London, three worked 50 hours or more each week.

Traditional assumptions regarding the gender division of domestic labour

We found an overwhelmingly traditional division of domestic labour. Even cases where both partners were highly qualified high-earners working long hours, the mother was almost invariably the one who organised the household, although there was some sharing of the domestic tasks that were not marketised (see Chapter 7). To some extent, this division of labour was objectively or economically rational – reflecting the different gender wage profiles. Key decisions regarding the gender division of labour seem to have been made without much, if any, thought (Bourdieu, 2001; Butler, 1993). When asked whether they had ever considered reversing their roles, mothers in couples following a one and a half earner or one earner model, in which the man was the primary earner, usually replied 'no' – ' well he couldn't' – 'his firm wouldn't understand' . . . often ending in 'well actually, I don't think he would'. It has to be cautioned that these findings rest predominantly on mothers' accounts.

A more equal sharing of domestic work and childcare was usually the result of rather specific circumstances: in one case (Amanda, see Table 8.2a), the mother was a high earner and her partner was self-employed, running a home-based web start-up firm, and so he could adjust his working hours around school times and his partner's physical presence. Non-professional, dual earning households would often try and offset their hours and holiday arrangements so that they could manage childcare or school holidays without incurring extra costs (for example, Janette, see Table 8.2a; also see La Valle et al., 2002). This finding is supported by Jay Gershuny's (2005) analysis of time use data which shows that in the last 20 years, when paid and unpaid work are added together, men in non-professional occupations and women professionals have experienced increases in total hours, whereas total working hours have declined for other groups. Customarily, however, it was mothers that directly faced the complex problems of scheduling.

Spatial logistics

One major constraint reported by almost all respondents, and especially those in London, arose from the patriarchal and heteronormative assumptions embedded in the urban fabric (Booth et al., 1996), together with inaccessible or unaffordable childcare cover. The spatial organisation of cities complicates any coordination between geographically distant schools/childcare facilities, workplaces and housing.[17] Common concerns included the difficulties in managing journeys in different directions in order to take children to and from their various forms of care, in addition to the work journey.[18] A further common concern was the continuing difficulties of using public transport with young children. The following comment made by Diana (see Table 8.2b) was typical and found across all social groups:[19]

> 'I hate buses, I really do, they just, like, they've designed all these new buses with the nice little lowering ramp, but unless you're disabled he's not lowering the ramp, he's just not lowering it, you have to literally arch up the pram and . . .'

While there is a gender dimension to the way that the problem of over-coming spatial logistics rests primarily with women, the extent of the difficulties posed by this barrier to employment varied critically both geographically and by social class.

Logistical difficulties were resolved in various ways reflecting individual characteristics, particularly qualifications and earnings (especially mothers' earnings), which perhaps can be summarised as social class, but also by more dynamic factors such as partnership status, the number and age range of children, employment type (public or private) and whether or not the employee had any control over their actual working time.

Ideas and expectations regarding what constituted a feasible journey and what form of childcare, school or extra-curricular activities were considered essential ranged widely between households. The extent and the manner in which the expectations were fulfilled also varied by social class in particular, as some of the cases discussed below illustrate. We should emphasise that we are not arguing that spatial logistics are determinant, but they provide one means of cutting through the complexity of our data in order to discuss the way that employment outcomes are influenced by both contingent and contextual circumstances, few of which are permanent at the individual level. We first discuss the different ways in which particular cases manage work–life balance practically, and then pay attention to more experiential issues, including ambivalence, stress and 'busyness'.

Practicalities of daily life

Tables 8.2a and 8.2b have provided details of the households that we focus on in this particular chapter in terms of their occupational status (professional and non-professional, public or private sector) and working hours, as we found these factors to be important in influencing how work–life arrangements were decided upon and how they were experienced. The common criterion in all cases was being a parent with at least one child under 10.[20] The illustrations were chosen because they are indicative of broader patterns in our data. Establishing whether these factors are representative of broader trends requires further research based on large-scale quantitative analyses.

Logistical problems are particularly intense for lone parents who typically have nobody else within the household with whom they can share the physical burden, irrespective of the emotional and educative work increasingly expected of contemporary parents. Indeed, the physical presence of a relative to assist with childcare was the critical difference between the two lone parents, Diana and Jenny, discussed below, who in terms of their age, qualifications, ethnicity (both belong to minority groups) and expressed attitudes towards childcare, were very much alike in 'care capital' (see Chapter 9).

Of the 24 lone parents in our study, the majority were in paid employment, including six who were working long full time hours (over 40 per week). Similar to national trends, educational qualifications and the age of the youngest child were positively related to the likelihood of being in paid employment. All of those whose youngest child was over three years of age and who had a university degree were in paid employment. The majority of lone parents not in paid employment were from our London population which again corresponds to London's comparatively low employment rate, compared to other regions. By comparatively analysing the transcripts, it is possible to examine more closely the processes leading to these outcomes.

Lone parent Diana is the mother of one child under two years old, currently living in inner London and working two full days a week at a gym, in addition to studying – with a view to getting a more fulfilling job in the future. Her arrangements depend critically on the proximity between her home and workplace and the willingness of her own mother to take care of her child, along with other grandchildren. Diana manages the logistics by using a private car to transport the child to her mother's house and occasionally by working through the night to complete her college work. Diana receives little financial or other support from the father of her child or his family, something she regrets. She states that money is the prime motivation for working and stays with her current job primarily for logistical reasons.[21]

> '. . . 'cos it's convenient and I'm so bloody lazy! It's just convenient because it's amazing how I've got a flat round the corner from my workplace, so I don't think the chance of that happening again . . .'

The key difference between Diana and another lone parent Jenny, who is not in paid work, is the proximity of flexible work and the presence/absence of the grandmother, rather than any particular orientation towards paid work. Jenny could not afford childcare and her immediate family was unable to assist as they were all working. She too was studying part-time to increase her career options for the future.

For people in low paid jobs, simply managing the physical task of travelling between home, school and work on public transport is complex and may lead to withdrawal from employment, even for those in dual adult households. Melissa has three school-aged children and works part time on a fixed term contract as a nursery nurse in a local authority play-group centre. She had recently given up a full time job in order to work closer to home. Her problems arose from the routing of public transport and the journey time, rather than straight geographical distance, and were compounded by her husband's shift work, which made it impossible for him to provide childcare on a predictable basis.

The significance in taking local jobs for which people are over-qualified has also been noted in the EOC's (2005) report on the hidden brain drain. There are several parallel illustrations in our survey. Caitlyn, for example, was a highly qualified mother in Manchester who similarly opted out of a higher paid and more permanent job which had entailed a 12-hour day, including travel time, indicating the difficulty in obtaining jobs locally to match skills. This problem is greater in Manchester, which had a more limited range of jobs for the highly qualified.

In terms of qualifications, age and number of children, Melissa and her partner can be contrasted with Janette, living with her partner in Manchester, and working full time for a private firm. Janette's job is more permanent than that of her husband's, whose work is temporary and with varied hours. In the relatively recent past, her husband might possibly have been an unskilled manufacturing worker but had so far been unable to find regular permanent employment for someone without formal qualifications. This couple manage, however, as both their jobs are closer to home and they have access to a nearby low-cost child centre. Overall, they juggle their working hours, make use of a comparatively low-cost, local and state-provided care facility, and generally take their holiday at separate times to cover school closures.

Melissa might also be contrasted with Frances, whose three children are considerably younger, but is highly qualified and able to pay for a whole range of marketised services including childcare, transport (including taxis) and domestic help, as well as living in her own high-cost house not far from work. Frances's lifestyle indicates how high earnings facilitate and sustain paid employment, something also very clearly evident in the case of Clare, a highly qualified lone parent with one pre-school child and a very demanding, permanent full time job. She uses a private nursery five days a week but also has a live-in au pair who collects her child in the late afternoon and takes care of her until Clare arrives home, as well as doing all the child's cooking, cleaning and washing, and errands for Clare, such as fetching clothes from the dry cleaners. Live-in assistance is essential for Clare, owing to her long and unpredictable working hours and because she often works away from London. Clare also makes occasional use of a baby-sitting agency and has used the emergency crèche at her ex-partner's workplace (also a city finance firm). Similarly, if her usual arrangements break down, she would call upon an ad hoc network created by her ex-nanny and her ex-partner's au pair, but this would all be paid support.[22]

Even with paid domestic support, some mothers find the complexities of childcare overwhelming, especially when they have more than one child and when the ages of children means that their care or schooling is in different locations. Zoe, for example, is currently a 'housewife' with three children (twins aged 4.5 and a toddler of almost 2 years) and a partner who works very long hours, being away from the house between 6.30 a.m. and 10 p.m. Zoe returned to work following the birth of her twins but had remained at home ever since her toddler was born. She had employed a nanny on several days a week to assist with the twins, though they also attended a private nursery school. The private school/nursery was one and a half miles from the house and considered unmanageable by public transport. Zoe explains: 'I just logistically can't do it. I would be to-ing and fro-ing and to-ing and fro-ing.' She goes on to point out all the equipment that her children require for school and after-school activities and, given her partner's work hours, why she needs additional paid help:

'What I'm looking for in fact was two days a week, but then three mornings as well, 8.30–10.00, just so I don't have to take Henry (the toddler) on the school runs really. Because it's quite a lot to have to get three children in, to school . . . and Zed and Jay both have a library book bag each. They've got to have a lunchbox because there's no kitchen in the school, so they've got to have a packed lunch each day. Then they go swimming. I think they're starting music in the new year, so they'll have a music bag, and you know . . . your hands are completely full of bags.'

Zoe and her partner also employed a cleaner and outsourced shirt ironing. At the time of the interview, however, she was also overseeing the modernisation of her house and, given the rate at which house prices were then rising in London, was probably earning as much from this as she would have done if employed as a professional in the public sector.[23] Another graduate mother, with two young children and currently not seeking paid work, was similarly involved in house reconstruction, but with no domestic support, likewise regarded paid employment outside of the home as simply too complicated. She was one of the few respondents to express unequivocally a desire to remain out of the labour force until her children were older.

Clearly, interpretations of these circumstances may vary and it could be argued that the two cases referred to above are less work-centred than many others, whose anxieties stem from juggling different jobs and childcare locations, rather than lunch boxes and swimming kit. However, preference theory (Hakim, 2002) and research using this perspective implies some degree of permanence in orientations and behaviour and tends to neglect the way that people make adjustments relating to a whole range of factors, only some of which are under their control.[24]

Busyness, stress and happiness

Having looked at some of the impacts of spatial and temporal logistics, we now consider how people expressed satisfaction or anxiety about their current work–life arrangements. Consistent with aggregate attitudinal data (Crompton & Lyonette, 2005, 2006b), working mothers reported a sense of well-being, though with very busy lives, combining a range of activities throughout the day and with little time for independent thought or leisure. Almost without exception they reported that their paid work was important to maintaining a sense of themselves, as well as offering opportunities for socialisation. There was a tendency for mothers to mention money as their major reason for working, as in the case of Diana above, but without much probing they would generally go on to discuss other advantages in terms of self-esteem. This finding raises a possible limitation about the use of attitudinal data when it is based on the response to a limited number of questions. Hakim, for example, defines work-centred women as being focused on competitive activities, planning their careers and work for intrinsic satisfaction as well as money (Hakim, 2000, 2002, 2004). Without probing, this last factor would have included the majority of working mothers in our survey, and yet it is clear that they considered that employment provided a range of other benefits.

Paralleling the findings of Crompton and Lyonette (2005), some of the most troubled were those who were not currently seeking work. Zoe, for example, points out how she feels isolated and something of a social misfit:

'I've felt very, very isolated, it's very difficult, So when I go to toddler groups and stuff . . . it's very difficult, because I'm instantly on a different level because of the way I speak. You know where my children go to school or whatever. So I can't kind of share what a lot of the non-working mums in the local area are like. And then in other places it's all nannies, and nannies aren't particularly keen to get chatty and friendly with mums so it is, it feels like a double whammy in a way, like great, Peter (partner) does earn a lot of money in a way, and maybe it's not absolutely essential that I work. But then it's isolating that I don't work . . . and if we didn't have a choice, and I just had to do it, then there wouldn't, sometimes choices aren't always helpful, I suppose!'

She also expressed reservations about her current division of labour with her partner.

'Well, it feels like I'm doing all the home stuff, and Peter's doing all the work stuff, which is not my preferred way of doing it. It's quite difficult to alter that much. But we'll have to see whether we can try and address that a bit. Um, certainly, when I did work, it did feel as if, rather than me working and things changing in terms of the demands on me, the demands on me remained the same and I worked.'

Clearly, there was inequality in the domestic division of labour when she was in paid work and, although the reason she withdrew was not discussed at length, being the lower earner was considered obvious or 'natural'. In her husband Peter's work in private sector finance, flexible working or even standard full time hours are not currently practised, something that the highly qualified mothers also commented on. While formal equal opportunities and leave arrangements existed in practice, they were more limited and were reported as being 'for the secretaries, not us'. Two women working in finance, Sandra and Nasrin, commented that they were the first mothers their firms had ever employed at their level and some allowances were made for their new status, such as being able to complete work at home.

While the glass ceiling has been cracking a bit, sticky floors remain firmly in place, owing to a mixture of continuing discriminatory practices, but also to some degree because of self-selection by women. It is this area of self-selection where the debate between choices and constraints re-emerges. Some women do make decisions which take them away from the most highly paid jobs, not because they do not like the work, nor because they lack the capabilities, but because that they are aware that time demands associated with current work practices means that full-time demanding employment is not a viable option if they want to have any kind of life away from their place of work. Time demands are particularly strong for younger workers in their twenties and thirties, where the demands of career and family formation coincide.

'All the girls leave corporate' is a common expression among city lawyers where work practices are notoriously long and unpredictable.[25]

Professional employees in the public sector were more likely to experience regular working hours, have access to flexible working arrangements which they felt able to take as a right, rather than as a favour, even though it would have a detrimental impact on their career at a future date. Brenda and Dawn work long part time and standard full time hours in London and Manchester respectively as professional workers in the public sector and manage by juggling their working times around school events and by using a range of after school and school holiday clubs, together with help from grandparents, especially during school holidays. Thus both are able to work professionally and still have time to spend with their children in the evenings and weekends.

A further difference, which again is job and class specific, is the way that higher earners are more likely to have task- rather than time-specific jobs which allow them to manage their own time. In other words, even though they may work long hours, there is nonetheless some porosity or space in the working day, during which they are able to check that household arrangements are working smoothly. Typically, they are more able to arrive late or leave early to attend school events from time to time, conditions which would not be possible with the stricter time-based regimes experienced lower down the employment hierarchy.[26] This informal form of flexibility has been reported to be more widely practised than more formal arrangements for flexible working on a regular basis, made possible by the law passed in 2003, giving parents of young children in the UK the right to request flexible work arrangements (CIPD, 2005).

In lower paid occupations, employees generally have less discretion in their use of time, are more likely to have closely monitored hours, and pay is closely related to hours worked. Some mothers organised their own flexibility by selecting certain work patterns to fit around their caring commitments, but worked intensely during these hours, as employment patterns are determined around the flow of work. Typically, there is little porosity in their working days. Sarah, a cleaner in Manchester, is paid for three hours a day for the time spent actually cleaning houses, but not for the time spent travelling between them, indicating some differences by social class in the way flexibility is experienced. Similarly, Cara in London had a contract to work 16 hours a week at a 'Supermarket Local'. While pointing out that the firm benefited from this arrangement as she often worked more hours than this, even though her holiday and sick pay would be calculated on the contracted minimum, she none the less appreciated having some control over her working hours.

What was also apparent from our interviews was that while many mothers were clearly very stretched in terms of time (and some also for money) and constantly holding together what was sometimes a very fragile balancing act in combining the dual life of work and caring – having an income, socialising and utilising their training, as well as playing a direct role in their children's lives, was clearly their preferred way of being. Optimistically, they were perhaps carving out a trajectory that in the future may be shared by fathers with benefits all round, as portrayed, for example, in Nancy Fraser's (1996) universal carer model.[27]

Crompton and Lyonette (2005) find that congruent liberals (those mothers who had liberal attitudes about mothers of young children being in paid employment and a 'less traditional' division of domestic labour in the home) were found to have the highest degrees of personal and family happiness, as measured by life in general, satisfaction with family life and lower stress at home. By contrast, women defined as congruent traditionals (those with the opposite characteristics to those above, with respect to mothers' attitudes towards paid employment and the domestic division of labour) were less happy on all three counts. As a result of their analysis, Crompton and Lyonette (2005: 615) conclude by stating that 'the evidence we do have suggests that for women (but not for men), gender traditionalism in attitudes or practice (as indicated by gender role attitudes and the domestic division of labour) is not associated with greater general or family happiness, but indeed the opposite'. In general we concur with their findings. While people may report work–life 'stress', this term is often used, not in its medical sense to reflect anxiety, but rather to portray a sense of time pressure, work–life conflict and the way that people in this situation have to manage a whole range of issues simultaneously. However, it could also be that busyness is almost a status symbol – the new badge of honour of the middle classes (Gershuny, 2005). One finding, especially among those working very long hours, was a strong sense of ambivalence and sometimes guilt, arising from a sense of incapacity to do paid and unpaid work as effectively as they would like to. These women expressed a desire for there to be more hours in the day so that they could contribute more to both work and home life.

Conclusions

On the basis of our analysis, we suggest that exploring the specific circumstances within which mothers make their 'choices' with respect to labour market participation, shows that in the UK, where there is a lack of universally available, affordable and accessible childcare, particular influences, especially incomes and logistical complexity, intersect and generate recurring patterns that make some choices more likely or more rational than others. Our data therefore indicate the continuing role of structural factors in shaping outcomes, although in highly complex and differentiated ways.

Our findings are largely consistent with the trends from aggregate data in relation to working patterns and the attitudinal data relating to the desirability for mothers of young children to be in paid employment (Himmelweit & Sigala, 2004). What our findings add to existing studies is a greater understanding of the class-specific, differential conditions of employment which in some ways make it easier for high earning women to manage competing pressures in ways that are more likely to secure their economic well-being as individuals. They suggest that social class and gender, together with geographical context and individual preferences, each play a role in shaping individual decisions and in accounting for aggregate, social outcomes. People in different geographical and social locations, formed by the way different structural factors intersect with each other and with individual characteristics, including age, qualifications and number of children, are confronted in practice with systematically different 'choice sets' or constraints within which they make their decisions. These choice sets and constraints are in turn the intended or unintended outcomes of existing policies and as a consequence, potentially may form the basis for future, more gender-equitable policies.

We also find that these decisions, taken in the context of widening inequalities in the labour market and the continuation of inadequate childcare, tend to reinforce the emerging inequalities based on social class divisions. Overall, we find that the impact of the feminisation of employment on gender equality has been less than might have been expected. Class divisions remain significant and are likely to be reinforced, as there is clearly a lower incentive for people with the prospect of low earnings to enter paid employment. Providing both incentives and penalties is one reason why the British Government introduced policies to 'make work pay' – policies that have expanded since the research was carried out. However, while such policies make the monetary returns from employment more attractive, they do not include the questions of time and space. What the research has shown is that low earners find it more difficult to overcome the complex and time-consuming journeys to work which severely constrain the range of employment options open to them.

Overall, we conclude that women do indeed make history or shape their own futures, but not in circumstances of their own choosing. Social expectations concerning the roles of mothers have clearly changed, almost becoming the antithesis of those established from the late 19th century, based on the ideal of the bourgeois housewife that gradually percolated through all social classes as an ideology if not a practice, and never reached the poorest groups at all. What is apparent, however, is that the infrastructure necessary to meet these revised expectations for women is inadequate. Furthermore, men have not adjusted their behaviour in significant ways to meet the new expectations placed on parents. Mothers, consequently, are left to negotiate these changes in ad hoc ways, according to their precise circumstances – including qualifications, occupations, the number and age range of children, partnership status and so on. In many cases, they do so in extremely resourceful ways, holding together the complex logistics of scheduling arrangements in space and time. These arrangements are shaped strongly by social class, which is contributing to widening inequalities between women, while only affecting gender equality in more moderate ways.[28]

Notes

1. The Equal Opportunities Commission has published a series of reports which demonstrate continuing gender inequalities in the labour market, (see EOC (2005) and their website: www.eoc.org.uk).
2. (see Gambles et al. (2006) and Crompton & Lyonette, 2006b).
3. Lewis, J. (2003).
4. Crompton and Lyonette (2006b).
5. This latter debate has been addressed extensively elsewhere so is not rehearsed in detail here.
6. The research material comes from an ESRC funded study on 'Living and Labouring in London and Manchester' (grant number R000239470). In this chapter, emphasis is placed on the London part of the study.
7. See for example the study by Bell et al. (2005) on lone parents.
8. The participation rate of lone parents has increased (by 11 per cent to 55.8 per cent since the introduction of the tax credit policies, DWP 2005).
9. In recognition of the high costs of living and working in London new in-work credits are to be introduced in 2005 but for a limited period (DWP 2005).
10. The scale of in-work benefits boosts entry into paid employment but this form of support is means tested on the basis of family income – thus couples are assessed jointly and the current system means that the financial return from having a second earner is now lower on average than it was in 1997 when the Government first came into power. Consequently there is a disincentive for the lower earner in any household, generally the female partner, to enter the labour

market, even though in the longer term labour market inactivity will have a negative impact on their lifetime incomes (see Brewer and Shephard 2004).

11. See Nolan and Salter (2002) who identify this trend but do not fully explore the gender dimensions.
12. See Charles and James (2005).
13. In financial services for example the gender pay gap in London is 60 per cent compared to 40 per cent in Manchester.
14. See Charles and James (2005) for a critique and Bell et al. (2005) where the concept of orientation is used to define household types in an otherwise rich discussion of the constraints faced and decisions made by lone parents.
15. This is one of a number of papers arising from this research project.
16. Overall, we interviewed a high proportion of professional and managerial households which in part reflects the changing composition of the population especially in central London (Hamnett, 2003), but also reflects the way that the interviewees were contacted via playgroups, nurseries, local libraries, etc. which are more likely to be attended by the middle classes, or increasingly by their nannies.
17. See Skinner (2003) and Jarvis (2005).
18. See Jarvis (2005) and McDowell et al. (2006).
19. Problems cannot always be eased in London with private transport as parking can be extremely expensive or not even possible. In addition the congestion charge has increased the relative cost of private transport.
20. Otherwise the sample is rather unstructured but as Catherine Hakim argues (Hakim, 2003), this does not hinder our discussion of preference theory.
21. On Hakim's typology this would mean that she was not work centred. On the other hand studying to improve her career in the future would suggest that she might be.
22. See Blair-Loy and Jacobs (2003).
23. Clearly these 'earnings' would only be realised when the house was sold but this also indicates how staying at home does not mean that work is not being done.
24. Defenders of preference theory might argue that such illustrations correspond to the adaptive category. It may however be more helpful to identify the circumstances that influence the choices actually made.
25. See Baker (2003) for a US comparison.
26. See Perrons (2005) and Rubery et al. (2005) for further exposition of the role of porosity in the working day.
27. In Gillian Rose's (1993) terms this model might enable women to cease to be simultaneously prisoners of but exiles in a physical and social world that continues to embody the priorities of a male breadwinner model.
28. Gender equality has increased marginally between women and men at both ends of the earnings distribution as more qualified women are able to enter but not reach the top levels of high paid professional and especially managerial occupations. At the lower echelons the decline of manufacturing has removed many of the better-paid opportunities for relatively low skilled men, so their incomes have declined and become more similar to those found in occupations where women are over-represented.

9
Care Capital, Stress and Satisfaction

Anneli Anttonen and Jorma Sipilä

Introduction

Our aim in this chapter is to study the family-related stress and satisfaction that women and men experience in their home lives, using data collected in Finland and Norway for the International Social Survey Programme (ISSP, 2002). The study will focus on families with children under 18, because our aim is to evaluate the usefulness of the concept of care capital in the context of work–life balance research.

In all post-industrial societies there is a pressure to increase life-long labour market participation of all adults, and especially women's engagement in paid work. Finland and Norway represent the Nordic welfare state model in which the state and local governments have assumed an extensive public responsibility for the care of children, as well as for other people who need help and care (Anttonen & Sipilä, 1996; Bettio & Plantenga, 2004). Women's labour market participation rate is already at a high level, and parents of young children are entitled to both work-related and care-related social rights (Leira, 2002), helping them to combine work and care and to relieve the tensions they face in today's society of mass consumption. Despite the support, even in such well-developed welfare states, parents often care for their children under strained conditions (for example, Kröger & Sipilä, 2005). State-sponsored childcare services do not cover all care needs, such as parents having to work during evenings and weekends.

In this chapter, we will employ the concept of 'care capital', which refers to the total amount of resources needed in childcare. Our main argument is that there has to be a certain amount of care capital available to avoid care poverty or care deficiency. In all post-industrial societies, care deficiency is a social risk which may reduce quality of life and increase stress and dissatisfaction. Care capital consists of different elements: first, there must be *people* who are willing and capable to care. Secondly, there has to be *time* to care for others: care is an activity that is based on human interaction and is time-consuming. If time for caring activities is limited, stress and other feelings of frustration may follow. Thirdly, there has to be *financial resources* to arrange the care that is required. The fourth dimension is the *place*: good care requires an appropriate place. The availability of people, time, financial resources and place are all important for care capital to accumulate, and for this reason, care capital depends on working times, social relations, and the financial resources available to families.

The huge amount of research devoted to the issue of reconciling work and family in present western societies can be seen as a consequence of the fact that care capital is often insufficient. Working life has become increasingly demanding and there is plenty of research to show that the length of working time is positively related to work–family conflict (Major, Klein & Erhart, 2002: 427). It is often difficult for parents to arrange all the childcare required, particularly as many countries still lack reliable childcare services which are affordable for middle- and lower-income families (for example, Anttonen, Baldock & Sipilä, 2003; OECD, 2001c). Even if such a service does exist, it may not always be used because of child or parent sickness, as well as other exceptional circumstances. In addition, evenings, weekends and holiday periods are not covered by day care centres or schools.

Therefore, a necessary condition for the continuity of childcare is that there should be more than one carer available, but even two parents can often feel pressurised. Everybody is affected by illness at some point, and not everyone can, or wants, to be at home all the time. Lone parents, in particular, often find difficulty in finding other people to help with childcare (Le Bihan & Martin, 2004). Families are generally smaller than in previous generations; couples split up more often and as a consequence, there are more lone parents. For these parents in particular, care capital in the form of helping relatives, ex-partners, neighbours or friends is extremely valuable. Although care can also be purchased, the market price of non-state sponsored care services is so high in Northern Europe that only a limited minority of parents are able to afford them.

In this chapter, we will examine the kinds of conditions which are associated with stress or satisfaction among respondents with children under 18 living in the household. Our main objective is to explore the extent to which different elements of care capital help to make family life a more positive experience. We begin our exploration by making some assumptions, based on previous research. The prevalence of work–family conflict is well documented and several social and psychological outcomes of this conflict have been identified. For example, research has shown that work–family conflict leads to higher stress, lower life satisfaction, and lower quality of family life (Higgins & Duxbury, 1992; Adams, King & King, 1996). However, it has not been proven that one parent remaining at home to care for children is a better solution than both parents working outside the home. One school of researchers supports the scarcity hypothesis, claiming that individuals who attempt to balance work and home life experience objective conflict, and that the demands of one domain are incompatible with the demands of the other domain. They tend to support the role conflict model, where work interferes with family life (Adams, King & King, 1996: 7; Grant-Vallone & Donaldson, 2001: 216). Another school of researchers supports the enhancement hypothesis, claiming that role accumulation is a positive phenomenon, and multiple roles are therefore multiple sources of gratification (Higgins & Duxbury, 1992). Men with working spouses were also shown to experience increased marital satisfaction and other advantages. In their famous paper, Baruch, Biener & Barnett (1987) remark upon the role conflict of mothers staying at home, with women's family roles viewed as stressors, but they also refer to studies which demonstrate the mental and physical advantages for women who are employed outside of the home.

Researchers are more unanimous about the finding that the number of children within the family is positively related to increased feelings of pressure in marriage, and also contributes to stress and lower satisfaction with family life (Kinnunen & Mauno, 1998: 168–70; Grant-Vallone & Donaldson, 2001: 221; Major, Klein & Erhart, 2002: 428). Marital conflict and marital dissatisfaction are also major stressors for women, and negative interactions with husbands are strong predictors of depression for wives. Social support and help from the family, especially the participation of the husband, has a beneficial impact on employed women's mental health (Baruch, Biener & Barnett, 1987). Similarly, emotional sustenance from family members is positively related to life satisfaction (Adams, King & King, 1996).

In applying the findings from previous research, we assume that people are less stressed and more satisfied with their family lives if they have more care capital: time, capability, money, and good social relationships. If the conditions are fine and resources match their needs, parents will feel better about caring. Thus, if a family has fewer children to be cared for and more adults to do the caring, we expect parents to be less stressed and more satisfied. Second, we assume that parents are less stressed and more satisfied if they have *enough* time to spend at home, although we do not wish to claim here that the more time they have at home, the better they feel. Third, we anticipate that parents are more satisfied and their lives are less stressful if they have more money available, for example, in order to provide good conditions for childcare or to purchase services to support it. Fourth, we consider that good social relationships relieve parents' stress and increase satisfaction. Finally, we anticipate that stress and satisfaction will be negatively correlated, in that more stress will mean less satisfaction.

Methods

Data

In the analyses presented here, we use data from the 2002 International Social Survey Programme (ISSP) for Finland and Norway. These two countries are Northern, Protestant, Scandinavian welfare states, investing a relatively large part of their GDP in family policy, with their public family policy expenses among the highest in the OECD (Adema & Ladaique, 2005: 28). There is a long tradition of women's equal participation in working life in both countries (Kinnunen & Mauno, 1998; Leira, 2002). In Finland, women have also traditionally worked full-time when they have small children, whereas in Norway it has been more typical for women to work part-time (Ellingsæter, 2003). Crompton and Lyonette (2006b) describe Finland and Norway as countries where work–life conflict is lower than in Britain, France and Portugal. This is related to the fact that full-time workers have a shorter working week, gender role attitudes are more liberal, and the governments have implemented policies to facilitate dual-earner families in both countries.

The childcare policy models of these two countries are exceptional, providing state-sponsored childcare services for nearly all parents, and financial support if parents want to arrange care of their children in some other way. This combination is based on the principle that the care of young children should be well supported, irrespective of how parents want to arrange childcare: parents should be able to choose between different childcare arrangements (Ellingsæter, 2003; Kröger, Anttonen & Sipilä, 2003). In contrast to the two other Nordic countries, Denmark and Sweden, parents have access to subsidised day care centres for children, as well as receiving financial support if they want to take care of their children themselves or use the money to purchase private services. Since 1990, the local councils in Finland have been obliged to provide day care places for all children under the age of three (since 1995 under the age of seven), whose parents wish to choose this service. As an alternative, all guardians of children under three have the right to take a home care allowance (Kröger, Anttonen & Sipilä, 2003). In her 1992 book, Leira described Norway as a latecomer in childcare policy among the Scandinavian welfare states. However, Norway has caught up fast and can now boast one of the highest proportions of children in public day care. In addition, since 1999, Norway has had a generous system of home care allowances (Leira, 2002).

The ISSP 2002 sample as a whole includes 1353 Finnish and 1475 Norwegian respondents but our analysis concentrates on those 1070 respondents who have at least one child under 18 in the household. The data includes 188 Finnish and 277 Norwegian respondents who have at least one child under six or seven (under compulsory school age), and respectively 356 and 450 respondents with a child aged between six and seventeen in Norway, or between seven and seventeen in Finland, living at home. Similarities in childcare policies have had an impact on how we analyse the Finnish and Norwegian data. As the sample of families with children, and particularly with small children, is so small, we have worked with the combined data where possible. Comparing Finland and Norway is therefore not the main aim of this article.

Measures

Our analyses concentrate on the relationships between care capital, stress and satisfaction with family life. We measure care capital by

- people available: the number of adults in the household,
- time: working time spent in the labour market,
- financial resources: incomes, and as a compensatory variable, education, and
- adult co-operation: sharing household work and making decisions together.

After experiments with stress scales consisting of several variables, we decided to use one item only: 'My life at home is rarely stressful.' The response scale ranges from five ('strongly disagree') to one ('strongly agree'). Thirty per cent of the respondents got scores of four or five ('disagree' or 'strongly disagree'), reflecting high levels of stress. Among the respondents who had children, the mean stress score was 2.81 (s.d. = 1.00).

Satisfaction with family life was measured with the standard question: 'All things considered, how satisfied are you with your family life?' The highest score of seven represents high dissatisfaction ('completely unhappy'). Ninety per cent of the respondents with children were more or less satisfied (scores one to three) with their family life (mean score 2.46; s.d. = 0.97).

Most of the data analyses were conducted using ANOVA to compare group means and to test for significant differences. Linear and multi-nomial regression models were also used on occasion, as well as Pearson correlation coefficients, contingency coefficients and chi-square tests.

Results

Country and gender

Before we go into a more detailed analysis of families with children, we report some general findings. The ISSP data for Finland and Norway as a whole supports the well-documented finding that women in general are slightly more satisfied with their lives than men (mean score for women 2.85 and for men 2.94). However, when asked specifically about satisfaction with family life, women are a little less satisfied than men (mean for women 2.53 and for men 2.48). And finally, Table 9.1 shows that, when only those respondents with children in the household are included,

Table 9.1: Country, gender, stress and satisfaction (means)

Respondent's sex	Country	Stress at home	Dissatisfaction with family life
Male	Finland	2.39	2.39
	Norway	2.84	2.37
	Total	2.65	2.38
Female	Finland	2.81	2.57
	Norway	3.07	2.50
	Total	2.96	2.53
Total	Finland	2.62	2.49
	Norway	2.96	2.44
	Total	2.81	2.46

A two-way ANOVA was performed with sex and country as independent variables and stress at home as the dependent variable. The post-hoc pairwise comparisons were Bonferroni corrected. The main effects for sex and country on stress at home were both significant $p < 0.001$. The model explained 5 per cent of the variation in stress at home ($R^2 = 0.05$).

The main effect for sex on dissatisfaction with family life was significant $p < 0.01$, for country it was not significant. Variation in dissatisfaction was weakly explained by the model ($R^2 = 0.01$).

the difference is even larger (mean for women 2.53 and for men 2.38). It appears that for men in particular, family and children improve satisfaction.

Women in families with children are on average both more stressed and less satisfied than men. If we compare respondents with children to the data as a whole, which also includes single people, we get results which are challenging for gender equity. Living with children seems to add more to the stress levels of women (difference = 0.33) than those of men (difference = 0.21). The presence of children in the household makes a positive impact on men's, but not on women's, satisfaction with family life.

In all categories in Table 9.1, Norwegian respondents express more stress than Finnish respondents, with Finnish men the least stressed of all. It is also worth noting that single men are remarkably dissatisfied with their family lives (mean 3.34), whereas single women are much less dissatisfied (mean 2.80).

The amount of work: numbers of children and parents

We now examine how the numbers of children and adults in the family influence the experiences of stress at home and satisfaction with family life (Table 9.2).

Table 9.2:   Household composition, stress and satisfaction (means)

Household composition	Stress at home	Dissatisfaction with family life
Single household	2.39	3.05
1 adult, 1 child	2.55	2.71
1 adult, 2 children	2.89	2.92
1 adult, 3 children+	3.84	2.68
2 adults	2.31	2.35
2 adults, 1 child	2.67	2.49
2 adults, 2 children	2.88	2.38
2 adults, 3 children+	2.80	2.38
3 adults	2.41	2.58
3 adults, 1 child	2.86	2.54
3 adults, 2 children	2.46	2.22
3 adults, 3 children+	2.87	2.25
Total	2.54	2.50
N	(2593)	(2634)

Stress by household composition: $p < 0.001$, $R^2 = 0.06$. Dissatisfaction by household composition: $p < 0.001$, $R^2 = 0.05$.

In general, people without children report lower stress at home. Childless couples and single households confirm this in Table 9.2. The presence of children increases stress at home, and the higher the number of children, the more stress there is, especially among lone parents. In families with three adult persons, however, the number of children seems not to be related to stress in any consistent way. Satisfaction with family life is not connected to household composition in the same way as stress. Not only are single households least happy with their family life, but also the respondents with several children tend to be slightly more satisfied than those with one child only. Broadly speaking, stress at home does not mean dissatisfaction with family life.

Stress and satisfaction levels do not appear to be affected by whether the children are young or old (Table 9.3). Parents who have small children are slightly more stressed but they are also more satisfied than those who have older children. Having both older and younger children does not relieve stress. It could be assumed that the children in the age group of between six/seven and seventeen help their parents in taking care of younger children and therefore add to the care capital, although this is not confirmed by our data.

Time for household work

If there is more time to spend at home, there might be less stress at home and more satisfaction with family life. Table 9.4 shows that people report lower stress if there are no children in the household, but being out of the labour force and staying at home does not relieve stress at home. It is interesting to note that in families without children, full-time employment does not increase levels of stress.

Satisfaction with family life appears extremely stable, irrespective of respondents' work status and of children being at home or not. In other

Table 9.3: Older and younger children, stress and satisfaction (means)

Young and older children in household	Stress at home	Dissatisfaction with family life
No children	2.36	2.53
Younger children only	2.88	2.34
Older children only	2.73	2.51
Younger and older children	2.97	2.47
Total	2.54	2.50

Stress by young and old children in the household: $p < 0.001$, $R^2 = 0.05$. Dissatisfaction by young and older children in the household not significant.

tables, children have generally been shown to add to the satisfaction with family life, but Table 9.4 show that adults who are working full-time and have children are somewhat more satisfied than those without children, but people outside the labour force present contrary feelings. One explanation for their particular situation is that plentiful time at home is often linked to financial difficulties. Obviously, this issue must be explored more closely. Indeed, when more accurate work status categories are used, and comparisons are made between two kinds of respondents (homemakers and unemployed persons) who both have children in the household and are outside the labour market, we find quite different answers. Those taking care of the household (n = 64, 62 of whom are women) report high stress (mean 3.06, also higher than the female average), while the mean score for the unemployed (n = 27) is low (2.53) for both women and men. On the other hand, satisfaction with family life appears to be almost the opposite: the mean score for the housewives is the most positive of all the work status categories (mean 2.34), but for the unemployed (mean 2.71), the score is more negative than the average (mean 2.45). Perhaps we could even conclude that the housewives are stressed but satisfied, whereas the unemployed are not stressed but dissatisfied.

Table 9.4:   Respondent's work status, stress and satisfaction (means)

Respondent's work status	Children in household	Stress at home	Dissatisfaction with family life
Full-time	no	2.34	2.55
	yes	2.79	2.43
	Total	2.55	2.49
Part-time	no	2.41	2.53
	yes	2.97	2.46
	Total	2.66	2.50
Not in labour force	no	2.36	2.46
	yes	2.86	2.52
	Total	2.49	2.47
Total	no	2.35	2.51
	yes	2.82	2.45
	Total	2.54	2.49
N		(2478)	(2529)

Stress by children in the household: $p < 0.001$, $R^2 = 0.05$. Dissatisfaction by interacting variables children in the household and respondents' work status: $p < 0.05$.

Money

Money is a resource that can be used to improve the conditions of child-care and to relieve the burden of household work. On the one hand, money is earned in paid employment for most people, reducing the time resources which could be used at home. In the Finnish ISSP data, but unfortunately not in the Norwegian data, there is information on incomes, which means that the next analyses are based on the Finnish respondents only. In order to learn if money is a positive resource and a part of care capital, we focus initially on respondents' incomes. When inspecting the Finnish respondents' incomes, however, there does not appear to be a clear connection between money, stress and happiness. The expected association only exists among those respondents who are outside the labour force. There is also a small group (n = 7) of full-time working respondents with low earnings, whose stress is low and level of satisfaction very high (mean 1.86).

Another alternative is to look at family incomes instead of individual respondents' incomes. Three categories are used here: low = 0–2999 €, medium = 3000–3999 €, and high = 4000 € and over, per month. This alteration makes the picture more explicit. Table 9.5 shows that dissatisfaction with family life clearly decreases with increasing family incomes; this also applies to stress but to a lesser extent. Income means care capital, but it is the family income that counts.

Other adults

Table 9.2 showed that the number of adults in the family has an impact on stress and satisfaction. There is less stress and more satisfaction in a family with children if there is more than one adult person living in the household. With three adults in the household, the results are not very consistent – apparently, the score depends very much on what kind of a

Table 9.5:   Family incomes, stress and satisfaction, Finnish data only (means)

Family income	Stress at home	Dissatisfaction with family life
Low	2.77	2.83
Medium	2.72	2.53
High	2.56	2.36
Total	2.66	2.52
N	(371)	(374)

Stress by family income not significant. Dissatisfaction by family income: $p < 0.01$, $R^2 = 0.03$.

person the third adult is. In a nuclear family with two parents, the amount of stress and satisfaction is unlikely to be independent of the quality of the parents' relationship. We now examine two popular topics: do the partners share household work, and do they make decisions together in their everyday lives? A summary variable for 'sharing household work' was constructed from responses to the question 'In your household, who does the following things . . .?' A binary code (those answering 'about equal or both together' were coded as co-operative) was constructed for each of the six items, which specify the division of labour between the spouse/partner and the respondent. After coding, the items were added up. The other summary variable, 'deciding together,' was based on questions relating to 'Who usually makes the decisions?' The five items concern bringing up children, choosing weekend activities, buying major things at home, pooling the money, and agreeing about the sharing of household work. Before summing the items, they were recoded to create a binary code: those who had said 'we decide together' and who 'rarely' or 'never disagree' about household work were counted as co-operative.

Women in families with children spend 13 hours a week on average on household work (not including childcare and leisure time activities), whereas men spend six hours. On average, the respondents said that they share 1.4 of the six household tasks. Sharing decision-making, however, appears easier. In our data, the partners reported that they make 1.7 of the five possible decisions together. (It is no surprise that men reported 0.4 more shared tasks and 0.2 more shared decision topics than women.)

The data in Table 9.6 includes both Finland and Norway. Sharing of household work and making decisions are significantly correlated, and both are associated with decreased stress and increased satisfaction. If causal interpretations are allowed, making decisions together appears to have a stronger influence on stress and satisfaction than sharing of

Table 9.6:   Sharing household work, deciding together, stress and satisfaction (correlations)

	Stress at home	Dissatisfaction with family life	Sharing of household work
Stress at home	—	—	—
Dissatisfaction with family life	0.26(**)	—	—
Sharing of household work	−0.05	−0.13(**)	—
Making decisions together	−0.13(**)	−0.31(**)	0.42(**)

** Correlation is significant at the 0.01 level (2-tailed). N = 1024.

household work. It is important also to note that, although stress and dissatisfaction have correlated inversely in several of the earlier tables, here both variables are positively correlated.

We also find that people in general are less stressed and more satisfied if they share a few household duties together. However, if men and women are viewed separately, stress and sharing duties vary congruently for women only (see Crompton & Lyonette, 2005). Almost one-third of the male respondents say that they share no duties equally. These men are the least stressed of all respondents (mean 2.58); on the other hand, they are also the men who are least satisfied with their family lives (mean 2.57). Similar dissatisfaction is true for women who do not share duties (mean 2.69), but they are also the most stressed of all women (mean 3.02).

The situation is quite different if, instead of examining household duties, we turn to common decision-making between couples (Table 9.7). Both male and female respondents are generally less stressed at home and more satisfied with their family lives if they make decisions together. Even here, however, there is a large group (one-fifth of all men in families with children) who on average feel no stress and yet make no decisions with their partner. As in the previous table, avoiding stress does not make them happy, however, as they are the most dissatisfied of all men with their family lives.

Stress and satisfaction

How are we to understand the varying interaction between stress and satisfaction? In some cases, the respondents who feel high stress also report satisfaction with their family lives, but in other groups, highly stressed respondents report that they are dissatisfied with their family lives. In order to clarify this, we now concentrate on the ends of the scales. Firstly, we examine only those respondents who are the least or the most stressed. The least stressed are persons who 'strongly agree' that their life at home is rarely stressful, while the most stressed 'strongly disagree' or 'disagree' with this statement. To characterise these two groups, we use ANOVA and observe that the most stressed people are more likely to be women than men (eta = 0.20), and feel more often that they do more than their fair share of household work (eta = 0.27). But how satisfied are they with their family lives?

Table 9.8 shows that between the least and most stressed persons there is a large gap in satisfaction with family life. Stress and dissatisfaction correlate strongly (eta = 0.29). Although this result is important, it does not explain the differences in the interaction between these variables,

Table 9.7: Decisions made together, stress and satisfaction (means)

Respondent: Sex	Decisions made together	Stress at home	Dissatisfied with family life
Male	None	2.57	2.82
	1	3.13	2.42
	2	2.74	2.46
	3	2.50	2.31
	4	2.69	2.08
	All decisions	2.32	1.94
	Total	2.65	2.38
Female	None	2.92	2.87
	1	3.47	2.86
	2	3.12	2.61
	3	2.96	2.38
	4	2.77	2.11
	All decisions	2.35	1.95
	Total	2.96	2.53
Total	None	2.79	2.85
	1	3.31	2.66
	2	2.91	2.53
	3	2.76	2.35
	4	2.73	2.10
	All decisions	2.33	1.94
	Total	2.81	2.46
N		(1024)	(1058)

Stress by decisions made together: $p < 0.001$ and by sex: $p < 0.001$, $R^2 = 0.08$. Dissatisfied by decisions made together: $p < 0.001$, $R^2 = 0.11$.

Table 9.8: Satisfaction and the extreme levels of stress (means)

Stress at home	N	Dissatisfied with family life
Least stressed	67	1.96
Most stressed	309	2.78
Total	376	2.63

Dissatisfaction by extreme levels of stress: $p < 0.001$, $R^2 = 0.09$.

which has been found previously. We therefore continue by cross-tabulating the extremes of two variables, stress and satisfaction. We code as most satisfied those respondents who say that they are 'completely satisfied' with their family lives. The other end consists of those who are 'fairly' or 'very' or 'completely' dissatisfied.

Table 9.9: Stress and satisfaction, extreme cases only

		Satisfaction with family life		
		Completely satisfied	Dissatisfied	Total
Stress at home:	least stressed	27	3	30
	most stressed	19	25	44
Total		46	28	74

Chi-Square < 0.001 Contingency coefficient = 0.43.

The number of cases in Table 9.9 remains small. However, the information is clear and the discrepancy between stress and dissatisfaction becomes somewhat easier to understand. Almost all the respondents who report very little stress are also completely satisfied with their family life. Lack of stress goes together with strong satisfaction, whereas the most stressed respondents can be found at either end of the satisfaction scale. Strong stress is compatible both with the feeling of satisfaction and with the feeling of dissatisfaction.

Care capital

Our intention is to find out if we can explain variations in the experiences of stress and satisfaction with the use of care capital as a summary variable. How does the availability or lack of time, financial resources and another adult person influence stress and satisfaction levels? One solution is to inspect the three central dimensions simultaneously by cross-tabulation. Another method is to construct a summary variable of the three variables operationalising these dimensions. Once again, we use the Finnish data because of the need for information on family incomes.

After several experiments, it was shown that working time is not related to stress and satisfaction in the anticipated direction. Our original assumption is therefore wrong: parents are not less stressed and more satisfied if they have a lot of time to spend at home. Also in the combined Finnish/Norwegian data, long working hours correlate positively with non-stress at home and satisfaction with family life. For this reason, we concentrate on the two remaining variables and transform them into a binary code: parents have the highest possible care capital if they live together and have a family income of at least 4000 €. Those living alone and having a smaller family income have the lowest capital.

Cross-tabulations produced logical results: those respondents living with a partner and having a higher family income were less stressed at home and more satisfied with family life, but the differences were not statistically significant (probably because there were too few lone parents.) A decision was then taken to test the impact of care capital in a three-variable linear regression model, with sex and age as the other variables. When explaining stress at home, sex was the only significant variable ($p < 0.001$). However, when explaining dissatisfaction with family life ($R^2 = 0.05$) both age and care capital were highly significant ($p < 0.001$) while sex was not. Adding shared decision making to the model raised the predictability of the model to a higher level ($R^2 = 0.17$). Shared decision making, age and care capital were highly significant, and sex also became significant ($p < 0.005$).

But what should we think about the lack of significance of working time? The Finnish and Norwegian respondents simply did not connect long working hours to stress at home or to dissatisfaction with family life. This finding did not change, although we varied the measures of working hours, looking at individual respondents, their partners, and also couples working for shorter or longer hours. The only exception was that couples whose combined working hours were very short were slightly more stressed and less satisfied than the other groups.

As a result, should we therefore insist that time is not a part of care capital at all? It seems that the importance of time cannot be measured by examining respondents' stress and satisfaction levels. This is because people already take into account their caring duties before they decide how many hours they spend at work. For instance, 51 per cent of the unmarried parents worked less than 35 hours a week, compared with only 27 per cent of the married respondents. In other words, the presence of small children has little effect on married women's working hours, whereas unmarried women's working hours tend to be reduced.

An interesting outcome was demonstrated when examining extreme dissatisfaction with family life, using a multinomial regression model. Sex remained insignificant when the variable 'decisions made together' was included in the model. In other words, women were no more likely than men to be very dissatisfied with their family lives, on condition that decision-making was shared.

Discussion

The central topic in this study is how certain dimensions of care capital are related to stress at home and satisfaction with family life. We found that the central resources (time, money and other people) are all connected with stress and satisfaction scores, but not always directly. Time without money does not reduce stress and dissatisfaction. Money without time has a stronger effect, but there are still exceptions, because higher than medium income levels seem not to add to satisfaction with family life. Another adult in the family is an extremely significant resource, assuming that there is good cooperation in decision-making and household work. If not, another adult may be one more person to be cared for. The best outcome is multidimensional: people need time, money and adults with whom they can share housework and childcare.

By and large, the associations between care capital and satisfaction with family life were as expected. However, there were some exceptions. Our main result seems to contradict earlier research which has supported the scarcity hypothesis and emphasised role conflict between work and family. The Finnish and Norwegian parents who were employed simply felt less stress at home. There are three possible explanations for this result. First, it is quite possible that our finding is related to factual childcare arrangements: work–life conflict must be influenced by context, and a Scandinavian welfare state certainly helps in relieving the childcare dimension of the conflict. Second, our result certainly depends on how the concept 'stress at home' is understood by the respondents. Stress at home in this study seems to be largely ascribed to the amount of household work undertaken. A similar result was also found by Frank, Harvey and Elon (2000: 138). As a consequence, the respondents do not necessarily associate stress with dissatisfaction with family life, particularly if living together with small children is the factual reason for stress. Indeed, this might be the explanation for our unexpected result: the missing correlation between stress and dissatisfaction.

When discussing the connections between care capital, stress and satisfaction in our study, it is necessary to remember that all our respondents live in welfare states, with relatively generous support for families with children and childcare. A large part of the care capital is embodied in state benefits and in municipal institutions (Crompton & Lyonette, 2006b), which leads us to think that the care capital possessed by individual families and persons might not be so relevant in Finland and Norway as in societies without active family policies (cf. Rothstein, 1998). This is a good reason to use larger, cross-national data when studying care capital in future.

In the ISSP 2002 survey, Norway and Finland appear to be countries with liberal gender role attitudes, encouraging men to do more household work and child-care (Crompton & Lyonette, 2006b). In spite of all this, our investigation reminds us that traditional gendered practices have not vanished in these two countries. Although our summary variables describing partners' co-operation in household work and in decision-making were based on rather demanding criteria, the amount of more equal sharing was low, and there was also a minority of men not co-operating in anything and feeling less stressed than the others. The image of the egalitarian Finnish family found in the study of Kinnunen and Mauno (1998) is not supported in our findings. There still are remarkable gender differences in experiencing work–family conflict.

Finally, what should we think about the concept of care capital? First, it certainly is a pragmatic way to speak of care resources as a totality. We have also shown in this chapter that it can be operationalised for empirical research. Although care capital as a summary variable was not the best possible variable to explain variation in stress at home or satisfaction with family life, it would still be of great importance to study care capital more fully, and the resources families have available to them in arranging care for their children in such a way that good care becomes possible. Unfortunately, this test cannot be made with the ISSP 2002 data.

The advantage of using the concept of care capital can be found elsewhere. Firstly, this concept may help to bring the discourses around care closer to the discourses on social capital (Sevenhuijsen, 2002a). If we discuss social capital without demonstrating its connection to family and care, the old fallacy, which undermines the importance of care, will continue. It should be thoroughly accepted that economy is embedded in social reproduction and eventually, in taking care of dependent human beings. Second, we think that a concept like care capital invites researchers to measure the capital, to assess its productivity, and to define how much care capital is needed in a society. It calls on citizens, including politicians and economists, to understand that care is an element which must be taken into account if societies are to be sustained. The concept of care capital emphasises that care is based on resources that must be created, accumulated and distributed as equally as possible. We need alternative ways to study social capital in contemporary societies (Stolle & Lewis, 2002).

The concept of care capital also leads us to theoretical paths. One example of such a path is the question: who possesses the care capital? Is the care capital actually money and time acquired and controlled mainly by women and then consumed in the tasks of caregiving? This point of view would mean that women spend money earned by both them and men, and that women abstain from other activities in order to have the time to care. Another alternative is to think that women, instead of being the main owners, are low paid workers who perform duties for care capital to accumulate. Whereas our results confirm the old finding of social research that men, in particular, benefit from marriage and children (Baruch, Biener & Barnett, 1987), we need to ask: do women still in an archaic sense somehow constitute a distinct part of the capital possessed by men? Although this might be the truth in some cultures and some families, mercifully there are better ways to create and use care capital: men and women also seem to create and manage care capital by sharing resources and decision-making.

Conclusions

Our aim was to examine the use of the concept of care capital when studying stress at home and satisfaction with family life in families with children. Care capital is a concept that allows us to study care resources in a multidimensional way. We think that a certain amount of care capital is needed to make family life a positive experience for both women and men. In this study, we operationalise care capital so that it includes the following dimensions: the number of adults in the family (social relations), working time and labour market participation (family–work relations), family incomes (financial resources) and the co-operation between adult partners in the family (sharing of housework and childcare). While concentrating on respondents from Northern Europe only, the importance of individualised care capital could not be studied. In the Nordic welfare states, a considerable amount of care capital is embodied in state-sponsored services and benefits paid to parents to combine care and work. It would be of great interest to compare the Nordic countries with those European countries where public support for childcare is much more limited. We found that the central dimensions of care capital (time, money, and other persons) were all connected with the scores of stress and satisfaction, but not always in a direct way. Those respondents who had more time to spend at home (and less money) did not report lower amounts of stress and dissatisfaction. In spite of this, we could not exclude the importance of time. Money had a stronger positive effect, but higher than medium incomes seemed not to add to satisfaction with family life. Another adult in the family was an extremely significant resource, assuming that good co-operation existed between partners in decision-making and in household work. People need time, money and co-operation with the adults they are living with. This explains why parents staying at home do not necessarily feel happy or satisfied.

When discussing the usefulness of the concept of care capital, we suggest that the concept may help to bring the discourses around care closer to the rich discourses on social capital. We also think that a concept like care capital invites researchers to measure the capital, to assess its productivity, and to define how much and which kind of care capital is needed in a society. The concept of care capital underlines for citizens, including politicians and economists, that care is based on resources which must be created, accumulated and distributed, not only individually but also collectively.

10
The Workplace as an Arena for Negotiating the Work–Family Boundary: a Case Study of Two Swedish Social Services Agencies

Margareta Bäck-Wiklund and Lars Plantin

Introduction

The Swedish welfare state has for a long time been distinctive in developing radical social policies in the area of reproduction, particularly as far as children are concerned. For more than 30 years, the government has implemented a family policy with the clear aim of gender equality, with *parental insurance* and *public childcare* being two of its most important developments. The potential for working parents in Sweden to successfully combine work and family life is good. The number of working mothers has increased in recent decades, and at the same time, relatively high fertility rates (see Chapter 4) have been maintained, although with considerable fluctuations. For many years, Sweden has had a high percentage of working mothers, and 80 per cent of women aged 25–54 with two children or more are currently in work, with 60 per cent of them employed in the public sector (Fagnani et al., 2004).

However, at the beginning of the 1990s, Sweden experienced a severe economic crisis, resulting in mass unemployment and reductions in welfare benefits. For the first time, support to families was reduced, meaning that many families with children suffered financially. Combined with rising unemployment, this led to a drop in the fertility rate (see Chapter 4). A new pattern of class-differentiated family formation began to emerge, where employed people were more likely to have children, especially if they were well-educated and well-paid. The reverse was true for lower-educated, lower-paid or unemployed people, who tended to put parenthood on hold. This trend of 'no job no kids' still exists today. Thus, it is possible to argue that we are witnessing a new parental identity where a secure job is one of several prerequisites for parenthood.

These developments indicate that family life, as well as individual autonomy, is tightly coupled with both the welfare state and the labour market. According to Esping-Andersen, 'the Nordic welfare state regimes remain the only ones where social policy is explicitly designed to maximize women's economic independence' (1999: 51). In this respect, the welfare state reinforces the general trend towards individual autonomy.

Against this background, we now focus on the workplace as an intermediate organisation between the welfare state and the family, where individual independence and family responsibilities meet. The Swedish welfare state is supposed to function as a buffer between the family and the labour market, but how does it affect the way workplaces and working parents handle work–family boundaries? Except for the rights guaranteed by the state, what kind of support do working parents get from their employers? In what way do employers' management practices help or hinder employee strategies for combining work and family life? We know from previous research that Swedish employers have far fewer policies in this area than many other western European countries (den Dulk, 2001; Haas, Hwang and Russell, 2000; Jämo, 1999; 2000). The aim of this chapter is to examine these questions and to study the workplace as an arena for negotiating the work–family boundary. We will do this by presenting the results from a case study based on two social service agencies in one of Sweden's largest cities.

Research strategy and design

The case study includes two social service agencies which belong to the same municipal welfare organisation, named after their geographical locations within the city, *Centre* and *Periphery*. Although their history of organisational change is somewhat different, their present structure is similar. In both places there has been a gradual adaptation to an interorganisational 'buy and sell' system, as well as strategies to reduce costs. From an international perspective, this trend has been defined as *New Public Management* (see, for example, McLaughlin, Osborne & Ferlie, 2002). Both organisations have a high rate of people on sick leave, at almost one month per person, per year. The Periphery has more people temporarily employed and also more people working part time than the Centre.

Case studies help to explore the working practices which facilitate or block employees' strategies for integrating paid work and personal life. They are particularly appropriate for studying the complexity of organisations by incorporating multiple methods and perspectives. Case studies also include a research strategy whereby data is generated from several levels within the organisation (employers and employees), as well as from the organisational environment, (for example, family members of employees) (Lewis, Das Dores Guerreiro & Brannen, 2005).

Following this research strategy, the study is based on a variety of material: focus group interviews, individual interviews, documentation from the organisations about different policies, statistics, organisational charts, and a well-being questionnaire. The material includes individual interviews with the two directors from both agencies, as well as the two human resource managers and 14 unit managers (eight in one agency and six in the other), totalling 20 interviews in all. The material also includes six focus group interviews with working parents (three groups at each agency), with a total of 26 participants. By using this strategy, the aim was to get a broad view of the organisation and how employees in different positions negotiate the work–family boundary. In order to achieve this, we included respondents from different settings in the organisation, and from different social backgrounds, education, employment, ethnicity and housing status. The respondents were recruited through the human resource managers, according to specific criteria. Four of the focus groups included exclusively professional social workers, and one included only unit managers and one low skilled worker from the cleaning and maintenance service. Eighteen of the interviewees were women and eight were men. Most of them were married, although ten were cohabiting and one was living alone. There were also differences in levels of education among the participants, as 19 had a university degree, six had upper secondary school education and one had compulsory school education only.

The age of the interviewees in the focus groups ranged from 26 to 40 years, with a majority in their early thirties, and almost all had children under six years of age. In both the focus groups and the individual interviews, a guide with three distinct foci was used: the transition to and experiences of parenthood; organisational well-being and workplace practices; and work–family boundary strategies.

Family friendly policies

Parental insurance is, along with public child care, the welfare state's most important support for working parents. It entitles parents to 480 days' leave from work at different replacement rates. It is allocated on a quota basis, so that the mother and father each have 60 earmarked days, while the remaining days, guaranteed by statute, can be shared between them. This principle was introduced to encourage men to stay at home to care for their young children. The parental insurance also includes a temporary benefit (VAB) which allows parents to stay at home to care for a sick child (up to the age of 12) for up to 60 days per child per year, with a 20 per cent reduction in salary. The Swedish Association of Local Authorities, which covers all those employed in local authorities, has added extra compensation for parental leave, such as two days paid time off to attend childbirth classes or medical examinations related to pregnancy. If more days are needed, the parental insurance also allows for the possibility of using 60 days before the anticipated birth of the child. The Local Authority employees in the case study organisations also had a flexitime contract that allowed individuals some control over their working hours.

Both agencies have an official equal opportunity policy, based on the requirements of The Equal Opportunities Act from 1980. The purpose of this Act is to promote equal rights for women and men in matters relating to work, the terms and conditions of employment, and other working conditions and opportunities for development in work. Every employer in Sweden with more than ten employees is obliged to have an equality plan including measures on how to promote equality in working life. The equality plan is supposed to cover active measures in several areas, for example, to ensure that working conditions are suitable for both women and men, to facilitate the combination of gainful employment and parenthood with respect to both female and male employees, and to take measures to prevent sexual harassment and sex discrimination. Employers must also carry out annual surveys and analyse regulations and practice concerning pay and pay differentials between women and men.

For all social workers employed in municipal welfare organisations, there is also a special scheme known as the 'model for competence development'. This model is a bottom-up initiative, designed to raise the status of social workers as a profession, with extensive further education and individual competence factors to be recognised in relation to wages and discretion. The model comprises five steps, according to education level and professional experience (Byberg & Lindquist, 2003). This emphasis on education goes hand in hand with the ideas expressed in the latest revision of the Social Service Act from 1998, the requirements of the National Board of Public Health, as well as local managers' use of education as a managerial tool.

Policies and practices

Even though policies in many areas can be linked with the preconditions for successfully combining work and family life, it is primarily the policy on flexible work hours and the equality plan which, apart from parental leave rights, most clearly concern working parents. The following section will therefore focus on these policies, using selected accounts from employers and employees in different contexts within the workplace.

Flexibility, economy and workload

Most parents use flexible working hours, which are viewed as crucial in combining work and family life. Flexibility allows parents to stay at home for whole days, to leave early, to arrive late, or to leave in cases of emergency. At the same time, flexible working time acts as an important economic buffer to ease the financial losses incurred by the use of temporary benefit (VAB). Almost all respondents describe that when their children are sick, they would rather use previously earned compensation time, or try to coordinate their working time with partners in order to avoid the 20 per cent loss of salary when using parental leave for sick children (VAB):

'It means I don't need to use as much VAB or be away from work. For my daughter I have not used one single VAB-day and for the boy maybe only 2 days. If I am in an emergency it's usually solved by my sister or mum coming to the rescue.' (Female social worker)

Interviewer: How come?

'It's good economically since I don't lose money. I already lose a certain amount, since I'm on sick leave for 50 per cent and work for 50 per cent of the time.'

The use of compensation time can also be a way for managers to meet an increasing work-load. Even if both employers and employees report an increasing workload, the use of paid overtime is still uncommon, due to budget restrictions. In these situations, some unit managers feel that they have to handle contradictory and unclear signals from their managers:

'They expect things to be done in time and sometimes that means you'll have to work long hours. But on the other hand, the general rule here is that you shouldn't have too much overtime or compensation time. So, it's a bit contradictory.' (Unit manager)

Nearly all unit managers said they were aware of, and fully sympathised with, the problems in combining work and family life. As a result of this, they also tried to be as understanding as possible towards employees with work and family-related problems. As an example, managers said that they always tried to meet requests for part-time employment. However, although this might seem generous on their part, in Sweden all parents with children under 12 have a legal right to part-time work, which means that employers cannot deny such requests from parents.

Many of the respondents in the focus groups who had experienced part-time work also confirmed the unit managers' reports. Requests for part-time work were generally accepted, but to reduce one's workload accordingly was often very difficult. None of these respondents had received any help from their managers with the transition to part-time working, and often found themselves in situations where they were still expected to work full-time. Due to a lack of managerial guidance in relation to the whole work team, the part-time worker often ended up in ambiguous situations with conflicting demands and dependence upon his or her team members:

'My employer has had a very positive attitude to my part-time work. After all, I was recruited to this social agency even though I told them that I was working part-time from the very beginning. And my fellow workers have also given me support, taking over some of the things I couldn't take on because of my reduced working hours. But, there hasn't been any clear practical structure [in that attitude]. Instead, a lot of work, which I haven't been able to take, has suddenly been loaded on to my colleagues. And some work hasn't been done because of poor planning and a gap between attitude and practice. It causes both me and others a lot of irritation.' (Unit manager)

Gendered discrimination

As mentioned above, the equality plan was poorly implemented within the organisations. Most unit managers were well aware of its existence, but no one could actually fully explain its contents. The working parents had no knowledge of the plan or its content. Some employees also reported their own experiences of discrimination. A single mother reported that she had had to face negative attitudes:

'As a single mother – I do not recognise your description of an equality plan. I have tried to do my best – and I have adjusted my time schedule . . . it is taken for granted that you should always be available. But when I have failed to do this, people have shown how disappointed they are in me.' (Social worker)

One man felt that there was a level of gender discrimination, in that men are not supposed to be absent because of family issues:

'The employer is slightly more tolerant towards women in a traditional way . . . I sometimes get comments in relation to my absence from strategic meetings – you must come . . . after all, there are two parents in the house. They obviously think that it is more appropriate that my wife stays at home. There seems to be a hidden agenda.' (Social worker)

Gender, therefore, seems to matter in various subtle ways. When talking about parental leave, one human resource manager referred to general principles and discourses that men 'must have' the experience of caring for their child/children. She did not present any ideas on how to encourage men to take leave, but claimed that it was 'extremely important that men take parental leave' – that is, that men should be 'encouraged' to be carers. However, other managers saw men working in social services as 'caring men', just as competent as women in handling parenthood. This was emphasised by a third unit manager who claimed that 'men as well as women are parents':

'Men in Social Services are generally very caring. They look upon themselves as parents, prioritise their children, and stay at home to care for their children when needed.'

The accounts above demonstrate how discrimination might be perceived in relation to workplace policies, but there is also a more subtle dimension embedded in the official discourse about fathers taking parental leave and 'the new fatherhood'. By some managers, men's parental responsibilities are interpreted as a state concern, contrary to women's responsibilities which are seen as a private family matter.

The parents in the focus groups showed a similar pattern to Swedish parents in general, regarding the use of parental leave. Women have primary responsibility for home and children overall, with the women in the study using about two-thirds or more of their parental leave. Around half of them also worked part-time, whereas all the men worked full-time. The gendered use of the parental insurance has also been recently confirmed in an official evaluation (RFV 2004).

Practices relating to family issues

The unit managers claimed to be understanding and obliging when employees needed to be absent from work because of acute family issues.

Some of the managers felt that the organisation within a social agency must be built on flexibility in order to meet unexpected situations:

> 'Our jobs must be organised in a way that allow people to suddenly leave for different reasons. If this is because of acute situations in your private life or if it's related to the job and the clients, it doesn't matter.' (Unit manager)

The effects of employees being absent from work were often mentioned in a general way. However, it also became clear that if an employee was away from work a lot, for whatever reason, he or she might feel that they were letting their colleagues down:

> 'They can feel as if they're not doing enough, primarily in relation to their colleagues and not to the work itself. But I used to be supportive and tell them it's more of an organisational problem than an individual problem.' (Unit manager)

Several unit managers underlined that resolving situations like those above, or other kinds of clashes relating to work and family life, cannot be considered the sole responsibility of the employer. Employees also have a responsibility to be flexible and to try and solve such situations by various means in their private lives. In accordance with the prevailing discourse around gender equality in Sweden, some of the unit managers also recognised the importance of both parents being equally involved in everyday family life:

> 'I think I've only been irritated once in this respect and that was when I had a female employee, whose child often was sick, and her husband never stayed at home. All the time it was her and my responsibility to solve the situation. I think it was wrong . . .' (Unit manager)

But there were also many situations where the unit managers were not involved, as an informal culture seemed to have emerged among the employees:

> 'I used to plan my visits to the doctor at times of the day when I know we have less to do in the kitchen. I negotiate and plan it with my colleagues. And then I support my colleagues another time.' (Cook)

> 'Yes, it is important to get on with your colleagues because when you are away, they are the ones who have to do your job. It's not the manager. The manager doesn't do anything in this respect.' (Porter)

The picture of the employers being tolerant and obliging in relation to family crises was also confirmed by most of the social workers in the focus groups. However, it appears that most situations related to family crises were often resolved within the framework of the flexible time contract, and were negotiated with close fellow workers, rather than with the unit manager. This means that the majority of employees converted their overtime work into compensation time within the flexible time arrangements, rather than into paid overtime work.

Do policies matter?

The implementation of family-friendly policies was not a priority area for top management. Let us listen to what the director for Centre says about policies in general, and equality and flexibility in particular:

'Actually they are not that important. Managers use them "when needed". I very seldom give them a thought and I think that we govern more through education.'

All interviewed unit managers also claimed that, except for the general rights given by the state, it was more important to have a supportive manager than specific employee policies relating to different local workplace policies. While managerial decisions directly affect workplace practice, many policy agreements, they claimed, often turn out to be 'empty documents'.

The social workers also discussed the relative importance of the general rights guaranteed by the state and those facilitated by a supportive manager. However, it was obvious from their discussions that the problems and negotiations involved in combining work and family life were mostly handled at the periphery of the organisation between the social work employees, and without interference from managers. For this reason, many had experienced, as one of the social workers said: 'neither support nor resistance from the manager'. Instead, they mentioned the support from fellow-workers as most important:

'It would have been worse if colleagues were negative because you rarely meet the manager.' (Social worker)

In general, the use of flexible hours was not negotiated with the unit managers, but with colleagues in the work unit. This had clear advantages, since the decision making process was shortened. At the same time, the parent was then dependent on the colleague's goodwill and understanding of the situation when negotiating temporary absence. Sweden has recently faced a rising number of people on sick leave. Women, especially young women, seem to have more problems than other groups, and those women employed in the public sector appear to be the most vulnerable. This is sometimes explained by a general imbalance between family and work, but more often by workplace factors.

The organisations in this case pride themselves on 'looking after their employees', which is the general image presented at different levels within the organisation. However, when moving down the organisational hierarchy, different pictures were presented. The human resource managers often talked about principles 'in general' but gave few, if any, examples:

> 'The organisation is caring – even if we do not target working parents in particular – I would say that the attitude in general is very supportive.'
> (Human resource manager)

The unit managers seemed to have worked out their own principles and standards and also illustrated them with examples from their everyday practices. Members of the focus groups, acting on their behalf, had a more reflective view of their workplace. The management's general caring attitude towards employees included working parents, who were said to be treated on the same terms as other employees, within a 'comprehensive' framework. The unit managers' accounts gave a general impression of a caring organisation, but these were expressed rather vaguely. When asked if the organisation was indeed caring in its attitudes towards its employees, more than one of the managers replied: 'I should think so!' None of the managers suggested that it could be otherwise, in other words, that the social service organisation could be non-caring. When asked if the organisation was a good employer for working parents, it became quite obvious that this was not an issue discussed by the management or covered by a local workplace policy. However, it was also obvious that managers were concerned about the impact of working parents, as they often stayed at home to care for a sick child and caused disruptions to everyday work routines.

> 'I think that the unit managers have to look at the balance between working parents and the organisation – business must go on as usual – no matter what. But we do not have special agreements for working parents – and I sometimes hear unit managers complain about them being absent from work too often.' (Human resource manager)

The unit managers did not talk about working parents as a particular problem, but often referred to 'the state' and general rules and regulations:

'We do not talk about it – it is not even mentioned in our group meetings. We follow the entitlements regulated by the state, and that is it.' (Unit manager)

In practice, the unit managers set the standards for the work group, but any actual problem-solving was left to the work group. This was a recurring theme in many of the focus group discussions presented later.

'This is how I see it. My strategy as a manager is to handle certain sensible matters myself – but leave the rest to the work-group.' (Unit manager)

Experiences of the organisation

What factors influence managers in establishing work practices? All the unit managers claimed that their own experience of being parents was important in order to perform good management and that the organisation was to be regarded as a 'caring organisation'. On the other hand, they also confirmed that there were few, if any, specific management strategies to support working parents. One team manager reflected on her management strategies before and after she became a mother:

'Looking back I feel bad – because my understanding of working parents was not very good. But now with my own experiences, I realise that when someone is on leave, their workload has to be reduced. The organisation of everyday work routines must include preparation for unexpected events.' (Social worker and team manager)

Managers had different opinions about the importance of gender, but the general impression was that everybody should be treated on equal terms, regardless of sex. However, family and work were seen as different spheres and it was important to draw a dividing line between them. The family belongs to the private sphere and should be respected as such, with no outside interference. The unit managers presented different strategies for family/work balance in general, and sick leave in particular. When the employees reflected on their own situations, they generally took different positions when voicing their opinions, such as: state entitlements, management practices, colleagues and the individual situation. It was not possible to discern whether or not individual managers were more or less family-friendly, or more or less sympathetic towards working parents.

Paula is the mother of two teenagers and a six year old boy. She has been working for ten years in the same organisation on a permanent contract. She reflected upon her working conditions as a mother and the support she received from the organisation:

> [Dream of!?] 'Working life is so demanding, and to make ends meet you need to find all the loop holes yourselves. There is no time for private life. I do not have a hobby – I do not have the time – but I am happy, even though it is hard. I have developed an emergency plan – just in case. Every morning I memorise a list of people to call if anything should happen. It is OK to work part time, but when I changed from full time to part time, I was supposed to do the same job. I put myself under a lot of pressure. To reduce working hours does not automatically reduce the work load! As a matter of fact, I was left without any support at all.' (Social worker)

Paula reflects on what it is like to be a working mother in general, but she also describes how it triggers a family 'counter-culture' with private strategies to make ends meet. Her account is an example of how working parents have to be disciplined, and, as one of the unit managers mentioned earlier, become 'efficient and well structured'. Her account covers issues of importance for working parents, both in general and in relation to the work-place presented here. It appears to be acceptable to work part time if you are a working parent, but the idea of a local policy for working parents is just something you can 'dream of'. Paula emphasises the lack of management support in organising work tasks, in her case after returning from parental leave. She is ambivalent towards management, but positive in her attitude towards her team colleagues. She describes many hardships but in spite of all this, she is happy. Her attitude is in accordance with findings reported by Bäck-Wiklund and Bergsten (1997), in which a young working mother describes the hardships she has to face, but then adds 'This is what life is all about – and I do it for them! (husband, but most of all the children).'

To balance family and work is for Paula an individual and a family matter, an attitude shared by several others:

> 'I do not think that the employer is responsible for the balance between family and work: that is my own responsibility. I think it is a relief that family life draws the line between family and work. That's the way it's always going to be. I can't work overtime. But of course the flexible time is a great help.' (Social worker)

We now turn to Emrik and Sally, and their perceptions of management strategies:

> Emrik: They can ease our situation by just being cooperative. Working eight to five is not the right formula for everybody with small children. One way is to help parents to adjust their working time, for example when the children have school holidays.

> Sally: I do not think they can do anything about our situation.

> Moderator: Do you have any knowledge about the manager's jurisdiction?

> Sally: No . . . I don't!

> Emrik: I still think it is possible for them to find solutions.

Emrik takes a critical stand towards the employer, while Sally seems to have resigned herself to her situation without considering any alternatives. Neither of them seems to regard the balance between family and work as an individual or family matter, belonging only within the private sphere. They refer instead to 'the system'. The discussion below takes a different turn from what we have learned above and demonstrates an ambivalence towards the organisations as being caring in general, but not supportive in practice. These accounts are in direct response to the unit managers' strategy to rely on the work-group to make their own work–family arrangements, and the gap between words and deeds.

> 'When I came back from parental leave I started on 50 per cent. But I got no help to adjust my work load to part time. I mean, for example, was I supposed to take part at the counselling meetings . . . or? I needed help – but was left alone . . . (Social worker)

> Moderator: But do you get any support then?

> 'Of course there is support . . . in my work-group!' (Social worker)

Discussion and conclusions

In the empirical data presented above, some themes are clearly discernible and merit further discussion. In the following discussion, we will therefore describe the main empirical findings and discuss some of the emerging themes in more depth.

Professionals or working parents?

Managers at different levels talked about management from different perspectives. The top level of management tended to focus on education as a managerial tool, both to retain personnel and to direct change. This approach was in response to official policies relating to adequate employee education, but also to the social worker's struggle to develop discretion and professional status. It was also a response to the bottom-up, locally-initiated model for competence development, an officially recognised career path in which employees can rise from beginners to experts, through further education. The different steps on the career path entitle the employee to a higher salary, as well as taking on more qualified tasks.

For employed parents (often working part-time), further education often has to be postponed because of a lack of time and energy. In organisations like the one studied here, this is a potentially discriminatory factor towards young parents (notably mothers). The move towards professionalisation puts younger parents under a lot of pressure. Managers want professional social workers with updated qualifications, but they never mention this as a source of discrimination towards working parents. It was also surprising that this was rarely mentioned in the focus group discussions.

All of the interviews with managers revealed a discrepancy between intentions and practices. On an official level, they all remained consistent with the general, prevailing discourse in Sweden on 'equality' and 'the healthy organisation'. They viewed their organisation as caring, providing generous allowances for its employees to further their education, as well as tolerance towards working parents. In spite of this, parents often referred to examples of discrimination. As an example, young parents sometimes encountered an attitude from managers that 'your time will come' when new and time-consuming tasks were introduced.

When talking more specifically about family friendliness, all managers claimed to be against a work culture in which people worked long hours, stressing the importance of encouraging parental leave for working fathers, as well as being positive to requests for part-time working. Furthermore, they regarded themselves as tolerant and empathic towards employees who were absent due to family matters, and understanding of working parents when scheduling time off during the summer vacation. In general, the managers also underlined the importance of not discriminating against working parents, but instead, treating them like all other personnel. This family and gender-neutral policy runs the risk, however, of regarding men's parenthood as a state matter and women's parenthood as a private family matter.

In spite of this, the material also shows that the managers' intentions were often weakened or were only vaguely expressed as far as the employees' everyday work is concerned. In fact, actual practices sometimes even ended up being contrary to their expressed intentions. As an example, most managers did not have any concrete ideas on how to improve family friendliness within the organisation, except for 'being complaisant in individual cases'. There appeared to be very little interest in working out a local policy initiative in the equality plan. Although both agencies in this study had an equality plan, they were, as previous research has also shown, often vague and lacking in concrete ideas (Jämo, 2000). The equality plan appears to be a document with no impact whatsoever on everyday working life. The Swedish ombudsman for equality argues that this demonstrates the very low priority placed by employers on questions regarding equality and work–family boundaries (Jämo, 1999).

Further examples of how poorly policies and intentions were implemented emerged in the study. Contrary to the often expressed intention from managers to get more men to take parental leave, they all reported a general lack of local policies and efforts in this area. All commented that the organisation offered no extra economic benefits, on top of the replacement from the state, to employees on parental leave. This was somewhat surprising, as the majority of public sector organisations now give extra benefits to encourage parents, both men and women, to take a longer parental leave. However, the managers' statements became even more surprising when it became clear that a local agreement existed between the union and the employers that all parents at the social agencies were in fact entitled to an extra economic benefit when on parental leave. Apparently, there were either communication problems between the different levels in the organisation, or a lack of interest among the different managers in implementing existing policies.

This general lack of clear strategies to encourage more men to take parental leave is not unique to this case study. Haas, Hwang and Russell (2000) found, for example, in their study of 200 major companies in Sweden, that only 3 per cent of employers had developed supportive measures relating to employees' parental leave rights. The rest had taken isolated measures or accepted, albeit passively, their employees' needs and rights in this area. Tyrkkö (1997) also found in her study that even if many employers were talking positively about parental leave, they actually showed little interest in encouraging or helping employees to take leave.

Yet another example of contradictory behaviour at the managerial level is that the managers had, on the one hand, very positive attitudes to requests for part-time working, but on the other hand, little interest in helping people to restructure their work so as to become truly part-time. Several part-time working employees in the focus groups complained about stressful working situations in which they had to 'work full-time but only get paid for part-time'. According to these experiences, it was easier to work 50 per cent than 75 per cent, as the less time you are there, the more the employer has to reorganise the work.

This picture of the managers' low interest in creating local family friendly policies and their conviction to treat working parents as 'anybody else in the organisation' shows similarities with Kugelberg's (2000) study of a large private company in Sweden. Kugelberg found, for example, a clear tendency at managerial level to look upon and treat working parents only as workers (especially the men). Parenthood was primarily seen as a private matter and rarely something that the organisation should have to deal with. However, as in our study, the working parents expressed a contrary point of view as they often regarded working life through, and in relation to, their parenthood. This also is in line with the results of Haas, Hwang and Russell's (2000) study which concluded that most employers primarily regarded the balance between work and family life as something for the state and the family to deal with, and not a question for employers.

The workplace – between the state and the family

Social services in Sweden are dominated by women with professional ambitions – this case study is no exception. To understand how work–family boundaries are developed in this context, the gender dimension is crucial. The management strategy of leaving the work group to organise everyday work, within certain limits, was another crucial dimension. The employees become dependent on each other in the work group but are also dependent on the organisation and its representatives – the managers. It is in the area between these dependences that collective strategies are developed. The results of our study indicated the different ways in which parents managed to identify with the work group and to establish trust and reliable relationships with their work colleagues. By doing this, they created important preconditions, as well as an arena to handle clashes between work and family life. It was clear that in all of the focus groups with the employees, parenthood formed a clear basis for solidarity. This was often expressed by the participants in how they agreed with each others' descriptions of parenthood, especially regarding the hardship of combining work and family life. Furthermore, the participants often used 'we' to describe themselves and 'they' to describe colleagues without children, or colleagues with adult children. In this way, the common connections between parents with small children were underlined.

However, in spite of this, the working parents often said they ended up in a dilemma where they had to prioritise between family and work. Professional social workers are not easy to replace instantly when there is an emergency situation at home – for example, a sick child. Professional social work, like parenthood, is based on long-lasting relationships. To be a 'good enough parent' sometimes meant that they had to jeopardise a professional ethic and risk the blame from colleagues for abandoning a client in need. At the same time, when leaving a client to a colleague, their professional management of cases was exposed and open to criticism from other professionals.

As mentioned before, the combination of parenthood and profession creates various dilemmas related to the work–family balance. Most of these were exposed and sorted out in the work group. Therefore, the workplace becomes an arena between the state and the family, where gendered negotiations about the family–work balance take place.

Informal solutions in a formal system – the family in focus

When talking about family and work, the respondents referred to different value systems emerging from everyday routines. It was obvious from the interviews that the managers in practice delegate most of the responsibility for setting the preconditions and potential for combining work and family life to each separate work group. If someone needs to stay at home with a sick child or has to go to the dentist with the child during the workday, they negotiate this with their colleagues and make use of the possibilities within the flexible time arrangements. From the managers' point of view, this was a way of reducing bureaucracy and creating more flexibility for individual employees. From another point of view, however, this could be seen as a way for the managers to get rid of, and deny the importance of, these questions in the employees' everyday life. By pushing the responsibility further down the organisational hierarchy, this also prevents the establishment of more institutionalised and generalised local rights around work–family boundaries. An alternative, informal value system develops, forcing employees to balance individual and collective responsibility.

Therefore, even if the working parents in our study underlined the importance of support from the state in balancing work and family life, they also, as a result of the managers' strategy, placed a strong emphasis on their colleagues. However, many of them claimed that it is important to have a supportive manager, or at least a manager who does not discriminate against you because you are a parent. In practice, however, most of the working parents rarely put their trust in the manager to solve problems between work and family life, relying primarily on support from the state, their partner and work colleagues.

Looking more closely at partner support from a gender perspective, this appeared to have different meanings for men and women. All interviewees, irrespective of gender, were united in a belief that gender equality had increased within society over the last decades and that today's fathers were more active at home than previous generations, especially with children. Moving down from the discursive level to practical experiences, however, the picture changed somewhat. When describing their own situations, it was obvious that the women still had the main responsibility for children and household labour. In spite of support for parenthood, the family is still an arena where the strategic family–work negotiations take place. This is a well known fact in most of the gender literature, showing that male hegemony and traditional gender contracts still dominate modern family life. This leads to unequal power positions and reduced possibilities for women to negotiate work–family boundaries. While men can generally rely on their partners in this matter, women are left to try to negotiate with their partners. On the other hand, it seems as if this traditional gender contract is being increasingly challenged, as the interviewees often described everyday family life as filled with constant negotiations and compromises to fit 'all the pieces together' (see further Connell, 1995; Bäck-Wiklund & Bergsten, 1997; Plantin, 2001).

The workplace in a welfare state context – a paradox

The aim of this case study has been to look more closely at the workplace as an arena for negotiating the work–family boundary. But what does it mean to be an intermediate organisation between individual independence and family responsibilities? Does the function of the strong Swedish welfare state, as a buffer between the family and the market, affect the way workplaces and working parents handle work–family boundaries?

The result is a paradox. The road to professional discretion and independence is often blocked by parenthood, which is why any national policy promoting individual independence is almost impossible to achieve. The gender-neutral policy to treat working mothers just like everybody else gives no support in easing the family–work balance. The national policy, with individual autonomy as an overarching goal, has little support at the workplace level. Instead, an informal value system offers guidelines for negotiable outcomes for individual autonomy in situations of involuntary absence, caused by children or other family responsibilities. It appears that individual autonomy within a workplace context transforms itself into a family issue. To conclude, even in the Swedish case, the negotiations surrounding family–work boundaries are still questions to be dealt with in a family context that is still characterised by a persistence of traditional gender roles.

11
Women's Occupational Patterns and Work–Family Arrangements: do National and Organisational Policies Matter?

Maria das Dores Guerreiro and Inês Pereira[1]

Introduction

This paper focuses on women's occupational patterns and work–family arrangements. It draws upon a study carried out in Portugal on various service organisations, in all of which a significant number of women are employed in different occupations.[2] The main aim of the study was to identify and analyse i) the different work–family policies and practices existing in those organisations, ii) their relationship with the working parents' strategies and attitudes towards their jobs and family life, and iii) the parents' main difficulties and expectations in reconciling these two spheres of life. Methodological procedures used in the study combined interviews with male and female employees and Human Resources managers, the purpose of which was to highlight how the culture of the organisations perceives the roles of women and men, both as workers and parents; how far employers provide the same career development opportunities for men and women; and whether or not this reflects the existence of specific working agreements. The study also focused on the strategies developed by workers to combine work and family life and on their 'sense of difficulties' and expectations. A twin-track approach was developed, directed at individuals and employing organisations, to ascertain the factors which are conducive to a work–family balance, the main areas of policy intervention, and the impacts of each sphere on the other.

Thus, in this chapter, we focus on different levels of action: (1) the framework provided by the state; (2) the organisational context and its policies, cultures and values; and (3) work–family arrangements. All these dimensions are marked by gender, as gender particularly shapes the strategies for combining the work and family spheres. The purpose is, therefore, to combine an analysis of macro-level structures, such as the state, with meso-level dimensions of the organisations providing work and the social support networks for working parents. These related factors frame the interviewees' range of possibilities and their individual strategies for balancing work and family.

Work–family relationships and gender

In contemporary societies, work and family are considered two important but distinct areas of social life. Different authors have shown how these two social spheres interact and repeatedly influence each other (Friedman & Greenhaus, 2000; Brannen, 2005; Coltrane, 2004). When we speak about work and family relationships, we can see the need to balance two worlds that sometimes seem to be profoundly disconnected, involving different norms and behaviour patterns, different languages and demands, and great time pressures, making equal participation in the two spheres extremely difficult. Throughout this text, we will present different forms, and ways of interaction, between work and family.

The work–family relationship has become an important issue in our societies following recent changes in the labour market and within families, in particular the increasing involvement of women in the labour market and the changing forms of employment (Crompton et al., 1996) emerging in all countries. The 'gendered social contract', as a typical industrial society model of the sexual division of work – men as breadwinners and women as carers – has declined and, despite the current forms of gender segmentation, families are no longer characterised by a single male breadwinner. Since the second half of the twentieth century women have participated widely in the employment system and the dual-earner model has predominated.

This new family model, consisting of a dual career, or dual earner, couple (Rapoport and Rapoport, 1971; Gilbert, 1993), has involved large changes in the family and the workplace and has created new work–family demands. Though women have entered the labour market, various constraints still mean that men do not take on much of the work in the family. Women remain the main carers and are responsible for the majority of household tasks, thus bearing a double burden of work. On the other hand, partly as a reflection of the organisation of private life, horizontal, vertical and transversal segregation (Ferreira, 2003) is still the common experience for female employees. It is therefore necessary to debate the changing forms of work, the work–family relationship and its impact on women's working patterns.

There are three typical approaches to combining work and family, as far as gender roles are concerned (Lewis, 2001; Wall & Guerreiro, 2005). In the traditional model of industrial societies, prevailing in the first half of the twentieth century, the balance between family and work was achieved by means of a segmented approach, based on different gender roles: the man was the wage provider and the woman the carer and housekeeper. A second perspective, still centred on 'essentialist' principles, though more moderate with regard to women, recognises the participation of women in the labour market, but with a less prominent role than men, as the family remains primarily a woman's responsibility. Labour policies such as female part-time work and long maternity leave follows this concept of a work–family balance, allowing women to have more time for the family. For example, absence from work for family reasons tends to be seen as exclusively for women. A third, more egalitarian, perspective considers that men and women have similar roles, both in paid work and the family. Following this perspective, work–family policies should allow men and women to fulfil their roles as parents and employees on an equal basis. This model considers that 'the combination of work and family is primarily seen as a condition to create real gender equality on the labour market' (den Dulk, 2001) and it sees employers as providing arrangements for the work–family balance, taking full advantage of a more qualified female workforce that is not just involved in care duties. At the same time, it provides a new fatherhood role, with men being able to assume family and care responsibilities. This is mostly an idealised model, not fully implemented, although present to a limited extent in organisations with good practices.

Work–family balance results from a multiplicity of structural and cultural factors and dynamics (Crompton, 2003), including the state, as responsible for the general establishment of policies; employing organisations, implementing state measures and specific regulations; managers and team-members, who informally adapt the practices proposed; and the individual, who makes choices according to his or her field of possibilities and sense of entitlement (Lewis, 1998).

The state is a key agent, framing the general policy for reconciling work and family, while also providing care services and supporting other care institutions. The role of the state coexists with different agencies in the workplace, the family and the community. In the workplace, there are various arrangements which are usually perceived as good practice as far as the work–family balance is concerned. Of note is the good use of time (Parcel & Cornfield, 2000) and space, since much of the incompatibility between work and family results from the conflict between the working

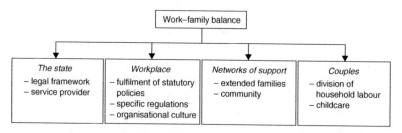

Figure 11.1:   Agents influencing the work–family balance

hours and locations implicit in these two spheres (Guerreiro, 2000). Organisational and professional cultures also play an important role in recognising that all employees, regardless of sex, are entitled to attend to family duties. Many, however, still tend to assume that a physical and controlled presence in the workplace is an indispensable characteristic of good employees, and mandatory for career progression (Lewis, 1998). Furthermore, the infrastructure available in the community, such as childcare and other services, public transport and household services (Cancedda, 2001), is an important element of work–family balance. Within the home, men and women's responsibilities for childcare and domestic tasks are still governed by enduring traditional gender roles, not yet emerging as symbols of equal obligations and rights. In addition, the role of informal networks should be taken into account, since they may provide important support for work–family balance.

Figure 11.1 identifies the various agents involved in work–family balance, and provides a framework for the topics discussed in this chapter.

The Portuguese context

Until the 1970s, Portugal was characterised by a political and legal model that represented the traditional image of the family, where women were not involved in public life. The Civil Code regulated the family and considered the man as the head of the family, to whom the woman and children owed respect and obedience, while the woman was responsible for care of all family members. After the April Revolution of 1974 and the publication of the new Constitution of the Portuguese Republic (1976), a space was opened up for a new gender contract, where men and women would be considered to have equal rights and obligations. Since then, the 'male head of the family' model has been abandoned and both parents should have similar responsibilities in providing care for their children.[3]

As a result of a multiplicity of social, economic and political factors, such as the colonial war and massive emigration, Portugal appears among southern European countries as a society with a high rate of female employment, at around 65 per cent.[4] Another distinction of the working pattern among Portuguese women is the high proportion of full-time employees. Only 16 per cent of women work part-time (although this rate is still considerably higher than the figure for men, which stands at 7 per cent) (EC, 2003). Portugal is also one of the European Union countries where women work the longest hours – 37.4 hours per week, compared with the European average for women of 32.9 hours. Portuguese men work 41.3 hours per week, which is also above the EU15 average of 40.9 hours. The percentage of working mothers, and specifically mothers of children aged between six and fourteen years, is also quite high at 76 per cent for mothers between 20 and 49 years old (Eurostat-LFS, 2002).

Empirical research on values, as discussed in Chapter 6, underlines the general agreement within the Portuguese population on the contribution of both partners to the family budget, the importance of employment to a woman's independence and, at the same time, the more limited involvement of women in paid work when their children are small. This reveals the enduring duality in the norms relating to the role of women as individuals (citizens) and mothers (Almeida & Guerreiro, 1993). As the reconciliation of professional and family life emerged as an important issue, a number of Portuguese studies began to explore the strategies used by parents (Portugal, 1995; Torres & Silva, 1998; Guerreiro & Lourenço, 1998; Wall, 2000; Guerreiro, Pereira & Abranches, 2003). These studies explored how daily life is managed, and the organisation of housework, as well as childcare arrangements. For the latter, the combination of different arrangements made by families was demonstrated, as was the importance of family support, such as grandmothers, in caring for young children up to two years old.

With regard to men's participation in family and household tasks, various studies show that, despite the different models for dividing domestic work (Wall & Guerreiro, 2005), the degree of men's contribution in one way or another to domestic work (Guerreiro & Ávila, 1998; Torres & Silva, 1998) is rarely above 30 per cent.[5] A key Portuguese study on the use of time (INE, 1999) points out that the difference between male and female professional work time is one hour per day, while women spend three hours more on domestic/care work than men (Perista, 2002). This data demonstrates that women's greater participation in the labour market is not followed by greater male participation in housework. The studies identify specific arenas of male participation in family life – such as administrative affairs, shopping and gardening – while cooking meals and taking care of clothes remain female domains (see Chapter 7). However, father's participation in childcare is slowly increasing. The ISSP study of values also captures a snapshot of this 'light' male involvement when it reveals that more than 85 per cent of respondents agree that men should be more involved in childcare and domestic duties (Wall, 2001). If men cannot be persuaded to do more domestic work, this scenario suggests a major need for the provision of childcare, care for the elderly, and other household services by different agencies within the field.

The policy role of the Portuguese state with regard to the work–family relationship may be summed up in four main points: (1) the definition of general labour laws; (2) the regulation of sectoral collective work agreements; (3) the formulation of family and gender policies; and (4) the direct provision of services or the funding of community care structures. Labour, employment, working conditions and the rights and duties of employers and employees are regulated by labour law, which sets out rules on remuneration and career progress, the different types of working contracts (permanent, short term, full-time, part-time), the regulation and organisation of work time (schedules and holidays), absences and dismissal. Apart from this general legislation, certain sectors are ruled by specific collective work conventions and company agreements (Lima et al. 1999), with the state contributing to negotiations as the regulator. These particular instruments cannot be used to limit employees' rights and must give greater benefits than the general labour law, as will be outlined later.

Current labour law also regulates the protection of parenthood and the possibility of support being given to a family. According to the 'New Labour Code' (2003), mothers are entitled to 120 days' fully paid maternity leave and fathers to five (statutory) plus 15 (optional) days, also fully paid. Maternity leave can be extended to 150 days on 80 per cent of pay. Fathers are entitled to use part of this maternity leave (except for the first six weeks), as negotiated between the couple. After this period, parents may apply for three months' unpaid parental leave, part-time work for six months, or a combination of both. To facilitate feeding during the child's first year, the mother or father can apply for a two-hour reduction in their daily paid schedules.

The most recent revision to the Portuguese Constitution introduced the right to reconcile work and family obligations (1997).[6] In fact, the closing years of the twentieth century saw the emergence of a set of complex initiatives for the promotion of work–family arrangements, such as the Comprehensive Policy for the Family (1999), the

Comprehensive Plan for Equal Gender Opportunities (1998) and the National Plan for Employment, all of which contained measures for reconciling work and family. During the 1990s, the Portuguese government also promoted a huge expansion in childcare services, as a support for families as well as an educational goal. However, while the pre-schooling rate has reached 70.6 per cent, crèches only cover 23 per cent of young children (up to two years old) (PNE 2005). An increase in the availability of crèches is therefore another goal, and the National Action Plan for Employment foresees an increase of 50 per cent in the current capacity of crèches.

The cases studied

Different business sectors have specific conditions in the workplace and promote different opportunities and measures to balance work and family. This research focused on six national and multinational business organisations of various sizes, with operations in distinct areas (Table 11.1).

Two main subsets of companies can be identified: one with more traditional and less skilled occupations such as retail, hotel and cleaning services; and the other, more 'modern' group, with higher qualifications and greater possibilities of career progression, which includes consultancy, telecommunications and finance. Though all of these organisations are characterised by a significant female presence, women predominate in those sectors where poorly skilled jobs prevail. Interviews were held with a total of 51 employees (14 male and 37 female) with a wide range of occupations and qualifications, some of them with supervisory responsibilities. Most of them were parents but, to allow for comparisons, some people

Table 11.1:   Business organisations involved in the case studies

Organisation	Activity	Size	Prevailing gender	Type
A	Telecommunications	Large	M	National
B	Consultancy	Medium	M	Multinational
C	Finance	Large	M	National
D	General services (cleaning, temporary work)	Medium	F	Multinational
E	Hotel services	Medium	F	National
F	Retail/supermarket	Large	F	Multinational

without children were included. HR managers were also interviewed and asked to discuss their personal lives as well as company policy.

Organisational policies

In general, the principles of gender equality and a work/private life balance were not found in enterprise statements and employers did not have explicit arrangements for such principles. When the research team discussed these topics, the human resource managers who were interviewed recognised them as important. Within the framework of companies' social responsibilities, an emphasis on an improvement in working conditions and the introduction of so-called 'win–win' flexibility emerged as 'modern' good practices. However, they were still seen primarily as important for working mothers, rather than fathers.

When discussing the impact of workplace conditions on work–family reconciliation and women's occupations and career patterns, we examine (1) the existence of specific collective agreements, (2) the fulfilment of statutory regulations, (3) the organisational culture, which may (or may not) be supportive of work–family reconciliation and gender equity, (4) the informal practices devised by line managers and work teams, and (5) the employees' values and attitudes towards work.

In the group of business organisations studied, regulations include general labour law and company agreements. The various collective work agreements were analysed on the basis of a set of dimensions usually related with work–family reconciliation and gender equity: recruitment, work schedules, career progress, leave, facilities and other kinds of support. As regards recruitment processes and work schedules, the general statutory regulations outlaw gender discrimination and lay down a 40-hour working week. Collective agreements, however, can offer better arrangements, either in the number of hours worked per week (reduced to 35–38) or in the flexibility of time use. This occurs in three of these companies: those involved in telecommunications, finance and hotel services. In retail services and cleaning, part-time work and shift arrangements are not so much for the benefit of the female workers, but are instead an imperative of the business. Schedule flexibility, often presented as a good practice, appears to be quite problematic in most workplaces. Female hypermarket employees, with rotating shifts and weekend work, face difficulties in organising their lives and spending time with their families. This is related to the fact that, although flexibility may satisfy some employees' needs, thus representing an important measure for more successfully reconciling work–family demands, it is often used for the benefit of the organisation, as employees have no or little say in managing their schedules. As Gloria Rebelo points out (2002), it is difficult to promote work reorganisation schemes that satisfy both the enterprises and the employees.

In respect of recruitment, some traditionally male dominated jobs now receive more applications from women, as more women are getting the appropriate qualifications. This fact was mentioned as a problematic issue in certain enterprises (finance and consultancy), with the consequence that some positive discrimination favouring men had been introduced.[7]

Career advancement varies greatly from sector to sector and tends to combine qualifications, performance, length of service in a particular category and degree of absenteeism, even if justified (which generally affects mothers at the time that their children are born). The most polarised situations are, on the one hand, the telecommunications company, which is still state owned, in which every occupational category can include different levels through which employees progress, depending on their seniority and performance[8] – and, on the other, the general services company, where the (female) cleaning staff have no opportunities for advancement in their work.

Occupational training is the most developed in consultancy, banking and telecommunications – given the great changes and the consequent need for new skills that these companies have faced. Although various studies indicate limitations for women in the availability of training, gender differences could not be identified here. In terms of maternity leave, almost all the enterprises follow statutory law, with the same applying to paternity leave of five days (though not fathers' voluntary leave of 15 days). However, in some enterprises such as the telecommunications and banking companies, collective contracts go far beyond what is stipulated for short leave and arrangements for time to manage family and personal affairs. It is also the policy of some of the enterprises to provide allowances for childcare or children's education (telecommunications, finance and retail), an annual visit to a children's holiday camp (retail and telecommunications) and access for children to the company restaurant.

General regulations and specific policies particularly affect the issue of the work–family balance in that they shape daily times and rhythms. All interviewees in this research emphasised the importance of having enough time to be simultaneously good employees and good parents. However, employees do not always feel entitled to use some of their formal entitlements.

Corporate culture, gender and attitudes towards work

Our research showed that, although workplace policies and practices are shaped by national and local regulations and framed by the existing welfare-state model, there is a significant gap between formal policies and current practices and attitudes in the workplace (Den Dulk et al., 1998; Lewis, 1998). These practices reflect the different cultural patterns and values that are intertwined with corporate cultures. The application of work–family arrangements depends on organisational cultures and the potential for daily and informal negotiations within each workplace.

One of the most important elements is the daily schedule, with employees facing a culture of long working hours and occasional work peaks. A number of statements suggested that pressures were applied regarding time-use and leave, and that the 'culture of availability' led to an intense concentration on work, to the detriment of personal life. All of these factors can affect the renewal of a work contract, promotion or a rise in salary, and it is often considered that 'those who do not give maximum time to the firm [are] less productive and committed, and hence less valued than those working long hours' (Lewis & Taylor, 1996: 122). Thus 'unless the discourses of time are challenged, therefore, family-friendly policies alone will have little success in changing organisational cultures, and the reduction of work–family stress' (Lewis & Taylor, 1996: 123), as the following quotations illustrate:

'If you have no children, you take the risk, and like, and even do nights, which helps, and you move up in your grade. But if I do shifts, who looks after the baby at night? Of course, I see the difference in my pay . . . I didn't get a rise and they said it was because I wasn't available.' (Cashier, supermarket, female)

'. . . if you're absent, when there's promotion to be given, you don't get it . . . they don't give you certain tasks. I had to adapt my life to my work. I chose to get a home-help. Before my child was born, I had to lie down and I went to work so my boss at the time could go on holiday. During my maternity leave, I was completely available for them and I didn't benefit from the feeding time.' (Head of accounts department, hotel services, female)

'In my case, I can't stay late. I've already felt that I've lost out because of this . . . I stay until the normal leaving time. I work, fine, but I have to be there with my children. It's not worth pushing the family to the side.' (Bank employee, female)

However, this pressure is higher in specific sectors and occupations, for example, for those in supermarkets, in the front office in banking, or with supervisory responsibilities:

'At the management level, fixed working hours don't operate. I always get home around 8 pm. It even happens that I have to come to work on Saturdays or on weekdays until midnight.' (Bank manager, male)

'Our working week is 40 hours but that isn't to say that's how many we do. In general, the nature of our work means we go from eight in the morning till eight at night . . . And anyone who leaves before the boss is in his bad books.' (Line manager, supermarket, male)

On occasion, managers and employers neither understand nor support gender equity in the labour market for women or men, although their most common discourse is neutral. The tendency is to say that all employees are considered equal but, in spite of this, differences are apparent in attitudes towards men and women. Organisational culture is, therefore, a multifaceted concept that has a significant impact on the work–family relationship and gender equity (see Chapter 10). Difficulties were noted in the companies' ability to free themselves from stereotypes and adjust to new social and cultural forms, where men and women employees can have similar social roles as parents. This still represents a major handicap for work–family balance.

The managers who were interviewed accepted the lack of symmetry between the household responsibilities of men and women and the impact of this on women's careers. They generally admitted that career advancement is easier if an individual does not have many family responsibilities:

'Here, nowadays, a woman boss is perfectly accepted from the cultural point of view . . . but there is no doubt that availability is a conditioning factor. In the present day, the availability that a young woman must have at the counter is very significant.' (Human resources manager, finance, male)

'Maybe career progression is faster if the person has more freedom and is not so restricted by external factors. Maybe single men and women progress faster than married ones, but that is the same for men and women. We have this anecdote here: a person's girlfriend challenged him to choose between her and his career. He said: OK, I opt for my career. And he only married when he was forty . . . sometimes people just prefer to invest in their career.' (Human resources manager, supermarket, male)

These quotations illustrate both the assumption that opportunities are not the same for men and women and the idea that family duties interfere with career progress. Also, the anecdote relating to a male worker would have had a different end if it had involved a woman, as female workers have a greater tendency to give up their careers rather than their families. Women tend to feel that they are the main carers and housekeepers and therefore feel guilty if they cannot put family first. The gender stereotypes circulating in the culture of organisations are thus nourished, creating situations in which women are more likely to relinquish work obligations when faced with family necessity. An example given by a female professional from the consultancy illustrates this situation:

'It happened to me one day when my son had chicken pox. I had a very important meeting that I couldn't miss but, on that day, my husband couldn't miss work either. So it had to be me, I was the one that accepted the responsibility.' (Professional, consultancy, female)

This situation may also imply that it is not possible for men to assume their family responsibilities (Fried, 1998), as organisations do not expect (or tend to allow) men to take time off for family reasons:

'If a man missed work due to children, it would be a problem. For a woman, it's not such a big problem.' (Finance professional, male)

However, in many of the statements, we see the idea developing that gender roles are changing or at least will change in the short term:

'Some men say: I have to take my children to kindergarten. It's a role, I think, for both sexes. Or it is even a masculine task, now, to stay with them at home . . . For me, there's no problem in having a woman working in the storeroom, or a man doing the cleaning. We are moving towards equality. But I think it should be at all levels, and here we don't have any women in leading positions, and why not? Recently we had a vacancy for a finance director and I interviewed both men and women. I even think it would be good to have a woman here.' (Human resources manager, cleaning, male)

If organisational cultures show stereotypical, even if sometimes supposedly neutral, attitudes towards gender and the work–family relationship, men and women also have different attitudes towards occupations and careers. In this respect, there are both structural and cultural factors, as well as gender stereotypes, influencing men's and women's practices and attitudes. Men, in general, tend to consider themselves as the main breadwinners and usually do have better-paid professions. As for women, the less skilled their occupations, the more they tend to stress their identities as the main carers because, within the couple, they have an occupation of lower value and fewer career prospects. Some young women are not willing to give up their role as the partner mainly responsible for children. As an example, when asked about the possibility of sharing leave with a future partner when a child is born, this young woman said:

'To share the four months' leave . . . I don't know what my husband's relationship with the child should be like . . . well, I don't know if I would like to share this with him.' (Clerk, cleaning, female)

Both men and women tend to lack a sense of gender equity, an outlook that is especially strong among less qualified employees. In a few cases, we also noticed the inverse situation: where the women have good career prospects (and the men do not), the men tend to participate more in household responsibilities. What tends to be widespread, however, is the imbalance between men and women and their commitment (Schrimsher, 2004) to either work or family.

Our research focused on the workplace and men and women's careers, examining how family issues may affect their progress. The prevalent professional role model happens to be that of a man (a breadwinner) without family responsibilities, who is thus fully available for his career (Wajcman, 1998; Crompton & Sanderson, 1990). It was apparent during the interviews that, particularly in contexts where work pressure is higher, employees' careers tend to be constrained by a lack of availability. This was reinforced in various conversations and statements recorded during the interviews.

'Nowadays, it's not availability that is a distinguishing factor, it's the lack of availability. What do I mean by this? I mean that if someone is not very available everybody notices. It's quite natural in our business area. Everybody has their lives organized around work. That's the way it is . . .' (Manager, hypermarket, male)

Q. 'Do you think availability has an influence on careers?'

'Yes, it has. A lot, really. If a person takes a lot of days off, when there are promotions around, they won't be considered.' (Manager, hotel services, female)

If working time is a factor that greatly influences the work–family balance, career progression is also quite asymmetric between men and women. As women tend to have greater responsibility for family matters, they are less available in the professional sphere, which usually counts against them in performance evaluations carried out in the workplace. This seems to be a very important issue, as many interviewees highlight the impossibility of having both a career and a family without jeopardising one of them. Therefore, many interviewees think it impossible to reconcile career and family, with many women feeling that devotion to the family – mostly while the children are small – is definitely bad for a woman's career. Instead, they have a strategy of accommodation as far as their careers are concerned (Evetts, 1996), which is part of a traditional vision that defines those who do not give their maximum time to the firm as less productive, less committed and, hence, less valued than those working long hours (Lewis & Taylor, 1996).

In the companies studied, we noticed an enduring discourse on the huge impact of availability on career progression. Women are either seen as less professional than men or neutral, that is, they tend to be accepted if they are as dedicated to work as men. As a result, the gendered division of labour is reproduced in most organisations and women are still expected to be more concerned with solving work–family reconciliation problems, while men are seen as more career-oriented. Therefore, women tend to feel much more dissatisfied in the workplace than men, as they find themselves the main victims of the work–family imbalance. It is, however, also important to note that this gendered attribution of family responsibilities can also induce feelings of discomfort in men, as in some cases their roles within the family are not respected.

In conclusion, we may say that gender is still a key factor in understanding employees' life courses, particularly those involving parenthood. If it is true that women are now enjoying the same opportunities and success in their educational careers, it is also true that inequalities reappear as soon as they enter the employment system and start a family. However, the inequalities in these two spheres reinforce each other. Some statements suggest that women tend to see this orientation towards work or family as a personal choice, as they have deep feelings about the rewards of motherhood. On the other hand, it is important to note the difference between subjective experiences and structural contexts and to observe that these choices, even when recognised as individual, are socially constrained (Crompton, 2003), as people develop strategies within their own field of possibilities.

Household work and childcare arrangements

Portuguese women still face great asymmetries in the division of domestic work, assuming most of the responsibilities involving care (Wall & Guerreiro, 2005; see also Chapter 7). As has been seen, this circumstance is associated with the more limited opportunities that women have on the job market. Even when women are fully integrated into the labour market, men's careers are perceived as more important and men retain greater responsibility for work outside the home (Coltrane, 2004). Mothers tend not to work late to the same degree as men and also take more days off for family reasons than fathers, who, in turn, are not as involved in the household as women are in the labour market. Although interviewees tend to think gender roles are changing, a discrepancy is apparent between discourse and daily practice. Male participation in household tasks is generally low, quite specialised and very often perceived as extra help. However, as other research has shown (Wall & Guerreiro, 2005), it is possible to identify different ways of organising family life, which are associated with the different socio-economic profiles of families and attitudes to non-domestic work.

The typology developed is shown in Table 11.2 and distinguishes between four different methods of carrying out domestic work. In the first, the woman takes sole responsibility, combining work outside the home with domestic chores and childcare, without any contribution from the husband. In the second model identified among those interviewed in the various enterprises, both members of the couple participate in household work. This option has three typical sub-forms: the first is based on an egalitarian approach, reported very rarely by the interviewees, in which both members of the couple cooperate in a way that is understood to be equivalent; the second is based on specialised help, in which the man and woman are assigned certain tasks connected with the house – for example, doing the vacuum-cleaning or setting the table – or with the children – examples are giving them a bath or playing with them; and the third sub-form is based on what we have called 'unwilling cooperation', since the wife has to demand the partner's cooperation, given his unwillingness to

Table 11.2: The organisation of household work

Women as wholly responsible	Women double work shift	'My husband never helps. When I have split hours, I leave his dinner ready. When I arrive home, I wash the dishes and do the ironing . . .' (female, low-skilled, hotel services)
	Egalitarian participation	'My husband does nothing' (female, cleaner) 'I don't feel I have too much to do in the house. My husband sees to a lot of things and takes care of our child' (female, low-skilled, supermarket)
Couple who share the work	Unwilling cooperation	'My husband never takes the initiative to do anything . . . I always have to insist . . . I tell him "You're idle."' (female, professional, finance)
	Specialised help	'He hoovers, does the shopping, baths the children' (female, administrative employee, telecommunications)
Externalisation	Making use of paid work or household services	'I have a home-help. When my son was a child, I even had a home-help during weekends' (female, manager, finance)
Other supports	Family support networks	'It's my mother who helps me. Sometimes she makes dinner for us, baby-sits, gives us a bit of help' (female, professional, consultancy)

Table 11.3: Childcare solutions

Facilities – using only one institution	In a number of cases, parents can make use of private institutions that take care of children all day. This solution depends upon the hours of both parents and the childcare service.	'My daughters attend a private institution nearby. I chose this because of the hours they operate, and they're both there now' (F, professional, telecommunic.)
Facilities – using more than one institution	This is one of the most common solutions, mostly for children who are dependent but not very small, like those at school. Free-time activity facilities (ATLs) play a most important role.	'I have two children. The older one can already take care of himself, but the younger one goes to the ATL before and after school. They pick him up at school and he can have lunch there.' (F, manager, hotel)
Facilities and **extended family**	In many cases, kindergarten is combined with extended family help, mostly when the children are over three years old. This is usually seen as the best solution.	'My son goes to the free-time activity centre till 4 p.m. and then my mother picks him up and stays with him' (M, professional, banking)
Extended families – *grandparents*	This is the main strategy used by interviewees, and especially those with small children up to 2. Interviewees tend to recognise the importance of grandparents, and those who have this help appreciate it.	'My children are in the kindergarten. They go with me in the morning, at 9 a.m. and my husband picks them up in the evening. When he can't my mother does it. I arrive at home late, around 8:15 p.m' (F, professional, consultancy)
		'Even if I could get childcare, I wouldn't (…) my mother-in-law has a nice house with plenty of space, my child is her only grandson and, as she doesn't work, she can give him all her time' (F, sales, telecomm.)
Extended families – *others*	Other relatives may help, even older children – though this is not a common solution.	'When I started to work I left my child with a cousin. She was a great help!' (F, banking)
		'I have three children. One is 13 years old, one 16, and the youngest 6, and the older ones pick her up after school' (F, cleaner)
Informal paid work	Childminders are in many cases a solution for children under 2 years old.	'Until he was 2 he had a childminder.' (F, cashier, supermarket)

perform domestic chores. Returning to the original set of four modalities, externalisation (or 'outsourcing') refers to cases in which the family makes use of paid assistance by hiring professional help or availing itself of services on the market. Finally, other forms of participation correspond to informal support networks, generally at the level of the extended family. Some of these modalities can also be combined with others.

As illustrations of the above, the double working day predominated among employees with the lowest qualifications, in the cleaning and hotel sectors (although one couple shared work on the basis of egalitarian participation, as she was a supermarket cashier, a shift-worker whose husband had more school-friendly and compatible working hours for their son). Specialised help was found among non-managerial banking and telecommunications staff, and unwilling cooperation among some of the more highly qualified women in these same sectors. Externalisation is a constant among female executives' methods of reconciling work and family (see Chapter 7). Family support networks appear, essentially, to cut across all classes, although they are most notably connected with childcare, as shown in Table 11.3.

With regard to childcare, the strategies of Portuguese families are particularly complex in that, as seen above, female work is predominantly full-time, working hours are among the longest in Europe, and many parents travel long distances each day between home and work. However, the coverage rate of care services for the under-twos is still very low. Childcare solutions therefore reflect this difficult situation, which also involves shift-work and rotas, as well as the culture of being 'available' and working late in the enterprises studied.

The typology developed for childcare thus reveals a combination of facilities and informal support networks, paid and unpaid. The smallest children may be placed in crèches but many of them remain in the care of family members, in particular grandparents and childminders. For children aged three or more, facilities such as kindergarten, school and free-time activity centres predominate, as the most popular childcare or educational systems. This is generally, however, combined with other facilities, the extended family's informal support, or even paid support, so that the long period in which the parents are working and commuting is covered.

Conclusion – do policies matter?

We conclude by highlighting some of the major findings concerning gender, work–family arrangements and policies. In the preceding pages we have tried to explore how the relationship between family and work depends on a set of different factors and agencies. On the one hand, the state plays an important role in defining family policies and making laws that regulate the conditions for paid work, providing a setting for action. On the other hand, both workplace characteristics and family configurations also have a vital role to play, as they promote norms, practices and values that unquestionably shape gender working patterns and work–family arrangements. At this level, the way in which the work and family spheres depend on each other was also shown to be significant, as what happens in one clearly contributes to (or constrains) arrangements in the other, either reinforcing segregation or promoting conditions for a more balanced life.

Organisational cultures are a major factor in the promotion of gender equity and the combining of work and family life, as they regulate the interpretation and application of laws and policies. Generally speaking, however, measures promoting a better work–family balance are more likely to be found in organisations where there are collective agreements rather than those only governed by the general labour law, as policies enshrined in these agreements are more easily used and employees tend to feel more entitled to make use of their rights.[9]

In the companies studied, the telecommunications and banking sectors stand out as those whose collective labour agreements provide their workers with the best conditions and whose organisational culture is favourable to the use of these rights by parents, without having an impact on their careers. However, the 'glass ceiling' persists in these companies. The multinational consultancy firm has practices in Portugal which are below its international policy recommendations, and no specific collective labour regulations apply. The culture of long working hours and concentration on professional life, to the detriment of personal life, is highly accentuated in this situation, creating serious difficulties for working mothers in combining professional and family responsibilities. These women, therefore, tend to drastically reduce their working presence within the company, once they have children, and all the more so when higher positions are involved.

This culture of extended hours was also identified in the hotel trade and the distribution business, although in these cases it was associated more with specific departments or managerial styles. With regard to workers in the hotel trade, distribution business and cleaning services, even if shift work allows for the accumulation of a certain number of days off, the incompatibility of these days with other family members, in particular children's school hours, makes paid work difficult to reconcile with the responsibilities of private life. The women employed in the cleaning services – in many cases migrants and the only breadwinners in their households – had an even more difficult situation, having to divide their time throughout the day between different jobs.

Work–family reconciliation is dealt with via a complex set of arrangements. Besides the measures stipulated in the collective hiring instruments used in the enterprises where this study was carried out and which, generally, only consider exceptional or urgent family situations, parents must find day-to-day solutions that require sophisticated strategies for combining formal and informal support, according to their own range of possibilities. Moreover, there is a highly significant gap between societal expectations of women and men. Women are still expected, above all, to care for their children, while men are supposed to be more involved in their careers. It is important to note that objective conditions and professional values are extremely important, as women invest more in their careers when they feel more valued and rewarded.

However, despite the influence of organisational cultures on the exercise of rights and the structuring of women's and men's careers, there is no doubt that each economic sector's characteristics and the content of its collective labour agreements are decisive factors in the establishment of measures that balance work and family life and guarantee more equity in the workplace between women and men. In other words, policies really do matter and are all the more effective in their application when they apply to the specificities of workplaces and the staff who occupy them, particularly in gender and personal terms.

Notes

1. Maria das Dores Guerreiro, Inês Pereira: CIES, ISCTE, Lisbon, Portugal.
2. Guerreiro, Abranches and Pereira (2003).
3. Article 36, Portuguese Constitution.
4. Female employment in services corresponds to 64.6 per cent, in industry to 21.7 per cent and in agriculture to 13.7 per cent.
5. Activities with a major (near 50 per cent or more) male contribution are shopping, gardening, car maintenance and repairs, and administrative tasks.
6. Article 59, Portuguese Constitution.
7. On the basis of the argument that men are too immature at the age of 25, the age limit for applying for a job at the bank has been extended to 28, since women tend to get the best marks in the admission tests.
8. The size of the company also offers employees extensive opportunities to apply for another position once they get further qualifications like a first or a master's degree.
9. They are generally companies in whose sectors, since the revolution in April 1974, the trade unions have had a strong presence and have managed to negotiate favourable contractual agreements. However, the economic framework of globalisation and competitive pressure point towards significant changes in the short term, in terms of more restrictive measures that are already current practice in most private companies.

12
Employment, the Family and 'Work–Life Balance' in France

Nicky Le Feuvre and Clotilde Lemarchant[1]

Introduction

Once sufficient caution has been expressed with regard to the somewhat loaded terms often used to describe the gendered experiences of the work–life interface in any national setting (Junter-Loiseau, 1999; Lapeyre & Le Feuvre, 2004), the most noteworthy aspects of the 'work–life balance' question in France would seem to lie in the co-existence of apparently contradictory policy measures, social practices and attitudes. It therefore comes as no surprise that, in much of the existing literature on this theme, France continues to defy any straightforward classification in models of contemporary gendered welfare regimes (Fouquet et al., 1999). The country has long been characterised by a tradition of relatively high, full-time employment rates for women (particularly mothers) and by a relatively stable birth-rate (Le Feuvre & Andriocci, 2005). The combination of these two potentially contradictory phenomena has usually been explained by the traditional support for working mothers provided by the French state, notably through generous family allowances, tax relief on child-care and the extensive provision of full-time nursery education for the under-sixes (Hantrais & Letablier, 1996; Barrère-Maurisson, 2003). However, in recent years, both sides of this societal equation have undergone considerable change.

Firstly, levels of part-time work have increased considerably. Just under a third of all working women are now employed on a part-time basis. Secondly, the 3 per cent public debt constraints of the Maastricht Treaty have put considerable pressure on the public purse and there has been a clear attempt to use family policy measures as a tool for regulating the labour market. There has been a clear policy drive towards increased 'parental choice' with regard to child-care arrangements, including new measures to enable the parents of young children to take up to three years (poorly) paid parental leave. However, even on this issue, the situation in France is rather contradictory. Recent policy measures have included the Allocation Parentale d'Éducation (parental education grant), which has greatly reduced the activity rates of mothers of two or more children, but also measures, such as the AGED (Allocation de garde d'enfant à domicile – Home child-care allowance) and the AFEAMA (Aide à la famille pour l'emploi d'une assistante maternelle agree – Certified child-minder employment grant), designed to increase women's labour market participation rates, both at the upper and lower ends of the occupational hierarchy. Finally, France is one of the only European countries to have implemented a law to reduce the length of the working time for men and women, with an aim to create new jobs and to improve the overall 'quality of life', of which 'work–life balance' is recognised as an important component.

This chapter presents the main characteristics of the 'work–life balance' debate in France and aims to analyse some of the major characteristics of women's employment and family life experiences from a gender perspective. We begin with a rapid synthesis of some of the major policy measures that have contributed to the historical constitution of the 'work–life balance' debate in this particular national context over the past 60 years, before going on to consider the ways in which the framing of the employment–family interface in public policy terms is reflected (or not) in the opinions and practices of men and women from different social backgrounds. Data from the French national data set of the 2002 International Social Survey Programme's (ISSP) Family module will enable us to identify some of the major tensions around this question in France today.[2]

Work–life balance policies in historical perspective

As the results of a recent comparative research programme on family policy in Europe have confirmed, France is not only a country with a long history of State regulation of the family–employment interface (Hantrais, 2004), it is also a country where State intervention in the organisation of family life and welfare receives a high level of recognition and legitimacy (Büttner et al., 2002). In a survey carried out in February 2000, 58 per cent of a nationally representative sample thought that the existing level of State welfare intervention should be further increased and only 18 per cent agreed that it should be reduced (Forsé & Parodi, 2001). Despite the fact that public opinion shows considerable variation according to social class, geographical location, social integration and sex, there is good reason to believe that the state is seen as a legitimate social actor in the 'work–life balance' debate in France. However, there is no clear consensus about the precise role that the state should play in regulating the employment–family interface, particularly as far as women's employment is concerned. In a recent book on family policy in France (Commaille et al., 2002), the authors identify several successive periods in the relationship between family policy and employment policy in France.

The post-war period: a classic form of the 'male breadwinner/female carer' model

It has often been argued that work and the family have never really been framed in 'either/or' terms for women in France (Battagliola, 2000). However, from the post-war period and up until the end of the 1970s, France was characterised by a strong state-driven incentive for women to leave the labour market on marriage or on the birth of their first child. The strength of the 'male breadwinner/female carer' policy model adopted at this time in France is often underestimated in much existing comparative literature, notably because it was to be significantly weakened in subsequent years. It is true that, with the exception of the Civil Service during the Vichy period, the widespread imposition of a 'marriage bar' has never existed in France (Crompton & Le Feuvre, 2000). However, the adoption of the AMF (Allocation de mère au foyer – Housewife subsidy), in 1936, and the subsequent ASU (Allocation de salaire unique – single wage subsidy), adopted in 1941, undoubtedly reflected the desire of the French State, supported both by the Catholic church, reformist employers associations and trade unions, to encourage married women with children to leave the labour market, at a time when the foundations of the French welfare regime were being established.

The benefit levels of the ASU were raised in 1946, making labour market retreat an economically viable option for mothers of at least two children in most social categories, at least up until the early 1960s (Martin, 1998), when female activity rates started to increase again. In comparison to women's average wage levels, the relative value of the ASU fell throughout the 1960s and – partially in recognition for the potentially important economic role of women in an expanding economy and partly due to a declining national consensus on the subject of immigrant labour from the French colonies – the ASU was totally phased out in 1978. It should however be remembered that a large proportion of the post-war female labour-force in France was still involved in a (paid or unpaid) self-employed capacity in agricultural and family-run small businesses and was thus excluded de facto from the ASU benefit. The experience of combining 'work' and 'family' in this historically specific context undoubtedly influenced the ways in which women, and house-holds, experienced the transition to salaried labour in the following decades (Schweitzer, 2002).

The reformulation of the French 'gender contract'

In stark comparison to the immediate decades after World War II, the late 1970s and 1980s were characterised by the adoption of several meas-ures in favour of women's labour market participation throughout their child-rearing years. Following the demise of the ASU, the early 1980s saw the widespread adoption of the so-called childcare contracts (contrats d'enfance), aimed at increasing the capacity of collective child-care struc-tures and offering tax deductions to dual breadwinner households (see Chapter 4). However, one of the most important measures with regard to women's employment patterns is undoubtedly the level of state commit-ment to full-time nursery education for young children. Indeed, by the age of three, almost 98 per cent of all children have started attending an école maternelle, usually on a full-time basis. Alongside this commit-ment, public policies throughout the 1980s were progressively diverted away from collective, publicly-funded child-care facilities (crèches), towards more privatised and individualised solutions, but support for working parents was still in evidence, both through the AGED, intro-duced in 1986 and the AFEAMA, which came into operation in 1990.

The introduction of the APE (allocation parentale d'éducation), cre-ated in January 1985 for families with three or more children, has been interpreted as a major watershed in the 'work–life balance' debate in France. The APE was originally presented as a tool to reduce poverty amongst large families, mostly in households with a single (male) man-ual worker income. However, this measure has also been compared to the old ASU and seen as a tool specifically designed to encourage the mothers of large families to leave the labour market. It should be noted that, up until the 1994 reform of the ASU, there were just 154,000 recip-ients of this benefit, which was only paid until the youngest child reached the age of three. With a monthly benefit equivalent to half the national minimum wage, the APE was only paid to women with quite a long and continuous history of labour market participation before the birth of their third child (originally two years in employment during the

30 months preceding the APE application, this was reduced to two years during the past 10 years in 1986) (Afsa, 1998). Given the fact that mothers of large families had generally left the labour market on the birth of their first or second child, rather than on the birth of their third child (Lollivier, 1988), it seems reasonable to conclude that the 'inactivity incentive factor' of the first APE measures was fairly limited. As we shall see below, things changed radically after the 1994 reform of the APE.

The early 1980s also saw the first policy measures in favour of the development of part-time employment in France. Up until the beginning of the 1980s, employment on a part-time basis was seen as an exception and the legal rules around part-time employment contracts were very strict, making it impossible, for example, for a company to recruit someone directly on a part-time basis (only full-time staff already in employment could be transferred onto a part-time contract) (Maruani, 2000). The laws of 23 December 1980 (public sector employees) and of 28 January 1981 (private sector) and the decree of 26 March 1982 lifted the restrictions on the recruitment of staff directly on a part-time basis. However, it was not until the law of 31 December 1992 that the French state adopted a direct incentive for part-time work, via a 30 per cent reduction on employers social security contributions (increased to 50 per cent in January 1993, then brought back down to 30 per cent in April 1994) for each permanent part-time job of between 19 and 30 hours/week or 83 and 130 hours/month. In 1994, the duration of part-time jobs eligible for this reduction in employers contributions was widened to cover those between 16 and 32 hours/week or on an annualised equivalent duration (Audric & Forgeot, 1999). These financial incentives in favour of part-time work were abandoned in 2000, under the measures on the legal reduction of working time (Aubry laws). It is nevertheless clear that the incentives for part-time work modified what had previously been seen as the 'French exception' in relation to the increase in women's labour market participation rates throughout the 1970s and 1980s.

Unlike many other EU countries, the first stages of women's increased access to the labour market in France were accomplished on a full-time basis. It would seem that working-time policy measures have had differential effects on different sectors of the labour market. In the public sector, the proportion of women working part-time has remained relatively stable over time (an increase from 22 per cent in 1978 to 28 per cent in 2003) (INSEE, 2004), whilst part-time rates have more than doubled in some private sector jobs, with, for example, an increase from 28 per cent women part-timers in 1982 to 43 per cent in 1995 amongst shop workers (Maruani, 2002). Furthermore, part-time rates are highest amongst

Table 12.1:   Employment rates of women aged 25–49 years, according to marital status and number of children, 1962–2002, France

	Single, no children	Couple, no children	1 child	2 children	3 children and +
1962	67.5%	55.7%	42.5%	26.1%	15.9%
1968	71.8%	57.3%	46.8%	30.3%	17.8%
1975	78.2%	63.5%	59.4%	42.8%	23.2%
1982	83.0%	71.9%	70.1%	59.4%	31.6%
1990	87.6%	82.6%	79.7%	74.5%	44.5%
1997	88.6%	85.0%	83.8%	73.8%	49.6%
2002	—	89.0%	84.0%	80.0%	58.0%

Source: Maruani, 2000: 16, and for 2002 figures, Clément and Nicolas, 2003: 1.

Table 12.2:   Activity rates of men and women by age, France, 2001

Age group	Men	Women	Total
15–24 years	33.1%	26.5%	29.9%
25–39 years	94.6%	78.9%	86.7%
40–49 years	95.1%	80.6%	87.7%
50–59 years	80.5%	64.8%	72.5%
60 years and +	5.0%	3.3%	4.0%
Total	61.8%	48.3%	54.7%
N	14,109,633	11,934,200	26,043,833

Source: INSEE (2002) Enquête emploi 2001, INSEE Paris.

Table 12.3:   Rates of part-time work by age cohort and sex, France, 2001

Age	Men	Women
15–24 years	12%	34%
25–39 years	4%	29%
40–49 years	4%	31%
50–59 years	5%	31%
Over 60 years	20%	42%
Total	5%	30%

Source: INSEE (2002) Enquête emploi 2001, cited in Maruani, 2002: 93.

the under 25s and the over 60s, suggesting that this particular form of employment serves to regulate labour market entry and departure patterns, rather than playing a central role in the 'work–life balance' strategies of mothers.

The mobilisation of family policy measures for labour market objectives

It is generally acknowledged that, since the beginning of the 1990s, family policy has become dominated by employment policy preoccupations (Commaille et al., 2002). The extension of the APE to parents of two children is the most spectacular illustration of this new policy turn. In 1994, a new family law extended the APE to parents of two children and reduced the previous employment conditions for applicants. Thereafter, only two years in employment in the five years preceding the birth of a second child were required for admission to the APE benefit. The 1994 reform included periods of unemployment in the two year prerequisite rule. It also enabled parents to claim a 'part-time APE' and thus to obtain partial financial 'compensation' for a reduction in their working hours, following the birth of a second child. The overall rate of the APE benefit has remained stable over time: approximately 50 per cent of the minimum national wage. The reform was accompanied by changes to the parental leave policies already in existence in France. From 1994 onwards, small and medium-sized firms were required to provide up to three years unpaid parental leave to their staff, whilst granting their reinstatement.

The success of the new APE was much greater than expected. Within six years, the number of APE recipients increased dramatically, to almost 500,000 in 2001. Over the same period and for the first time in 40 years, the activity rates of mothers with two children and a youngest child aged less than three years dropped from 69 per cent to 53 per cent. In a detailed analysis of the new APE recipients (98 per cent of whom were mothers), Cédric Afsa has measured the influence of the APE on women's decision to leave the labour market. He distinguished between those women who had intended to give up work at the birth of their second child and who would have done so even without the APE benefit (effet d'aubaine) and those women whose decision was determined by the existence of the APE (effet incitatif). According to his calculations, the APE led 250,000 women who would normally have continued working after the birth of their second child to leave the labour market between 1994 and 1997 (Afsa, 1998). However, the most interesting results of his study concern the social characteristics of the APE recipients.

The results show a direct correlation between several factors, particularly women's difficulties in gaining access to the labour market and their geographical place of residence, and the decision to take up the APE-funded leave. Firstly, women who had experienced a period of unemployment prior to the birth of their second child are proportionately over-represented amongst APE recipients. No less than one-third of APE recipients were on unemployment benefit at some point during the year that preceded the birth of their second child. Women living in rural areas, where public-funded child-care facilities are notoriously scarce, were also disproportionately represented (Afsa, 1996). However, the take-up rate for the APE also varies according to the education levels of the mothers. Whereas the activity rate of qualified women has fallen by 13 per cent since 1994, that of the least qualified members of the female labour force has dropped by 17 per cent, thus increasing the gap between the activity rates of these two categories of women, from 13.5 per cent in 1993 to 17.5 per cent in 1998 (Bonnet & Labbé, 1999; see also Chapter 4).

It has thus been convincingly demonstrated that the new APE responded to the dual objective of: a) mechanically reducing the high (female) unemployment rate (Afsa, 1998) and b) lessening pressure on local governments and on the central State for the provision of child-care services for the under-threes. It is difficult to believe that the APE acted as an effective policy to enable parents to achieve a better 'work–life balance', since only 20 per cent of the APE recipients opted for the part-time option. For the remaining 80 per cent, the 'balance' was achieved through the good old solution of women simply leaving the labour market when their children were of pre-school age. The concerns expressed about the effects of this 'career break' on women's labour market participation patterns have been fuelled by a recent CNAF–CREDOC study which show that, at the end of their three years on APE benefit, 51 per cent of the recipients were out of work, whereas 71 per cent of them had a job when they decided to take the APE (results cited in Maruani, 2000: 56).

Similar misgivings have been expressed about the various measures adopted throughout the late 1980s and early 1990s to promote employment in the household services sector in France. These measures (tax advantages for households who employ a home help, essentially for cleaning, ironing, child-care or elder-care, reductions in employers social security contributions for service providers, etc.) were adopted with the explicit aim of increasing women's economic activity rates, and of promoting gender equality in the labour market, by facilitating women's access to higher level occupations, combating unemployment and promoting a better 'work–life balance' (Le Feuvre et al., 1999). In practice, they have actually contributed to the development of a significant number of flexible, low-paid, part-time jobs for poorly qualified women (Le Feuvre & Martin, 2001), whilst failing to address the essential question of the relatively low levels of domestic participation of men and fathers in French households (Gregory & Windebank, 2000).

The reduction in working time: a missed opportunity

The last set of policy measures to be mentioned in relation to work–life balance are the laws on the generalised reduction of working time, which were adopted by the socialist government in 2000. With an explicit aim of reducing unemployment rates and promoting job creation, the so-called '35 hours' measures were not explicitly devised to facilitate 'work–life balance'. However, they could have been expected to play some role in reducing the tensions between these two spheres. The first evaluations of the effects of the 35 hours legislation on the quality of life and on the working conditions of private sector employees show a high level of satisfaction with this measure. Almost 60 per cent of respondents say their quality of life has improved since the introduction of the 35 hours working week (Estrade et al., 2001). The satisfaction level is particularly high for women, with the exception of those in unskilled jobs. The results are slightly more ambiguous when the effects on working conditions are examined. Here, 28 per cent of respondents note a worsening of their working conditions and the most dissatisfied group is composed of women in unskilled jobs. A third of respondents declare that their 'work–life balance' has improved since the 35 hours (32 per cent of men and 38 per cent of women) and 57 per cent say that things are unchanged.

The results from a more specific study of the effects of the 35 hours on the parents of young children indicate that, more than other categories of beneficiaries, parents note an improvement in the ability to 'reconcile work and family life' (58 per cent claim that reconciliation is easier, 60 per cent of mothers and 55 per cent of fathers) (Fagnani & Letablier, 2003). However, more detailed analysis of the data shows that some parents have experienced new difficulties in synchronising their work and family life since the introduction of the 35 hours legislation, particularly due to the fact that their new 'reduced' working hours were imposed by their employer rather than negotiated and that they are more variable (from one day to another, from one week to the next, over the year) and less likely to be known a reasonable time in advance than before. There is also some indication that the intensification of working rhythms – and the 'mental fatigue' that goes with the less than proportionate reduction of work-loads – makes achieving a satisfactory 'balance' more difficult for some categories of parents than for others (Fagnani & Letablier, 2003).

Although childcare arrangements had generally not been affected by the reduction in working time, about half the parents of children under the age of 12 years say that they are able to spend more time with their children and there was no significant difference on this point between mothers and fathers (Estrade et al., 2001). However, there is a general consensus on the fact that the reduction in working hours has (as yet) done little to modify the dominant pattern of the gender division of household labour and caring activities. About 40 per cent of respondents claim to have increased the time spent on activities in the home and a large proportion say that they have changed the moment when they carry out their domestic chores, in order to 'free' their weekends or simply to be under less time pressure. It nevertheless remains the case that men have increased the time spent on DIY and gardening, whilst women have also increased the time spent gardening . . . but also spend more time tidying up the house.

Towards a 21st century 'gender contract' in France?

The 'Family Conference' of April 2003 largely confirmed the tendencies outlined above. However, this annual national event also introduced some interesting policy innovations, which seem to have been inspired both by the powerful 'family lobby' and by public opinion surveys. These measures include a simplification of the social benefits paid to parents on the birth of a new baby. Four of the existing benefits are to be unified within a new PAJE (Prestation d'accueil du jeune enfant – Young child benefit package) of approximately 800 Euros. This means-tested flat-rate benefit will be extended to cover 80 per cent of new parents, whereas only 50 per cent of households fell within the income ceilings of the previous measures (Hermange, 2003). Furthermore, in contrast to the pro-natalist criteria defined when they were introduced, complementary measures, such as the APE, AGED and AFEAMA are to be extended to include the first child. The government has also insisted on the need to give parents more 'choice' in managing their 'work–life balance'. Thus, parents of one child will have the option of taking six months parental leave (paid at the same flat-rate as the APE, about 300 Euros/month), or of receiving financial help to cover child-care costs if they both decide to continue working. The government claims that this measure will encourage families (mothers) to use the new APE on a part-time, rather than full-time basis. The amount paid to parents will vary according to their income levels and the type of child-care arrangements they adopt. Furthermore, tax incentives are to be offered to private companies who invest in child-care facilities for their staff.

This may either include work-place crèches or the pre-booking of a fixed number of places in a municipal crèche. They will be able to claim back 50 per cent of the cost of providing these services in the form of tax rebates. This measure comes in addition to the extra 200,000 places are to be offered in municipal crèches and to the new advantages offered to registered child-minders (assistantes maternelles), through an increase in basic wage levels and a public awareness campaign. The aim is to increase the number of women who register as child-minders and thus reduce waiting lists, particularly in rural areas.

From Jacobin centralism to regional variations

These measures are particularly interesting in the light of a recent study published by the CNAF, which reveals significant regional variations within France, both in terms of women's activity rates and of types of child-care solutions used by working parents (Clément & Nicolas, 2003). The extent of this regional diversity comes as something as a surprise in a country renowned for its centralist Jacobin heritage. At a national level, 11 per cent of the under threes are looked after in a collective crèche. However, this proportion varies from 2 per cent to 41 per cent according to geographical location. The highest levels of crèches are registered along the Mediterranean coast and in the Paris region. Likewise, 42 per cent of parents who benefit from the AGED reside in the Paris region, where income levels and women's activity rates are higher than elsewhere in the country. Paris is also the only region where the number of children looked after by a home-help, under the AGED scheme, is higher than the number cared for by a registered child-minder. On average, the number of children covered by the AFEAMA is 10 times higher than the recipients of the AGED (Clément & Nicolas, 2003). Largely due to the under-development of public child-care facilities, child-minders represent a particularly widespread solution for families with young children in the less densely urbanised regions of France (Brittany, Normandy, the Loire Valley). However, despite high levels of industrial development, regions in the East of France and along the Rhone valley (Lyon) are characterised by higher than average levels of female inactivity during the early years of motherhood and by the highest national levels of full-time APE beneficiaries. In Brittany and the Paris region, mothers are more likely to use the APE on a part-time basis. This leads the authors of the CNAF study to conclude that: 'Using the APE on a part-time basis is attractive to people living in the residential zones of urban areas, whereas using a full-time APE allocation is more likely for people living further away from the major urban poles'

(Clément & Nicolas, 2003: 2). Families in the North of France tend to use family networks for their child-care needs, although it should be remembered that the proportion of two year olds in full-time nursery education (écoles maternelles) is also high in this region, as it is in Brittany and the Massif Central. When analysing the French situation in a comparative perspective, it is therefore important to remember that: 'The French geography of child-care arrangements, with all its contrasts, is the product of an complex chemistry which combines local history, the distribution of particular family formations, the professional and educational aspirations of parents, demographic factors, the relative budgetary possibilities of local government institutions and the degree of urbanisation' (Clément & Nicolas, 2003: 4).

Despite these regional variations in work–life organisation patterns, the majority of young children in France now live in dual breadwinner households (Table 12.4). It would therefore be reasonable to believe that the relatively high activity rates of mothers would be reflected in the attitudes towards the 'work–life balance' issue. As we shall see below, this is not systematically the case.

Table 12.4: Distribution of young children (under 6 years) according to family composition and activity patterns of parents, France, 2001

Family composition and activity patterns of parents	*Children aged below 3 years*	*Children aged between 3 and 5 years*	*Children aged below 6 years*
Couples, of which:	93.2%	89.9%	91.6%
Dual-breadwinner	54.6%	57.4%	56.0%
1 child	27.1%	12.6%	19.9%
2 children	20.2%	30.9%	25.5%
3 children and +	7.4%	13.8%	10.6%
Male breadwinner	35.8%	29.5%	32.7%
1 child	6.5%	1.9%	4.2%
2 children	15.5%	12.3%	13.9%
3 children and +	13.9%	15.3%	14.6%
Father non-breadwinner	2.7%	3.0%	2.9%
Mother working	1.3%	1.6%	1.4%
Mother not working	1.5%	1.4%	1.5%
Single-Parent household	6.8%	10.2%	8.5%
Total	100%	100%	100%
Numbers	2,147,000	2,111,000	4,258,000

Source: INSEE (2002) Enquête emploi 2002, INSEE, Paris.

Attitudes towards 'work–life balance' in contemporary France

The data from the 2002 ISSP survey clearly indicate the contradictions and inconsistencies which characterise the 'work–life balance' debate in France. On the one hand, in line with the 'modified male breadwinner' model suggested for France by Jane Lewis (1992), women's employment outside the home is considered both desirable and legitimate by the vast majority of the adult population, at least before they have children.[3] Thus, 70 per cent of men and 75.5 per cent of women strongly agree that: 'Men and women should both contribute to the household income'. Furthermore, almost 80 per cent of men and 88 per cent of women agree that: 'After marrying and before having children, a woman should work full-time.' In much the same vein, over half the women (53 per cent) and 41 per cent of the men strongly agree that: 'Having a job is the best way for a woman to be an independent person.'

Nonetheless, once children appear on the scene, attitudes tend to favour mothers giving up work altogether or reducing their working hours, at least when children are of pre-school age. It is interesting to note the discrepancies between the ideal 'work–life balance' pattern that French mothers say they would like to adopt and their actual behaviour. Their discrepancies are clearly expressed in the ISSP data: 75 per cent of the mothers surveyed stated that they had continued to work when their children were below school age (50 per cent on a full-time basis, 25 per cent part-time), whereas 45 per cent stated that working part-time is the best solution for mothers of young children and over 38 per cent believe that it would be best for them to give up work all together (as against the 25 per cent who actually did this). Once the children reached school age, the full-time activity rate increased to 47 per cent, with 32 per cent working part-time and 21 per cent staying at home. These practices differ quite radically from the preferred options of the ISSP respondents, which testify to a much lower acceptance of full-time employment for mothers of school-aged children (21 per cent) and much higher aspirations for part-time work (72 per cent believe this to be the best solution). These aspirations disappear once the respondents are asked to envisage the ideal solution for women whose children have left home: only 17.5 per cent imagine working part-time at that stage in their life-cycle, whereas 70 per cent would choose a return to full-time employment and only 1.7 per cent would want to stay at home.

In total, 49 per cent of men and 44 per cent of women agree that: 'All in all, family life suffers when the woman has a full-time job'. These results are confirmed by a recent CREDOC opinion survey, where only 20 per cent of the respondents believed that the best solution at the birth of a child is for both parents to continue working as before (an increase from 14 per cent at the beginning of the 1990s). Respondents in 'male breadwinner' households are – logically – more likely to favour women leaving the labour market, whilst those in 'dual breadwinner' households (particularly with young children) would prefer mothers to work part-time (Damon et al., 2003).

Furthermore, it is interesting to note the continuing strong correlation between the 'work–life balance' aspirations of the ISSP respondents and their own family experiences (Lollivier, 1988; Ménahem, 1988, 1989). Men and women whose mothers never worked are twice as likely to believe that: 'A pre-school child suffers when his or her mother works outside the home' than those adults whose own mothers spent at least a year in employment before they reached the age of 14 (20 per cent, as against 10 per cent). In the same vein, they are also twice as likely to agree that: 'All in all, family life suffers when the woman has a full-time job' than those whose mother worked when they were young (23 per cent, as against 12 per cent). Furthermore, two-thirds of the respondents who agree with women with pre-school children working full-time come from families where their own mother worked.

Finally, French men are marginally more in favour of mothers with young children staying at home (48 per cent) than are the women themselves: 48 per cent of the later would opt for working part-time, whereas only 35 per cent would choose to stay at home. Furthermore, over half the men (56 per cent) agree that pre-school children suffer from their mothers working, as against just 35 per cent of the women. Men also tend to agree more with the idea that: 'Being a housewife is just as fulfilling as working for pay' (42 per cent) in comparison to the women, 35 per cent of whom agree with this statement.

Of course, there is also a generation effect in attitudes to the 'work–life balance' issue: 35 per cent of respondents aged over 65 disagree with the idea that: 'A working mother can establish just as warm and secure relationship with her children as a mother who does not work', as against only 13 per cent of the under-25s. However, 75 per cent of the older age group also agreed that: 'Men ought to do a larger share of household work than they do now', an opinion that is also shared in about the same proportions by the younger generations. This is perhaps an indication of the degree to which the increase in women's labour market participation in France has failed to make any significant changes to the domestic division of labour between the sexes.

The ISSP data confirms numerous studies on this question over recent years and illustrates the conservative attitudes to the domestic division of labour that would seem to characterise the country as a whole. To take just one example, almost three-quarters (76 per cent) of French women declare that they are solely responsible for the laundry, a task that is notoriously seldom shared within French households (Kaufmann, 1992). However, it is interesting to note that, despite the avowedly low levels of male participation in domestic chores, a large majority (70 per cent) declare that the domestic division of labour is never or rarely a subject of disagreement between spouses. Fewer than 20 per cent of the ISSP respondents declare frequent disputes about who does what at home, although women are more likely to recognise tensions around this question than are the men (25 per cent, as against 11 per cent).

Work–life conflict: the class divide

The ISSP questionnaire provides different kinds of data on the experience of work–life conflict in the different national contexts. Questions examine both the influence of the domestic division of labour on experiences at work and the effects of work pressures on family life. Given the unequal burden of domestic responsibilities that fall on women's shoulders, the results of the first aspect of this question are somewhat surprising: over two-thirds of French men and women declare that they are never (or rarely) preoccupied by their domestic and family worries at work. However, these results vary somewhat according to the family circumstances of the respondents and the negative effect of having at least one child in the household is much stronger for mothers than for fathers. Thus, 47 per cent of women with children declare having experienced occasional difficulties in concentrating at work due to family responsibilities, as against just 35 per cent of their childless female counterparts (Tables 12.5a and 12.5b).

The length of the working week does not appear to have a significant impact on the ability of women to concentrate at work, since 51 per cent of women working full-time with at least one child in the household state that they have never experienced such difficulties. Several hypotheses could explain these rather surprising results. On the one hand, women may refuse to recognise the difficulties they face in combining employment and family life, notably because these could be interpreted as 'personal failings', rather than as the result of structural tensions between the different spheres (Nicole-Drancourt, 1991). Secondly, women may anticipate the difficulties associated with the 'work–life balance'

Table 12.5a: Reponses to the statement: 'I have found it difficult to concentrate at work due to family responsibilities', from men and women (no child in the household)

	Several times a week	Several times a month	Once or twice	Never	Total
Male	1.1%	3.7%	· 26.1%	69.0%	268 (100%)
Female	0	5.8%	29.8%	64.4%	225 (100%)

Source: ISSP data set.

Table 12.5b: Responses to the statement: 'I have found it difficult to concentrate at work due to family responsibilities', from men and women (at least one child in the household):

	Several times a week	Several times a month	Once or twice	Never	Total
Male	0	3.6%	29.0%	67.4%	193 (100%)
Female	3.8%	7.7%	36.0%	52.4%	286 (100%)

Source: ISSP data set.

and choose those jobs which make it easiest for them to better manage these aspects of their lives (Duru-Bellat, 1990). Thirdly, women may also derive a certain sense of pride from having succeeded in overcoming daily difficulties on their own (Commaille, 1992). Finally, motherhood may provide women with a stamp of social and psychological 'normality'. The small minority of French women without children (who only represent about 10 per cent of the adult population) are often perceived as slightly 'odd', whereas mothers are generally seen as more 'responsible' and 'stable' (Gadéa & Marry, 2000).

Although the French ISSP survey reveals relatively low levels of impact of family life on work-related stress, there is nevertheless evidence of the considerable time pressure women experience at home, particularly when they are working full-time. Table 12.6 presents the responses to the following statement: 'There are so many things to do at home, I often run out of time before I get them all done.' Over 70 per cent of women with at least one child in the household agree with this statement. However, women in manual occupations are significantly more likely to experience these kind of time pressures at home than those in the other two occupational categories, even when they are working part-time.

Table 12.6:   Mothers' responses to the statement: 'There are so many things to do at home, I often run out of time before I get them all done', according to occupational status and working time (at least one child in the household)

Occupational status	Agree			Disagree		
	Total mothers	Mothers working FT	Mothers working PT	Total mothers	Mothers working FT	Mothers working PT
Managerial/ professional	70.5%	74.1%	60.0%	17.1%	14.8%	24.0%
Non-manual	70.9%	72.2%	66.7%	19.4%	18.6%	22.2%
Manual	81.5%	81.4%	75.0%	13.0%	11.6%	16.7%
Total	213 (72.7%)	165 (74.7%)	48 (65.8%)	51 (17.4%)	35 (15.8%)	16 (21.9%)

Source: ISSP data set.

It is also interesting to note that women in manual occupations also experience more difficulties in finding the time to complete their domestic chores than the other categories of women, even when there are no children in the household. Thus, 78 per cent of manual women without children agreed with this statement, as compared to 59 per cent of professional/managerial women in the same situation. This figure rose to 81 per cent amongst the manual women without children working full-time and still affected 70 per cent of those working part-time.

These results differ quite considerably from those obtained in the British case. Although women in manual occupations appear to experience the highest levels of time pressure at home in the two countries, the experiences of women in managerial or professional occupations appear to be significantly different in Britain and France. Thus, professional and managerial women working full-time with no children in the household are far more likely to run out of time for their domestic chores in Britain than in France (67 per cent, as against 58 per cent). This is likely to be a consequence of the fact that managerial and professional women in Britain work considerably longer hours than French women in the same occupational category. Furthermore, when they have at least one child in the household, the domestic time pressures on British managerial or professional women appear to be particularly strong (86 per cent agree that they run out of time), whereas the French professional and managerial women with children seem to suffer fewer pressures than their British counterparts and fewer pressures than women in other occupational categories in their own country (Table 12.7b).

Table 12.7a: Comparison of women's responses to the statement: 'There are so many things to do at home, I often run out of time before I get them all done', according to occupational status, working time and country (France/Britain) (no children in the household, full-time only)

Occupational status/country	France		Britain	
	% agree	Mean hours worked	% agree	Mean hours worked
Managerial/ professional	58.0%	39.9	67.0%	45.6
Non-manual	58.0%	37.2	68.0%	39.1
Manual	80.0%	37.8	80.0%	40.0

Source: ISSP data set.

Table 12.7b: Comparison of mother's responses to the statement: 'There are so many things to do at home, I often run out of time before I get them all done', according to occupational status, working time and country (France/Britain) (at least one child in the household, full-time only)

Occupational status/country	France		Britain	
	% agree	Mean hours worked	% agree	Mean hours worked
Managerial/ professional	74.0%	39.3	86.0%	43.9
Non-manual	75.0%	36.8	74.0%	36.8
Manual	81.0%	35.9	80.0%	39.1

Source: ISSP data set.

Discussion and conclusion

Part of the explanation for these cross-national discrepancies may well lie in the more systematic provision of affordable child-care solutions for working mothers in the French context. However, this explanation fails to account for the similar experiences of women in manual occupations in the two countries. It may well be that the child-care policy measures adopted in France are more readily exploited by women from privileged social backgrounds, particularly when they involve some kind of tax reductions (since only 50 per cent of French households pay any income tax and would thus be eligible for income tax rebates on their child-care expenditure). It is also the case that women in managerial and professional occupations are more likely to externalise some of their domestic responsibilities than those in other occupational categories. According to INSEE data, more than a quarter of professional/ managerial households pay for domestic services, as compared to under 4 per cent of manual households. This externalisation may also lessen the time pressures on women in managerial and professional occupations, despite the 'mental burden' involved in organising such services (Haicault, 1984). However, since the levels of domestic outsourcing would seem to be comparable in Britain and in France (see Chapter 7), this explanation fails to account for the different experiences of French and British managerial and professional women with regard to time pressures at home.

A more promising explanation for the cross-national differences probably lies in the nationally specific working time patterns identified in the two countries. Although women working full-time in all occupational categories tend to work longer hours in Britain than in France, the differences would seem to be particularly important for women in managerial and professional occupations. Although the mean hours worked by French mothers in these occupational categories exceed those of women in the non-manual and manual categories, the difference is significantly lower than for British managerial and professional women in comparison to their national counterparts. In full-time jobs, British managerial and professional women with children work on average nearly six hours a week longer than their French counterparts. The 'long-hours culture' of managerial occupations is obviously present in France too, but it would seem to take more limited proportions than in the British case. This is undoubtedly due to the effects of the national legislation on the 35-hour working week in France, which has contributed to a greater awareness of working time practices across the occupational hierarchy.

Thus, despite the fact that the French domestic division of labour tends to be rather more conservative in France than in Britain (see Chapter 7), the combination of the relatively widespread provision of child-care services and the public policy commitment to reduced working hours would indeed seem to have reduced some of the tensions associated with achieving 'work–life balance' in France. However, it is important to stress that the relative advantages of the French national model are not spread evenly over all occupational categories. As has been stressed elsewhere, working-class women in France are not only the least likely to benefit from a shared or non-traditional domestic division of labour, they are also restricted in their access to the financial and cognitive resources necessary for 'outsourcing' part of their domestic responsibilities. Furthermore, the adoption of the 35-hours legislation in France has had an uneven effect across occupational categories. Disruption to the standard, normative 'working week' has generally been more widespread in manual jobs than at the higher levels of the occupational hierarchy and this would seem to have increased rather than decreased the difficulties working-class women have experienced in achieving a satisfactory level of 'work–life balance' in France. This is an important issue to bear in mind when considering the policy tools best suited to promoting a better 'work–life balance' across Europe.

Notes

1. Clotilde Lemarchant wishes to thank Alain Degenne (CNRS) and Yannick Lemel (INSEE) for enabling her to take part in the French ISSP survey. Thanks also to Laurence Bouvard (centre Quetelet), Michel Force (CNRS) and Catherine Mason (University of Caen) for preparing the French ISSP datasets.
2. The authors thank Clare Lyonette for her contribution to the data analysis presented in this chapter.
3. The figures in this paragraph refer to the whole population, including those who have never had children.

13
Continuities, Change and Transformations

Rosemary Crompton, Suzan Lewis and Clare Lyonette

1. The complex and uneven nature of change and transformation

There have been recent, and dramatic, changes in the position of women and gender relations. In Europe, within living memory, discrimination in employment by sex has been perfectly legal, and married women have been formally subordinate to their husbands. For example, in England, rape within marriage was only criminalised in 1991, French men could formally forbid their wives to take up paid employment until 1965, and Portuguese women were by law subject to their husband's authority until the 1970s. However, the unravelling of the 'male breadwinner model' towards more egalitarian models of work–family articulation across Europe is a complex and very slow process. There is no doubt that the growth in the labour force participation of women, especially mothers, and the variety of national policy responses to support dual earner families have been associated with some changes in attitudes, expectations, behaviours and experiences, in the home and in the workplace, in different European contexts. However, the contributors to this book show that both structural and relational factors remain important in shaping work and family experiences, albeit in highly complex and differentiated ways. Changes and transformations are occurring at various societal levels, in different ways and at different rates both between countries and also within countries and within institutions, influenced by a plurality of factors. Nevertheless, gender continues to shape experiences of work and family everywhere.

'Gender' has recently been defined as:

> the division of people into two differentiated groups, 'men' and women', and the organisation of the major aspects of society along these

binaries. The binary divisions override individual differences and inter-twine with other major socially constructed differences – racial cate-gorisation, ethnic grouping, economic class, age, religion and sexual orientation – which interact to produce a complex hierarchical system of dominance and subordination. (Davis et al., 2006)

Thus the contributions to this book illustrate the complexities of changes or lack of change in attitudes, norms, decision making (about work and family patterns and also fertility), behaviours (including the domestic division of labour) workplace supports and barriers, gender equity at home and at work, and well-being, across diverse contexts. For example at the level of norms and attitudes, work and family expectations are shifting but not in a simple way. In Chapter 6, Karin Wall demonstrates that attachment to the male breadwinner model is declining across Europe, albeit at different rates, and a range of modern attitudinal patterns are emerging within different European countries. Although modern patterns are more prevalent in some countries, a diversity of attitudinal patterns exist even in countries usually considered more progressive in work and family attitudes. Moreover attachment to the male breadwinner/female carer-stay-at-home model has not totally disappeared even in countries with the most egalitarian policies. It is interesting that though endorse-ment of the male breadwinner model represents a minority attitude set, it is not limited to the older generations who were reared at a point in his-tory where full time female homemakers were the norm. Rather, it appears to be sustained for a minority of people across contemporary European contexts.

At the behavioural level, decision making about paid work and family care is also shaped by a multiplicity of interacting factors, including gen-der, social class, geographical and social location and historical context, as well as welfare state policies and provisions and employment conditions that influence the practicalities and ease with which paid work and child-care can be combined (see, for example, Chapters 8 and 12). Moreover, when we turn to the division of domestic labour, especially in respect of the most mundane tasks, it is clear that change is frustratingly slow and fragmented (Crompton & Lyonette, Chapter 7). Neither is it related in a simple way to welfare state policy or the availability of part time work. Indeed, the domestic division of labour is most traditional in Portugal and France, both countries with high a level of full time work amongst women. There are pockets of change, with higher status women being more likely to report a non-traditional division of labour, more so in some countries than others. Nevertheless, the relative ease or difficulty or reconciling employment and family life does appear to impact on decisions about family size, with the birth-rate falling across Europe, although not to the same extent everywhere (Fagnani, Chapter 4; Hašková, Chapter 5).

At the workplace level, many organisations in Europe also appear to be changing to support dual earner families in response to national social policy or by introducing 'family friendly' policies for a range of reasons (Den Dulk, 2001; Evans, 2001; Wood, Menezes & Lasaosa, 2003). Here too, however, fundamental change is slow, uneven and often superficial. The 'male model' of full-time, long-term work, predicated on outdated assumptions of separate and gendered work and family spheres (Bailyn, 1993; Lewis, 2001; Rapoport, Bailyn, Fletcher & Pruitt, 2002) continues to prevail and is intensified in contemporary settings. Nevertheless, some workplaces are more supportive of work–family articulation than others. This differs across national context, sector, specific type of workplace and for different occupations, influenced by combinations of national policy and its implementation, the nature of work and normative working practices. The qualitative studies reported in this book demonstrate that there are often multiple cultural layers within organisations and that while some workplace units may support work–family articulation, others within the same workplace are more resistant to change (Chapters 10 and 11). In these two very different countries (Portugal and Sweden), it is noteworthy that in both workplaces, the work of caring is largely seen as the paramount responsibility of women. Moreover, the impacts of changes purporting to be 'family friendly' are also far from clear as many current working practices, including flexible work arrangements, are often double edged (Lewis, Smithson et al., 2006; Smithson, 2005).

There is an assumption in the literature that support for work and family, both structural and relational, will enhance satisfaction and reduce stress (e.g. Allen, 2001; Kinnunen, Greuts & Mauno, 2004). Therefore, well-being can be expected to vary across national and workplace contexts. This appears to be true to some extent, but again the contributors to this book show that it is not simple. There are rising levels of sickness absence in many European countries and Bäck-Wiklund and Plantin (Chapter 10) note that sick leave rates are particularly high among young women in Sweden, despite social supports for working parents. It seems that well-being too is multi-dimensional and context dependent. For example, stress at home does not necessarily mean dissatisfaction with family life, and resources of time, money and people (care capital) interact in complex ways to contribute to well-being in dual earner couples (see Anttonen & Sipilä, Chapter 9). As Chapter 10 illustrates, it is possible to report hardships but still be satisfied. A recent European qualitative and comparative study of the transition to parent-hood suggests that well-being is more closely linked to expectations and sense of entitlement than to actual experiences (Lewis, Smithson et al., 2006). For example, women in Bulgaria, where the domestic division of labour is very traditional despite high levels of female labour force par-ticipation, reported little or no expectation of men's involvement in paid work, relying more on support from women in the extended fam-ily and were relatively happy with this (although we should note that Bulgarian women have joined the other Central and Eastern European countries in a 'fertility strike', see Chapter 5). Mothers in Norway, in contrast, felt entitled to more sharing of unpaid work by their male part-ners and were more likely to be dissatisfied if they felt that the men were not pulling their weight (these might be considered as examples of the 'adaptive preferences' discussed later in this chapter).

Finally, what has changed in terms of women's opportunities in the workplace after decades of European and national equal opportunities ini-tiatives? Women are certainly participating more than ever in the labour market, albeit still less than men (see Den Dulk & van Doorne-Huiskes, Chapter 3). This is the case even in countries where social policies aim to maximise women's opportunities to participate in paid labour and despite long standing policies on gender equality. However Den Dulk and van Doorne-Huiskes point out that other indicators of equality, such as earn-ings and advancement or breaking through the 'glass ceiling', paint a more pessimistic picture. Again, change is uneven. The wage gap remains stub-bornly in place and women advance more easily in some occupations than others (Crompton, 1994), but these outcomes are not necessarily related to national policies in obvious ways.

Nevertheless, despite these complexities, the chapters in this book also report many positive developments, albeit more evident in some coun-tries than others. For example, although men generally undertake less unpaid, family work than women, some men in some contexts are doing considerably more than in previous generations. There has been an increase in the availability of flexible and part time work in many con-texts, including a growth in 'good', protected part-time work, and fol-lowing EU initiatives, part-time workers increasingly enjoy equal rights to their full time counterparts. This too has the potential to support more egalitarian family patterns under certain circumstances, especially if taken up by men as well as women. While it remains true that the insti-tutional and normative frameworks that would facilitate an egalitarian model of work–life articulation have yet to be fully developed, more progress has been made towards this in some contexts than others. The comparative nature of this book enables us to identify some of the conditions and strategies that facilitate the more positive and equitable work–family adjustments.

On many counts, the social democratic countries offer the best opportunities for equitable work–family articulation. Social policies in the Nordic welfare state regimes, though varying in specific provisions, are designed to maximise women's economic independence and there is explicit recognition, through, for example, a father's quota of paid non-transferable parental leave, that this also requires men to change. Compared with mothers from other European countries, those in the social democratic welfare states spend the largest share of their total time on paid work. There is less gender inequality in domestic work in the Nordic countries than in the other European countries, and women have a higher sense of entitlement than those elsewhere to public, workplace and domestic support for combining paid work and care (Lewis & Smithson, 2001). These countries, along with France, have also sustained relatively high birth rates. However, if the ultimate goal is broader gender justice, the picture is not so straightforward. The social democratic model does not, at this point in its evolution, guarantee gender equality in earnings or occupational advancement, and this in turn holds back further social transformation.

2.   Equality, equity and the social embeddedness of 'choices' and 'preferences'

Above all, the contributors to this book highlight an apparent ongoing attachment to an 'ideology of domesticity' (Williams, 2000) that assigns primary responsibility for caring and domestic work to women, that prevails amongst many men and women, even in the Nordic countries. This could suggest that some women might 'prefer' or 'choose' to be more involved in care and less in paid work as compared to men, even if this undermines equality in the labour market. Indeed, a rhetoric of 'choice' underpins many national social policy initiatives on the reconciliation of work and family, particularly cash for care schemes which are being introduced in some of the most 'progressive' countries. However this raises questions about equality, equity and the nature of 'preferences' and 'choice', which are always socially embedded and constrained.

The objective of gender equality is often criticised for implying sameness in relation to an implicit male norm, for example encouraging women to work like men, rather than exploring diverse working patterns for men and women. The idea of gender equity rather than equality attempts to move beyond this 'sameness' and has been discussed in terms of fairness; for example, a fair distribution of rewards and constraints from paid work and family (see Gambles, Lewis & Rapoport, Chapter 2). This underlines the need for both men *and* women to change and a valuing of diversity in patterns of working and caring. Questions remain, however, about how to conceptualise what is 'fair', without recourse to a theory of individual preferences or implied biological essentialism. Jane Lewis and Susanna Giullari (2005) argue that one approach that might have the potential to move this debate forward, particularly in relation to issues of paid work and care, is the Capability Approach (CA) developed by Sen and Nussbaum (e.g. Nussbaum, 2003). The CA recognises human diversity, without getting embroiled in the sameness/difference debates, by shifting attention from inequalities in resources, outcomes and preferences to inequalities in capabilities, that is, the real freedom a person has to be or to do what s/he has reason to value (Lewis & Giullari, 2005). This approach helps to focus on the difficulties in ensuring real options for women, and also for men, to choose what to do or be in relation to care and employment.

Central to the CA is the concept of individual agency freedom, and a recognition that genuine freedom for a person to 'choose' has to be underpinned by resources and by personal, social and environmental factors that affect the ability to transform resources into opportunities. The CA has been criticised for this focus on the individual's agency freedom – which might smack of neo-classical economic theory – rather than on equality of resources or outcomes. However, Lewis and Giullari argue that the CA focuses on the individual's need to be in a position to make real choices, that is, a position where it is practically possible to choose a certain path (e.g. to work part time) or to choose not to do so. Individual agency freedom to 'choose' to care is of course, gendered. The persistence of the 'ideology of domesticity' means that it is more difficult for women to choose not to care, or for men to choose to prioritise care.[1]

Drawing on the capabilities approach, Lewis and Guillari account for diversity and gendered choices in relation to paid work and care, while recognising that these choices stem from different and unequal social contexts, in which 'preferences' are likely to be adaptive. For example, for a woman who has access to only low level poorly paid work in a context where there is little formal childcare support, a preference to prioritise care might be an adaptive response (see Crompton, 2006; Chapter 7). Preferences to undertake or prioritise informal care work are dependent on factors such as level of education, conditions of employment, and especially on assumptions about what is the 'proper' thing for women and men to do, which vary cross-nationally. As the chapters in this book demonstrate, decisions about working and caring are influenced by the dynamic interaction between social policy and cultural definitions of motherhood and fatherhood that contribute to a more or less guilt-inducing climate for maternal employment. Women face stronger pressure to care (Lewis, Kagan & Heaton, 2000; Finch & Mason, 1993), therefore they often express a desire to put care first (Duncan & Edwards, 1999). Moreover, a person's real freedom to choose also depends on the needs and actions of others, and where the position of men and women are unequal, the exercise of men's freedom to choose between work and care can serve to limit women's choices. As we discuss below, assumptions about the proper ways of doing work in workplaces can also constrain real 'choices' available.

For women and men to have the capabilities to reconcile paid work and care work in diverse ways, care work has to be recognised as both a legitimate opportunity/choice, as well as a necessary human activity to be shared among men and women, and valued equally with market work (Gambles, Lewis & Rapoport, 2006; Lewis & Giulliari, 2005). It follows that policies to encourage this will be those that promote conditions that not only enhance women's labour force participation, rewards and achievements, but also foster sharing of responsibility for caring and domestic work among men and women. The recognition that all decisions relating to the articulation of paid and unpaid work are socially embedded draws attention to structures designed to achieve gender equality or to enhance women's and men's capabilities to make genuine choices.

3. Which factors facilitate change towards gender equitable articulations of paid work and family?

It is striking throughout this book that, despite many cross-national and regional differences, there are also some strong commonalities and continuities. While aggregate measures suggest that the Nordic countries do 'best', at a more fine-grained level, we still find that women do more domestic and caring work everywhere. The gender wage gap remains across Europe and will be even more difficult to eradicate in a global context of competitive pressures leading to increased working hours and demands, found in all the countries discussed in this book, which will further undermine the capability to make relatively unconstrained choices about paid work and caring. So what can we learn from the contributions to this book about the factors facilitating change towards gender equitable articulations of paid work and family?

The chapters in this book work at different levels of analysis; from macro cross-national trends to micro snapshots of experiences within specific employing organisations; from a focus on social policy to a focus on individual attitudes. This enables us to explore both the big picture, as well as the specificity of diverse contexts. Perhaps most importantly, it demonstrates that further developments towards the unravelling of the male breadwinner role will involve attention to change at many different levels; in social policy, workplace practices and household relationships and behaviours.

Although there are certain basic provisions, such as childcare, that are crucial for combining paid work and care, the complexity of intersecting influences and of the nature of changes in the many dimensions of the work and family nexus that this book addresses, preclude simple recommendations of the way forward. Rather, it is important to tease out the combination of factors that can support transformations to gender equitable work and family articulation. National welfare state policy on childcare provision, leave arrangements, the availability of part-time work opportunities and other flexible working arrangements and employment policies, can make a huge difference. However, in many respects, policies do not change structures, relationships, attitudes, behaviours or experiences in simple ways and, crucially, attention also needs to be focused on organisational factors which determine whether and how policies are implemented at the workplace.

Affordable *childcare and leaves* provide an essential base for gender transformation. Where there is limited state childcare support, it is generally women who have to be resourceful and put together complex and often fragile arrangements, particularly but not exclusively women with fewest resources and hence the least capabilities to make genuine choices (See Chapters 8 and 11). Childcare is a necessary but not sufficient condition. It enables women to work and care – but not necessarily to achieve equitable rewards, nor does it address the domestic division of labour. Without affordable high quality childcare, along with legal provisions regulating work leave and work schedules, fertility levels are often a casualty (Chapters 4 and 5). Moreover, as is pointed out in Chapter 9, childcare issues are increasingly complicated by current workplace trends such as the growth of atypical and casualised work, and it is difficult for state-sponsored childcare services to cover all care needs and contingencies in a 24/7 society. Meanwhile, public debates on the quality of childcare and the desirability of long childcare days are growing across many European countries (Lewis & Smithson, 2006). With ageing populations across Europe, eldercare and other care services are also increasingly important (Williams, 2004).

Paid parental leaves can enable women to return to the labour market after having children, although the impact on women's capacity to make genuine choices is more equivocal than that of childcare provisions. Parental leave can serve to promote women's exit from the market or to promote equality (Deven & Moss, 2002). The take-up of parental leave is gendered everywhere, albeit less so in the Nordic countries, and in current contexts of rapid organisational change, the longer the leave, the more women's occupational careers are disadvantaged. A father's quota of paid non-transferable leave recognises that women's options for employment and caring are dependent on those of men and vice versa, and represents efforts to redefine the fatherhood role, in terms of active parenting and not just providing economically. Fathers' take-up of parental leave is growing where there is a fathers' quota. However, men still, on average, take considerably less parental leave than women, and recent research indicates that it is the amount of time that fathers take rather than whether or not they take some parental leave, that predicts the nature of involvement in childcare and renegotiation of fathers' and mothers' roles (Haas & Hwang, forthcoming.) Changes in workplace norms and practices will be necessary for real choices about working and caring to be available for men and hence also women, particularly in the current context of the intensification and extension of work (Brandth & Kvande, 2002; Crompton, 2006). Moreover, Haas and Hwang (forthcoming), in a survey of men in male-dominated organisations, found that women's employment situation remained a strong independent determinate of fathers' engagement in childcare, and argue that as long as Swedish women have fewer opportunities for well paid, fulfilling work than men, we might expect they will remain primarily responsible for childcare – both because of relative earnings and power and because many women are reluctant to give up the major power as parents without other compensations. This reinforces the importance of change at workplace levels.

The availability and affordability of part time work for mothers (and ideally fathers) emerges as very significant in the discussions in this book. However, the nature of part-time work varies very considerably across European states. There has been an increase, in many countries, in 'good' part-time work that is well protected, in well paid or high status jobs, and with equal employment rights. However, part-time work still has a negative impact on career development (Crompton et al., 2003). It remains a strategy used primarily by women, and, given the intensification of work, there is also a danger that part-time jobs may be characterised by unrealistic workloads (Chapter 10). Part-time work, in whatever form, is likely to remain double edged unless accompanied by shifts in the gendered division of labour, changes in workplace assumptions that only full time employees can be 'ideal workers', and take up of part-time work by men. In the absence of these changes, full time work often appears to offer more latitude for gender transformation. Full time work, however, is not inevitably associated with pay equity. The gender pay gap is relatively large in post-communist regimes where full time work has long been the norm but attitudes to gender roles and the domestic division of labour are both very traditional (Metcalfe & Afanassieva, 2005; Domsch, Ladwig & Tenten, 2003; Chapter 5). Shorter full time hours for both men and women may offer more opportunities for transformational change, but would require equally transformational, systemic change in workplaces.

Economic conditions, material and status resources also shape experiences of work–family articulation in diverse ways and there are many differences in experiences within, as well as between, national contexts, especially in countries with greater social class divisions and income inequality. Despite national variations, women in higher status jobs, with higher earning power are more likely to report non-traditional domestic division of labour everywhere (Chapter 7). This suggests that institutional arrangements that open up more opportunities for women to develop careers in well-paid jobs will facilitate more transformational change. Again however, status and resources interact with other factors. For example, we have seen that having the resources to outsource domestic work might make the practicalities of working and caring easier, but does not necessarily make life less stressful for women. It can absolve men from the need to change and perpetuate gendered assumptions of ultimate responsibilities for domestic work. This too varies by country. Crompton and Lyonette (Chapter 7) show that outsourcing domestic work does appear to reduce stress among higher status women in Portugal, but in the context of a high level of traditionalism that creates considerable stress for less advantaged women. However, outsourcing does not reduce stress for women in other countries. Resources thus interact with cultural and structural variables. Geographical context also makes a difference. For example, in the UK, resources go much further in regions outside London than in the capital (Perrons et al., Chapter 8) and Lefeuvre and Lemarchant (Chapter 12) describe the many regional differences that exist in France.

Finally, *workplace policies (if well implemented), cultures and practices* can, under certain circumstances, facilitate change toward more gender equitable articulations of paid work and family by providing flexibility and support for working and caring. Workplace systems interact with welfare state provisions in a number of complex and often contradictory ways.

There is evidence that organisations in states with the least welfare provisions are more likely to develop work and family policies (Den Dulk, 2001; Evans, 2001; Dex & Smith, 2002), with trade unions and collective agreements also playing an important facilitating role in some contexts (see Chapter 11; also Dex & Smith, 2002) – although these provisions fail to match the level of entitlements ensured as individual rights in the Nordic states (Evans, 2001). However, less is known about actual implementation, practices and assumptions cross-nationally. Even within national states it is not possible to generalise about the policies and practices across sectors or specific organisational units (see Chapters 10 and 11; Lewis, Smithson et al., 2006). The apparent high levels of policies in some UK organisations, for example, are partly to compensate for lack of state provisions such as childcare, and only rarely transform culture and practice (Lewis & Cooper, 2005; Bond, Hyman et al., 2002; Yeandle et al., 2003). Neither does state regulation guarantee fundamental workplace changes. There is a widespread implementation gap between policy (public and workplace) and practice everywhere (Haas & Hwang, forthcoming; Brandth & Kvande, 2002; Gambles et al., 2006). The implementation gap is exacerbated by current working patterns and pressures within global competitive capitalism in the private sector and the cost cutting strategies of 'new public management' in the public sector. It is also exacerbated by contemporary management practices that encourage the internalisation of employer demands and perceived 'choices' to work longer and harder (Lewis, 2003; Crompton, 2006; Perlow, 1998). Bäck-Wicklund and Plantin demonstrate that even in a public sector workplace in Sweden, where management is sympathetic to work–family needs and consider themselves to be supportive, actual strategies for putting policies into practice can be weak.

The extent to which welfare state and employer initiatives can enhance capabilities for women and men to make genuine choices thus depends on how they are implemented at the workplace level. This requires moving beyond quick fix solutions (Gambles et al., Chapter 2) towards fundamental shifts in workplace structures, practices and cultures, that is, systemic change (Bailyn, 1993; Rapoport et al., 2002). For flexible and part time work or shorter working hours to become a real choice that both men and women can opt in or out of, they need to be valued equally with the male norm of continuous full time careers, a concept that is itself increasingly challenged in contemporary workplaces. This draws attention to the gendered nature of organisations (Acker, 1990), which also underpins gendered decisions about working and caring.

4. Gendered organisations

Gendered organisations reflect the assumptions of separate, gendered, public and private spheres, which like the male breadwinner family model represents an increasingly minority phenomenon in the twenty-first century. The anachronistic assumptions that ideal workers do not have active family responsibilities, and that full time and uninterrupted work is a measure of organisational or occupational or professional commitment, underpins the devaluing and continued gendering of alternative working patterns. These assumptions are exacerbated in competitive global capitalism in private sector organisations, but are also manifested in female dominated public sector professions, as we see in the case of Swedish social workers (Chapter 10), for whom the concept of being a caring professional implies constant availability to clients.

Assumptions about the proper ways of doing work in workplaces constrain real choices available to women and men, and like assumptions about proper ways of being a mother or father, these are also gendered. Organisations are rarely gender neutral in their assumptions about the competencies of ideal workers, and stereotypically masculine competencies, such as aggressively competitive behaviour are often valued more than interpersonal competencies, that are more associated with women (Rapoport et al., 2002). Thus, just as care work (paid and unpaid), predominantly undertaken by women, is less valued than market work in the wider society, interpersonal or caring work in organisations, although essential for effective functioning, is often undervalued and rendered invisible (Fletcher, 1999). Greater valuing of 'feminine' competencies in the workplace may contribute towards a greater valuing of care work in households, perhaps leading to a recognition that men and women spending time with families can develop valuable workplace skills.

It is well recognised that gender inequality in terms of income and advancement is partly attributable to women's domestic responsibilities, but the impact of gendered organisational assumptions on women's labour market experiences has received less attention. Yet gender inequities at work reinforce the gendered division of labour and reduce the range of genuine choices available for women and men. Effecting systemic change in organisations to support social policy initiatives for gender equitable articulations of work and family is likely to involve intensive change initiatives at the micro level of work groups and teams, to supplant and replace gendered assumptions that undermine both gender equity and workplace effectiveness (Rapoport et al., 2002), rather than just policies. Evidence is emerging that such initiatives, for example through action research, can have favourable results, not harming and in some cases even enhancing organisational performance though win–win solutions (Rapoport et al., 2002; Lewis & Cooper, 2005). Various chapters in this book demonstrate that sector and specific type of workplace makes a difference. This implies that it will be important for workplace initiatives to focus on specific workplaces and specific occupational issues, rather than attempting to identify 'good practices' that overlook differentiated contexts.

Thus, state-provided entitlements, together with collective agreements, are necessary for setting standards for the articulation of paid work and family. However, the development of individual sense of entitlement to choose diverse work and family strategies, including a genuine choice to reject other possibilities, also depends on how these are implemented at the workplace level, which, in turn, requires challenges to deep-seated assumptions manifested in workplace systems and wider societies.

5.   Conclusions

The unravelling of the male breadwinner model to provide women and men with some genuine options for articulating paid work and family life requires a range of social entitlements. These include affordable care services, entitlements to family-related leaves and flexible working hours that men as well as women are encouraged and enabled to use, material resources and a range of employment rights, including the effective regulation of working time. These are necessary, but not sufficient, conditions for change and need to be backed up by challenges to prevailing, deep-seated, gendered assumptions within organisations. They may then ultimately challenge identities, assumptions and behaviours within households and contribute to more opportunities for women and men to choose, and be equally rewarded for, diverse employment patterns. We have seen that the process of change is uneven and differentiated across different contexts and future trajectories are likely to vary also. However, it is clear that action is needed at different levels, with attention to both welfare state arrangements and employer practices and cultures, to contribute to, and support changes in, gender relationships within families and more broadly. Initiatives within families and communities may also be important (Gambles et al., 2006).

To a considerable extent, however, all the facilitators of transformational change we have discussed are highly contingent upon other trends in the evolving global capitalist economy. Public childcare provisions may not be capable of meeting the demands for atypical work and long working hours, and it is debatable whether this would be a satisfactory solution. The intensification of work and increased permeability of work–family boundaries make it increasingly difficult to sustain full time jobs for two parents of young children, and at the same time undermines workplace policies and practices, such as shorter working hours, that might otherwise support dual earner families. These kinds of pressures from within the workplace will in turn have an impact on capacities for domestic sharing between men and women. Moreover, with the global spread of neo-liberalism, the pressures of competitive capitalism impact more and more widely, and well beyond the boundaries of Europe, including the developing countries. For example, these pressures are now affecting workers in the 'new economy' in India, where 'work-life balance' is articulated as a huge issue amongst these groupings (Gambles et al., 2006). All this reinforces the cycle of competition and intensification, and perpetuates gender inequities.

This raises questions about the social sustainability of current ways of working (Brewster, 2004; Webster, 2004; Lewis, Gambles & Rapoport, forthcoming). Declining birth rates, spiralling rates of stress manifested in sickness absence and early retirement in some contexts, and concerns about care deficits, suggest a social future giving as much cause for concern as (for example) the environment.

The spread of competitive capitalism, like the growth of environmentally damaging means of transport, appears virtually unstoppable at present. It is possible that gender arrangements might be more susceptible to change than organisational and economic policies, given that they depend on interpersonal relations between women and men, and that the evidence is that women are everywhere more 'gender liberal' than men, and in all 'western' countries the evidence of change is in a more liberal direction. If so, it is possible that 'creeping' change in the form of the emancipation of women may have more potential than major policy shifts to undermine current prevailing forms of workplace and social organisation that are potentially socially unsustainable in the long term. For example, it has been pointed out that the debate on work–life 'balance' only achieved widespread currency in the early 1990s, when a 'critical mass' of educated women in the workplace were able to make their voices heard.[2] But women cannot do it all alone. Social transformation, gender equity and positive articulations of paid work and family need underpinning by complex and interacting change in institutional arrangements at every level.

Notes

1. Indeed, Lewis and Guilliari (2005: 92) argue that ' . . . a conceptualisation of gender equality in terms of individual agency freedom (*as in CA*) is not so immediately helpful when it comes to the sharing of care work between men and women at the household level'.
2. Personal communication, Joan Acker. It may also be argued that it is the growing intensification of work more generally – i.e., for men and women alike – that brought about a focus on work–life issues from the beginning of the 1990s.

Bibliography

Aboim, S. (2006) 'Clivagens e continuidades de género face aos valores da vida familiar em Portugal e noutros Países Europeus', in K. Wall, L. Amâncio and A. Ramos (eds), *Atitudes Sociais dos Portugueses: Família e Género*, Lisbon: Imprensa de Ciências Sociais.

Acker, J. (1990) 'Hierarchies, jobs, bodies: a theory of gendered organisations', *Gender and Society* 4 (2): 139–58.

Adams, G. A., King, L. A. and King, D. W. (1996) 'Relationships of job and family involvement, family social support, and work–family conflict with job and life satisfaction', *Journal of Applied Psychology* 81 (4): 411–20.

Adema, W. and Ladaique, M. (2005) Net social expenditure, 2005 edition. More comprehensive measures of social support. *OECD Social, Employment and Migration Working Papers* 29. DELSA/ELSA/WD/SEM (2005): 8.

Afsa, C. (1996) 'L'activité féminine à l'épreuve de l'allocation parentale d'éducation', *Recherches et prévisions* 46: 1–8.

Afsa, C. (1998) 'L'Allocation parentale d'éducation: Entre politique familiale et politique pour l'emploi', *INSEE première* 569: 1–4.

Allen, T. D. (2001) 'Family supportive work environments: the role of organizational perceptions', *Journal of Vocational Behaviour* 58: 414–35.

Almeida, A. N. and Guerreiro, M. D. (1993) 'A Família', in L. França (ed.), *Portugal. Valores Europeus, Identidade Cultural*, Lisbon: IED.

Anttonen, A. and J. Sipilä, J. (1996) 'European social care services: is it possible to identify models?' *Journal of European Social Policy* 6 (2): 82–100.

Anttonen, A., Baldock, J. and Sipilä, J. (eds) (2003) *The Young, the Old, and the State. Social Care Systems in Five Industrial Nations*, Cheltenham: Edward Elgar.

Anxo D., Flood, L. and Kocoglu, Y. (2002) Offre de travail et répartition des activités domestiques et parentales au sein du couple: une comparaison entre la France et la Suède, *Economie et statistique*, no. 352–3.

Anxo, D. and Boulin, J-Y. (2005) *Working Time Options over the Life-course: Changing Social Security Structures*, Dublin: European Foundation for the Improvement of Living and Working Conditions.

Audric, S. and Forgeot, G. (1999) Le développement du travail à temps partiel, *Données sociales*. Paris: INSEE, pp. 177–81.

Bäck-Wiklund, M. and Bergsten, B. (1997) *Det moderna föräldraskapet: en studie av familj och kön i förändring*, Stockholm: Natur och kultur.

Bailyn, L. (1993) *Breaking the Mold. Women, Men and Time in the New Corporate World*, New York: Free Press.

Baker, J. (2003) 'Glass ceilings or sticky floors? A model of high income law graduates', *Journal of Labour Research* 24 (4): 695–711.

Barrère-Maurisson, M-A. (2003) *Travail, famille: le nouveau contrat*, Paris: Gallimard.

Baruch, G. K., Biener, L. and Barnett, R. C. (1987) 'Women and gender in research on work and family stress', *American Psychologist* 42 (2): 130–6.

Battagliola, F. (2000) *Histoire du travail des femmes*, Paris: La Découverte.

Bauman, Z. (1998) *Globalisation: the Human Consequences*, Cambridge: Polity Press.

Baxter, J., Hewitt, B. and Western, M. (2004) 'Post-familial families and the domestic division of labour', School of Social Science, University of Queensland.

Beck, U. (1992) *Risk Society*, Sage: London.

Beck, U. and Beck-Gernsheim, E. (1995) *The Normal Chaos of Love*, Cambridge: Polity Press.

Becker, G. (1991) *A Treatise on the Family*, Cambridge, MA: Harvard University Press.

Bell, A., Finch, N., La Valle, I., Sainsbury, R. and Skinner, C. (2005) *A Question of Balance: Lone Parents, Childcare and Work*, Department for Work and Pensions, Research Report No. 230, London: Department of Work and Pensions.

Bettio, F. and Plantenga, J. (2004) 'Comparing care regimes in Europe', *Feminist Economics* 10 (1): 85–113.

Bianchi, S. M., Milkie, M. A., Sayer, L. C. and Robinson, J. P. (2000) 'Is anyone doing the housework? Trends in the gender division of household labor', *Social Forces* 79 (1): 191–228.

Bivand, P., Gordon, B. and Simmonds, D. (2003) *Making Work Pay in London*, GLA, London: Centre for Economic and Social Inclusion.

Blair-Loy, M. and Jacobs, J. A. (2003) 'Globalization, working hours and the care deficit among stockbrokers', *Gender and Society* 17: 230–49.

Blood, R. and Wolfe, D. (1960) *Husbands and Wives: the Dynamics of Married Living*, Glencoe, IL: Free Press.

Blossfeld, H. P. and Mills, M. (2003) 'Globalization, uncertainty and changes in early life courses', *Zeitschrift für Erziehungswissenschaft* 6: 188–218.

Blossfeld, H. P. and Drobnič, S. (eds) (2001) *Careers of Couples in Contemporary Societies. From Male Breadwinner to Dual Earner Families*, Oxford: Oxford University Press.

Bond, S., Hymam, J. and Wise, S. (2002) *Family Friendly Working? Putting Policy into Practice*. York: Joseph Rowntree Foundation.

Bonnet, C. and Labbé, M. (1999) 'L'activité professionnelle des femmes après la naissance de leurs deux premiers enfants. L'impact de l'allocation parentale d'éducation', *Etudes et résultats* (37): 1–7.

Booth, C., Darke, J. and Yeandle, S. (1996) *Changing Places: Women's Lives in the City*, London: Paul Chapman.

Bourdieu, P. (2001) *Masculine Domination*, London: Polity.

Bradshaw, J. and Finch, N. (2002) A comparison of child benefit packages in 22 countries, Research report 174. London: Department for Work and Pensions. http://www.dwp.gov.uk/asd/asd5/rrep174.asp

Brandth, B. and Kvande, E. (2001) 'Flexible work and flexible fathers', *Work Employment and Society* 15 (2): 251–67.

Brandth, B. and Kvande, E. (2002) 'Reflexive fathers: negotiating parental leave and working life', *Gender, Work and Organization* 9 (2): 186–203.

Brannen, J. (2005) 'Time and the negotiation of work–family boundaries: autonomy or illusion?', *Time & Society* 14 (1): 113–31.

Brewer, M. and Shephard, A. (2004) *Has Labour Made Work Pay*, http://www.jrf.org.uk/bookshop/eBooks/1859352626.pdf

Brewster, J. (2004) *Working and Living in the European Knowledge Society: The Policy Implication of Developments in Working Life and their Effects on Social Relations*. Report for the project 'Infowork'. Dept. of Sociology, Trinity College, Dublin.

Burchell, B., Ladipo, D. and Wilkinson, F. (eds) (2002) *Job Insecurity and Work Intensification*, London: Routledge.

Burgess, A. and Russell, G. (2003) 'Fatherhood and public policy', in *Supporting Fathers: Contributions from the International Parenthood Summit 2003*, Bernard van Leer Foundation, www.bernardvanleer.org

Butler, J. (1993) *Bodies that Matter. On the Discursive Limits of Sex*, London: Routledge.

Büttner, O., Letablier, M.-T., Pennec, S., Bontemps, S. and Lurol, M. (2002) 'L'action publique face aux transformations de la famille en France', Paris: Centres d'études de l'emploi, Rapport national du projet IPROSEC.

Byberg, I. and Lindquist, A. (2003) *Kompetensutveckling inom socialtjänstens Individ- och familjeomsorg – Exempel och erfarenheter*. Stockholms Universitet. Institutionen för Socialt arbete. Rapport no. 107–2003.

Cancedda, A. (2001) *Employment in Household Services*, Dublin: European Foundation for the Improvement of Work and Living Conditions.

Castles F. G. (2003) 'The world turned upside down: below replacement fertility, changing preferences and family-friendly public policy in 21 OECD countries', *Journal of European Social Policy* 13 (3).

Central Statistics Bureau, the Netherlands (CBS) (2002).

Charles, N. and James, E. (2005) 'He earns the bread and butter and I earn the cream': job insecurity and the male breadwinner family in South Wales', *Work Employment and Society* 19 (3): 481–502.

Čermáková, M., Hašková, H., Křížková, A., Linková, M. and Maříková, H. (2002) *Podmínky harmonizace práce a rodiny*. Institute of Sociology, Academy of Science of the CR, Prague.

Chastenet, B. (2005). L'accueil collectif et en crèches familiales des enfants de moins de six ans en 2004. DREES, *Etudes et Résultats* no. 446.

CIPD (2005) Chartered Institute of Personnel Development 'Flexible working: the implementation challenge (written by Rebecca Clarke)' London: Chartered Institute of Personnel Development.

Clément, D. and Nicolas, M. (2003) 'Les disparités territoriales de l'accueil des jeunes enfants', *L'essentiel de la CNAF* (12): 1–4.

Coltrane, S. (2000) 'Research on household labor: modeling and measuring the social embeddedness of routine family work', *Journal of Marriage and Family* 62 (4): 1208–33.

Coltrane, S. (2004) 'Family man', in N. E. Sacks and C. Marrone, *Gender and Work in Today's World*, Cambridge: Westview Press.

Commaille, J. (1992) *Les stratégies des femmes, travail, famille et politique*, Paris: La Découverte.

Commaille, J., Strobel, P. and Villac, M. (2002) *La politique de la famille*, Paris: La Découverte.

Connell, R. W. (1987) *Gender and Power: Society, the Person and Sexual Politics*, Cambridge: Polity Press.

Connell, R. (1995) *Masculinities*, London: Sage.

Cousins, C. and Tang N. (2004) 'Working time and work and family conflict in the Netherlands, Sweden and the UK', *Work, Employment and Society* 18 (3).

Crompton, R. and Sanderson, K. (1990) *Gendered Jobs and Social Change*, London: Unwin Hyman.

Crompton, R. (1994) 'Occupational trends and women's employment patterns', in R. Lindley (ed.) *Labour Market Structures and Prospects for Women*, Equal Opportunities Commission.

Crompton, R., Gallie, D. and Purcell, K. (eds) (1996) *Changing Forms of Employment, Organisations, Skills and Gender*, London: Routledge.

Crompton, R. (ed.) (1999) *Restructuring Gender Relations and Employment. The Decline of the Male Breadwinner*, Oxford: Oxford University Press.

Crompton, R. and Birkelund, G. (2000) 'Employment and caring in British and Norwegian banking: an exploration through individual careers', *Work, Employment and Society* 14 (2): 331–52.

Crompton, R. and Le Feuvre, N. (2000) 'Gender, family and employment in comparative perspective: the realities and representations of equal opportunities in Britain and France', *Journal of European Social Policy* 10 (4): 334–48.

Crompton, R., Dennett, J. and Wigfield, A. (2003) *Organisations, Careers and Caring*, Bristol: Policy Press.

Crompton, R. (2003) 'Class and gender beyond the "cultural turn" ', *Sociologia, Problemas e Práticas*, 42.

Crompton, R., Brockmann, M. and Wiggins, R. (2003) 'A women's place . . . employment and family life for men and women', *British Social Attitudes: 20th Annual Report* Ch. 8, pp. 161–87. London: Sage.

Crompton, R. and Lyonette, C. (2005) 'The new gender essentialism: domestic and family "choices" and their relation to attitudes', *British Journal of Sociology* 56 (4): 601–20.

Crompton, R. (2006) *Employment and the Family: the Reconfiguration of Work and Family Life in Contemporary Societies*, Cambridge: Cambridge University Press.

Crompton, R. and Lyonette, C. (2006a) 'Research Note: some issues in cross-national comparative research on women's employment: a comparison of Britain and Portugal', *Work, Employment and Society*, 20 (2): 389–400.

Crompton, R. and Lyonette, C. (2006b) 'Work–life "balance" in Europe', *Acta Sociologica*.

Crouch, C. (1999) *Social Change in Western Europe*, Oxford: Oxford University Press.

Daly, K. J. (1996) *Families & Time*, London: Sage.

Daly, M. and Lewis, J. (2000) 'The concept of social care and the analysis of contemporary welfare states', *British Journal of Sociology* 51 (2): 281–99.

Daly, M. and Rake, K. (2003) *Gender and the Welfare State*, Cambridge: Polity Press.

Daly, M. (2004) 'Changing conceptions of family and gender relations in European welfare states and the Third Way', in J. Lewis and R. Surender (eds) *Welfare State Change: Towards a Third Way?* Oxford: Oxford University Press.

Damon, J., Croutte, P. and Hatchuel, G. (2003) 'Les opinions sur les modes de garde des jeunes enfants. Données CREDOC 2003', *L'essentiel de la CNAF* (11): 1–4.

Davidoff, L. and Hall, C. (1987) *Family Fortunes*, London: Hutchinson.

Davis, K., Evans, M. and Lorber, J. (eds) (2006) *Handbook of Gender and Women's Studies*, London: Sage.

Den Dulk, L., van Doorne-Huiskes, A. and Schippers, J. (eds) (1998) *Work–Family Arrangements in Europe*, Amsterdam: Thela-Thesis.

Den Dulk, L. (2001) *Work–Family Arrangements in Organisations. A Cross national Study in the Netherlands, Italy, the United Kingdom and Sweden.* Amsterdam: Rozenberg Publishers.

Den Dulk, L., Peper, B. and van Doornes-Huiskes, A. (eds) (2004) *Gender, Parenthood and the Changing European Workplace: young adults negotiating the work–family boundary: a state of the art report*, Brussels: European Commission.

Den Dulk, L., van Doorne-Huiskes, A. and Peper, B. (2005) 'Work and family in Europe: employment patterns of working parents across welfare states', in B. Peper, A. van Doorne-Huiskes and L. den Dulk (eds) *Flexible Work and*

Organisational Change: the Integration of Work and Personal Life, Cheltenham: Edward Elgar.

Den Dulk, L., Peters, P. and Poutsma, E. (2005) Employer involvement regarding work–family arrangements in the context of welfare state regimes. Paper presented at the Dutch HRM-Network Conference, University of Twente, Enschede, the Netherlands, 4 and 5 November 2005.

Department for Trade and Industry (2005) *Work and Families: Choice and Diversity. Government Response to Public Consultation,* London: HMSO.

Department for Trade and Industry/HM Treasury (2003) *Balancing Work and Family Life: Enhancing Choice and Support for Parents*, London: HMSO.

De Singly, F. (1999) *Sociologie současné rodiny*, Praha: Portál.

DWP (2004) *Opportunity for All Sixth Annual Report* (Cm 6239), Department of Work and Pensions, London: Stationery Office (available on the web at: http://www.dwp.gov.uk/ofa/reports/2004/summary/05.asp).

DWP (2005) *Pathways to work boost for lone parents*, http://www.dwp.gov.uk/mediacentre/pressreleases/2005/feb/emp2510-ndlp.asp

Deven, F. and Moss, P. (2002) 'Leave arrangements for parents: overview and future outlook', *Community, Work and Family* 5 (3): 237–55.

Deven, F. (2005) 'Assessing the use of parental leave by fathers: towards a conceptual framework', in B. Peper, A. van Doorne-Huiskes and L. den Dulk (eds) *Flexible Working and Organisational Change. The Intergration of Work and Personal Life*, Cheltenham: Edward Elgar.

Deven, F. and Moss, P. (eds) (2005) *Leave Policies and Research*, Brussels, CBGS-Werkdocument 3.

Dex, S. and Smith, C. (2002) *The Nature and Patterns of Family-Friendly Employment Policies in Britain*, York: York Publishing Services.

Dex, S. (2003) *Families and Work in the 21st Century*, York: Joseph Rowntree Foundation.

Diefenbach, H. (2003) 'Gender ideologies, relative resources, and the division of housework in intimate relationships: a test of Hyman Rodman's theory of resources in cultural context', *International Journal of Sociology* 43(1): 45–64.

Domsch, M., Ladwig, D. and Tenten, E. (2003) *Gender Equality in Central and Eastern European Countries*, Frankfurt am Main: Peter Lang.

Du Gay, P. (1996) *Consumption and Identity at Work*, London: Sage.

Du Gay, P. and Pryke, M. (2002) *Cultural Economy*, London: Sage.

Duncan, S. and Edwards, R. (1999) *Lone Mothers, Paid Work and Gendered Realities*, London: Macmillan.

Duru-Bellat, M. (1990) *L'école des filles. Quelle formation pour quels rôles sociaux?* Paris: L'Harmattan.

Duyvendak, J. W. and Stavenuiter, M. M. J. (eds) (2004) *Working Fathers, Caring Men: Reconcilation of Working Life and Family Life*, The Hague and Utrecht: Verwey-Jonker Institute.

Edwards, P., Armstrong, P., Marginson, P. and Purcell, J. (1996) 'Towards the transnational company?', in R. Crompton, D. Gallie and K. Purcell (eds) *Changing Forms of Employment*, London: Routledge.

Ehrenreich, B. and Hochschild, A. R. (2003) *Global Woman*, London: Granta Books.

Einhorn, B. (1993) *Cinderella goes to Market*, London: Verso.

Ellingsæter, A-L. (2003) 'The complexity of family policy reform. The case of Norway', *European Societies* 5 (4): 419–43.

Employment in Europe (2004) *Employment in Europe 2004*, Employment and Social Affairs, Luxembourg: European Commission.

EOC (2005) *Britain's Hidden Brain Drain. The EOC's Investigation into Flexible and Part-time Working. Final Report*, Manchester: Equal Opportunities Commission. http://www.eoc.org.uk/PDF/brain_drain_final_report.pdf

Escobedo, A. (2005) 'Spain', in F. Deven and P. Moss (eds), *Leave Policies and Research*, Brussels, CBGS-Werkdocument 3: 157–68.

Esping-Andersen, G. (1990) *The Three Worlds of Welfare Capitalism*, Cambridge: Polity Press.

Esping-Andersen, G. (1999) *Social Foundations of Postindustrial Economics*. New York: Oxford University Press.

Esping-Andersen, G. (2002) 'A child centred social investment strategy', in G. Esping-Andersen, D. Gallie, A. Hemerijck and J. Myles (eds) *Why we Need a New Welfare State*, Oxford: Oxford University Press.

Esping-Andersen, G. (2004) Inequality and the Welfare State in Europe, Ralph Miliband Lectures on Inequalities: dimensions and challenges, LSE, December.

Estrade, M.-A., Méda, D. and Orain, R. (2001) 'Les effets de la réduction du temps de travail sur les modes de vie : qu'en pensent les salariés un an après?', *DARES Premières synthèses* (21.1): 1–8.

European Commission (2003) *Employment in Europe*, Luxembourg: OOPEC.

European Commission. Eurostat (2004) *How Europeans Spend their Time, Everyday Life of Women and Men*. Data 1998–2002. 27 July. http://www.europa.eu.int/comm/eurostat

European Commission (2004a) *Towards a More Dynamic Approach to Implementing the Lisbon Strategy*: http://www.esc.eu.int/publications/pdf/booklets/EESC-2004-001-EN.pdf

European Commission (2005) *European Employment Strategy Guidelines for the Employment Policies of Member States* 2005/600/EC, Official Journal of the European Commission 1 (205), 21–27 http://europa.eu.int/eur-lex/lex/LexUriServ/site/en/oj/2005/l_205/l_20520050806en00210027.pdf

EuropeanPWN (2004). *European Board Women Monitor*, www.European PWN.net < http://www.EuropeanPWN.net >, accessed August 2004.

European Commission. Eurostat (2002) *Labour Force Survey*, Luxembourg: Office for the Official Publications of the European Communities. http://www.europa.eu.int/comm/eurostat

European Commission. Eurostat (2004) *Labour Force Survey*, Luxembourg: Office for the Official Publications of the European Communities. http://www.europa.eu.int/comma/eurostat

Eurostat (2003) *The Social Situation in the European Union*, Brussels: European Commission.

Evans, J. (2001) *Firms' Contribution to the Reconciliation between Work and Family Life*, Paris: OECD, Labour Market and Social Policy Occasional Papers.

Evers, A., Lewis, J. and Riedel, B. (2005) 'Developing child-care provision in England and Germany: problems of governance', *Journal of European Social Policy* 15 (3): 195–209.

Evetts, J. (1996) *Gender and Career in Science and Engineering*, London: Allen and Unwin.

Fagnani, J. (2003) *Context Mapping for the EU Framework 5 Funded Study: Gender, Parenthood and the Changing European Workplace'*, Manchester: RIHSC, Manchester: Manchester Metropolitan University.

Fagnani, J. and Letablier, M.-T. (2003) 'La réduction du temps de travail a-t-elle amélioré la vie quotidienne des parents de jeunes enfants?', *DARES Premières synthèses* (01.2): 1–10.

Fagnani, J. and the Transitions team (2004) *Context Mapping for the EU Framework 5 Funded Study, Work Package 3*, Report for the European Commisssion, Manchester Metropolitan University.

Fagnani, J. (2007) 'Family policies in France and Germany: sisters or remote cousins?', *Community, Work and Family*, 10 (1).

Ferreira, V. (2003) *Relações Sociais de Sexo e Segregação do Emprego*, Coimbra, FEUC.

Finch, J. and Groves, D. (eds) (1983) *A Labour of Love: Women, Work and Caring*, London: Routledge.

Finch, J. and Mason, J. (1993) *Negotiating Family Responsibilities*, London: Routledge.

Fine-Davis, M., Fagnani, J., Giovannini, D., Hojgaard, L. and Clarke, H. (2004) *Fathers and Mothers. Dilemmas of the Work–Life Balance, A Comparative Study in Four European Countries*. Dordrecht, Boston and London: Kluwer Academic Publishers.

Fletcher, J. (1999) *Disappearing Acts: Gender, Power and Relational Practice at Work*, Cambridge, MA: MIT Press.

Folbre, N. (1994) *Who Pays for the Kids? Gender and the Structures of Constraint*, London: Routledge.

Folbre, N. and Nelson, J. A. (2000) 'For love or money – or both?', *Journal of Economic Perspectives* 14 (4): 123–40.

Forsé, M. and Parodi, M. (2001) 'Un panorama des opinions à l'égard de l'Etat-Providence. Etude de l'enquête barométrique de la DRESS, vague 1', *Etudes & Résultats* (135): 1–8.

Fouquet, A., Gauvin, A. and Letablier, M.-T. (1999) 'Des contrats sociaux entre les sexes différents selon les pays de l'Union européenne', in B. Majnoni d'Intignano (ed.) *Egalité entre femmes et hommes: aspects économiques*, Paris: La Documentation française: 105–46.

Franco, A. and Winqvist, K. (2002) *Les femmes et les hommes concilient travail et vie familiale*, Statistiques en Bref, Brussels, European Commission.

Frank, E., Harvey L. and Elon, L. (2000) 'Family responsibilities and domestic activities of US women physicians', *Archives of Family Medicine* 9 (Feb): 134–40.

Fraser, N. (1994) 'After the family wage', *Political Theory* 22: 591–618.

Fraser, N. (1996) *Justice Interruptus: Critical Reflections on the Post-socialist Condition*, London: Routledge.

Fraser, N. (1997) 'After the family wage: a post industrial thought experiment', in her book, *Justice Interuptus: Critical Reflections on the 'Post-Socialist' Condition*, New York: Routledge.

Frejka, T. (1983) 'Induced abortions and fertility: a quarter century of experience in Eastern Europe', *Population and Development Review* 9 (3): 494–520.

Friedman, D., Hechter, M. and Kanazawa, S. (1994) 'A theory of the value of children', *Demography* 31 (3): 375–401.

Friedman, S. and Greenhaus, J. (2000) *Work and Family – Allies or Enemies?* Oxford: Oxford University Press.

Fuchshuber, E., Dulk, L. den and Doorne-Huiskes, A. van (2004) Explanations for differences in women's representation in managerial positions across countries: impact of welfare states. Paper presented at the workshop on female managers, entrepreneurs and the social capital of the firm. EIASM, the European Institute for Advanced Studies in Management. Brussels, 17–19 November.

Fuwa, M. (2004) 'Macro-level gender inequality and the division of household in 22 countries', *American Sociological Review* 69 (6): 751–67.

Gadéa, C. and Marry, C. (2000) 'Les pères qui gagnent: descendance et réussite professionnelle des ingénieurs', *Travail, genre et sociétés*, no 3.

Gallie, D. (2002) 'The quality of working life in welfare strategy', in G. Esping-Andersen, et al., *Why we Need a New Welfare State*, Oxford: Oxford University Press.

Gambles, R., Lewis, S. and Rapoport, R. (2006) *The Myth of Work–Life Balance: the Challenge of our Time for Men, Women and Societies*, Chichester: Wiley.

Geist, C. (2005) 'The welfare state and the home: regime differences in the domestic division of labour', *European Sociological Review* 21: 23–41.

Gershuny, J., Godwin, M. and Jones, S. (1994) 'The domestic labour revolution: a process of lagged adaptation', in M. Anderson, F. Bechhofer and J. Gershuny (eds) *The Social and Political Economy of the Household*, Oxford: Oxford University Press.

Gershuny, J. (2000) *Changing Times: Work and Leisure in Postindustrial Society*, Oxford: Oxford University Press.

Gershuny, J. and Sullivan, O. (2003) 'Time use, gender and public policy regimes', *Social Politics* 10 (2): 205–28.

Gershuny, J. (2005) 'Busyness as the badge of honour for the new superordinate working class', *Social Research* 72 (2): 287–314.

Giddens, A. (1992) *The Transformation of Intimacy. Sexuality, Love and Eroticism in Modern Societies*, Cambridge: Polity Press.

Gilbert, L. A. (1993) *Two Careers/One Family*, Newbury Park: Sage.

Ginn, J., Arber, S., Brannen, J., Dale, A., Dex, S., Elias, P., Moss, P., Pahl, J., Roberts, C., and Rubery, J. (1996) 'Feminist fallacies: a reply to Hakim on Women's Employment', *British Journal of Sociology* 7 (1): 167–74.

Glucksmann, M. (1995) 'Why "work"? Gender and the "Total Social Organisation of Labour" ', *Gender, Work and Organisation* 2 (2): 63–75.

Goldsen, K. I. F. and Scharlach, A. E. (2001) *Families and Work*, New York: Oxford University Press.

Goos, M. and Manning, A. (2003) 'Mc and Mac Jobs: the growing polarisation of jobs in the UK', in R. Dickens, P. Gregg, and J. Wadsworth (eds) *The Labour Market Under New Labour*, Basingstoke: Palgrave Macmillan, pp. 70–85.

Gornick, J. C. and Meyers, M. K. (2003) *Families that Work. Policies for Reconciling Parenthood and Employment*. New York: Russell Sage Foundation.

Grant-Vallone, E. J. and Donaldson, S. I. (2001) 'Consequences of work–family conflict on employee well-being over time', *Work & Stress* 15 (3): 214–26.

Green, F. (2006) *Demanding Work. The Paradox of Job Quality in the Affluent Economy*, Oxford: Princeton University Press.

Gregory, A. and Windebank, J. (2000) *Women's Work in Britain and France*, Basingstoke: Macmillan – now Palgrave Macmillan.

Gregson, N. and Lowe, M. (1994) *Servicing the Middle Classes*, London: Routledge.

Guerreiro, M. D. (org.) (1998) *Trabalho, família e gerações*, Lisbon: CIES-ISCTE.

Guerreiro, Maria das Dores and Ávila, P. (1998) *Confrata. Um Inquérito sobre Conciliação Família Trabalho*, Lisbon: CIES.

Guerreiro, M. D. and Perista, H. (1999) 'Trabalho e Família', in *Inquérito à Ocupação do Tempo*, Lisbon: INE.

Guerreiro, Maria das Dores (2000) 'Conciliação entre Vida Profissional e Familiar. Apresentação', in Comissão de Coordenação do Fundo Social Europeu,

Conciliação entre a Vida Profissional e Familiar, Lisbon: Ministério do Trabalho e da Solidariedade.

Guerreiro, M. D. (2002) 'Emprego em serviços familiares', *Sociedade e Trabalho* (12/13): 91–106.

Guerreiro, M. D., Abranches, M. and Pereira, I. (2003) *Conciliação entre a Vida Profissional e Vida Familiar – políticas públicas e práticas dos agentes em contexto empresarial*, Lisbon: CIES, ISCTE.

Haas, L. and Hwang, P. (1995) 'Company culture and men's usage of family leave benefits in Sweden', *Family Relations* 44: 28–36.

Haas, L., Hwang, P. and Russell, G. (2000) *Organizational Change and Gender Equity: International Perspectives on Fathers and Mothers at the Workplace*, Thousand Oaks, CA: Sage.

Haas, L. and Hwang, P. (forthcoming) 'The impact of taking parental leave on fathers' participation in childcare and relationships with children: lessons from Sweden', *Community, Work and Family*.

Haicault, M. (1984) 'La gestion ordinaire de la vie en deux', *Sociologie du travail* 3: 268–77.

Hakim, C. (2000) *Work–lifestyle Choices in the 21st Century*, Oxford: Oxford University Press.

Hakim, C. (2002) 'The search for equality', *Work And Occupations* 30 (4): 401–11.

Hakim, C. (2003) *Models of the Family in Modern Societies*, Aldershot: Ashgate.

Hakim, C. (2004) *Key Issues in Women's Work*, London: Glasshouse Press.

Hamnett, C. (2003) *Unequal City. London in the Global Arena*, London: Routledge.

Hantrais, L. and Letablier, M-T. (1996) *Familles, travail et politiques familiales en Europe*, Paris: Presse universitaires de France.

Hantrais, L. (2004) *Family Policy Matters: Responding to Family Change in Europe*, Bristol: Policy Press.

Harkness, S. (2003) 'The household division of labour: changes in families' allocation of paid and unpaid work 1992–2002', in R. Dickens, P. Gregg and J. Wadsworth (eds) *The Labour Market Under Labour: State of Working Britain 2003*, Basingstoke: Palgrave – now Palgrave Macmillan.

Hašková, H. (2005) 'Gender roles, family policy and family behavior: changing Czech society in the European context', in H. Haukanes and F. Pine (eds) *Generations, Kinship and Care. Gendered Provisions of Social Security in Central Eastern Europe*, Bergen: University of Bergen.

Hawkins, A. and Dollahite, D. (eds) (1997) *Generative Fathering: Beyond Deficit Perspectives*, London: Sage.

Hermange, M.-T. (2003) *La prestation d'accueil du jeune enfant*, Paris: Rapport au Ministre délégué à la famille.

Higgins, C. A. and Duxbury, L. E. (1992) 'Work–family conflict: a comparison of dual-career and traditional career men', *Journal of Organizational Behavior* 13 (4): 389–411.

Himmelweit, S. and Sigala, M. (2004) 'Choice and the relationship between identities and behaviours for Mothers with pre-school Children: some implications from a UK study', *Journal of Social Policy* 33 (3): 455–78.

Hobson, B. (ed.) (2002) *Making Men into Fathers*, Cambridge: Cambridge University Press.

Hochschild, A. (1989) *The Second Shift*, London: Piatkus.

Hojgaard, L. (1997) 'Working fathers: caught in the web of the symbolic order of gender', *Acta Sociologica* 40: 245–61.

Holt, H. and Thaulow, I. (1996) 'Formal and informal flexibility in the work-place', in S. Lewis and J. Lewis (eds) *The Work–Family Challenge*, London: Sage. http://caliban.sourceoecd.org/vl=4290427/cl=18/nw=1/rpsv/cgi-bin/fulltextew.pl?prpsv=/ij/oecdthemes/99980029/v2001n7/s1/p1l.idx (20.2.2006). http://www.cipd.co.uk/NR/rdonlyres/EBAA2100-EF46-43EE-9C6D-16577DCBC6DE/0/flexwork1005.pdf.

Huinink, J. and Kreyenfeld, M. (2004) 'Family formation in times of social and economic change: an analysis of the 1971 East German cohort', *MPIDR Working Paper* WP 2004-013, Max Planck Institute for Demographic Research, Rostock. «http://www.demogr.mpg.de/papers/working/wp-2004-013.pdf».

Humphries, J. (1982) 'Class struggle and the persistence of the working-class family', in A. Giddens and D. Held (eds) *Classes, Power and Conflict*, Basingstoke: Macmillan – now Palgrave Macmillan.

Humphries, J. (1984) 'Protective legislation, the capitalist state and working-class men', in R. Pahl (ed.) *Divisions of Labour*, Oxford: Basil Blackwell.

Hyde, M., Dixon, J. and Joyner, M. (1999) 'Work for those who can, security for those who cannot: the new social security reform agenda for the United Kingdom', *International Social Security Review* 52 (4): 69–86.

Immervoll, H. and Barber, D. (2005) *Can Parents Afford to Work? Childcare Costs, Tax-Benefit Policies and Work Incentives*, OECD Social, Employment and Migration Working Papers, No. 31.

INE, Instituto Nacional de Estatística (1999) *Inquérito à Ocupação do Tempo*, Lisbon.

Inglehart, R. (1995) 'Changing values, economic development and political change', *International Social Science Journal* 145: 379–404.

Inglehart, R. (1997) *Modernization and Postmodernization. Cultural, Economic and Political Change in 43 Societies*. Princeton: Princeton University Press.

INSEE (2002) *Enquête emploi 2001*, Paris: INSEE.

INSEE (2004) *Femmes et hommes: Regards sur la Parité*, Paris: INSEE.

Irwin, S. (2003) 'Interdependencies, values and the reshaping of difference: gender and generation at the birth of twentieth-century modernity', *British Journal of Sociology* 54 (4): 565–84.

ISSP (2002) International Social Survey Programme (2002) dataset: for a full description see Jowell, Brook and Dowds (1993) in Bibliography, or website: www.issp.org

Jämo (1999) *Jämställdhetsplanens betydelse för jämställdheten. Resultat från en enkätundersökning bland företag och myndigheter hösten 1999*, Stockholm: Jämo.

Jämo (2000) *Granskning av 22 IT-företags jämställdhetsplaner 1999/2000*, Stockholm: Jämo.

Jarvis, H. (2005) 'Moving to London time: household co-ordination and the infrastructure of everyday life', *Time and Society* 14 (1): 133–54.

Jaumotte, F. (2004) 'Labour force participation of women: empirical evidence on the role of policy and other determinants in OECD countries', *OECD Economic Studies* (37): 2.

Jenson, J. (1986) 'Gender and reproduction', *Studies in Political Economy* 20: 9–46.

Jowell, R., Brook, L. and Dowds, L. (eds) (1993) *International Social Attitudes: the 10th BSA Report*, Aldershot: Dartmouth Publishing.

Junter-Loiseau, A. (1999) 'La notion de conciliation de la vie professionnelle et de la vie familiale. Révolution temporelle ou métaphore des discriminations?', *Les Cahiers du Genre* (24): 73–98.

Kantorová, V. (2004) 'Education and entry into motherhood: the Czech Republic during the state socialism and the transition period (1970–1997)', *Demographic Research*, Special Collection 3, Article 10: 245–74. [www.demographic-research.org].

Kanter, R. M. (1993) *Men and Women of the Corporation*, New York: Basic Books.

Kaufmann, J.-C. (1992) *La trame conjugale, analyse du couple par son linge*, Paris: Nathan.

Kinnunen, U. and Mauno, S. (1998) 'Antecedents and outcomes of work–family conflict among employed women and men in Finland', *Human Relations* 51 (2): 157–77.

Kinnunen, U., Greuts, S., and Mauno, S. (2004) 'Work-to-family conflict and its relationships with well-being: a one-year longitudinal study', *Work & Stress* 18: 1–22.

Kocourková, J. (2002) 'Leave arrangements and childcare services in Central Europe: policies and practices before and after the transition', *Community, Work & Family*, 5(3): 301–18.

Kohler, H.-P., Billari, F. C. and Ortega, J. A. (2002) 'The emergence of lowest-low fertility in Europe during the 1990s', *Population and Development Review* 28 (4): 641–80.

Korpi, W. (2000) 'Faces of inequality', *Social Politics* 7 (2): 127–91.

Kremer, M. (2005) *How Welfare States Care: Culture, Gender and Citizenship in Europe*. Downloadable at: http://www.igitur.nl/igiturarchief/searchresults.php?language=nl&author=Kremer&title=

Kröger, T., Anttonen, A. and Sipilä, J. (2003) 'Social care in Finland: stronger and weaker forms of universalism', in A. Anttonen, J. Baldock and J. Sipilä (eds) (2003) *The Young, the Old, and the State. Social Care Systems in Five Industrial Nations*, Cheltenham: Edward Elgar, 25–54.

Kröger, T. and Sipilä, J. (eds) (2005) *Overstretched: Families up Against the Demands of Work and Care*, Malden: Blackwell.

Kuchařová, V. and Tuček, M. (1999) *Sociálně ekonomické souvislosti rodinného chování mladé generace v České Republice*, Praha: Studie národohospodářského ústavu Josefa Hlávky.

Kugelberg, C. (2000) 'Swedish parents at a multinational conglomerate', in L. L. Haas, P. Hwang and G. Russell (eds), *Organizational Change and Gender Equity. International Perspectives on Fathers and Mothers at the Workplace*, Thousand Oaks, CA: Sage.

Lahire, B. (2005) 'Patrimónios individuais de disposições: para uma sociologia à escala individual', *Sociologia, Problemas e Práticas* 49.

Lapeyre, N. and Le Feuvre, N. (2004) 'Concilier l'inconciliable? Le rapport des femmes à la notion de "conciliation travail-famille" dans les professions libérales en France', *Nouvelles questions féministes* 23 (3): 42–58.

La Valle, I., Arthur, S., Millward, C., Scott, J. and Clayden, M. (2002) *Happy Families? Atypical Work and its Influence on Family Life*, Final report, York: Joseph Rowntree Foundation.

Le Bihan, B. and Martin, C. (2004) 'Atypical working hours and childcare arrangements', *Social Policy & Administration* 38 (6): 565–90.

Le Feuvre, N., Martin, J., Parichon, C. and Portet, S. (1999) *Employment, Family and Community Activities: a New Balance for Women and Men in France*, Dublin: Report to the European Foundation for the Improvement of Living and Working Conditions.

Le Feuvre, N. and Martin, J. (2001) 'Les services de proximité aux ménages : De la solidarité à la précarité de l'emploi féminin', *Némésis* 3: 299–332.

Le Feuvre, N. and Andriocci, M. (2005) 'Employment opportunities for women in Europe', In G. Griffin (ed.) *Doing Women's Studies: Employment Opportunities, Personal Impacts and Social Consequences*, London: Zed Books, 13–63.

Leira, A. (1992) *Welfare States and Working Mothers*, Cambridge: Cambridge University Press.

Leira, A. (2002) *Working Parents and the Welfare State*, Cambridge: Cambridge University Press.

Lesthaeghe, R. (1995) 'The second demographic transition in western countries: an interpretation', in K. O. Mason and A.-M. Jensen (eds) *Gender and Family Change in Industrialized Countries*, Oxford: Clarendon Press, pp. 17–62.

Lesthaeghe, R. and Surkyn, J. (2002) New forms of household formation in Central and Eastern Europe: Are they related to newly emerging value orientations? In: *Economic Survey of Europe 2002/2*. Economic Commission for Europe, United Nations, New York and Geneva, pp. 197–216.

Lewis, J. (1992) 'Gender and the development of welfare state regimes', *Journal of European Social Policy* 2 (3): 159–73.

Lewis, J. (ed.) (1993) *Women and Social Policies in Europe: Work, Family and the State*, Aldershot: Edward Elgar.

Lewis, J. (2001) 'The decline of the male breadwinner model: implications for work and care', *Social Politics* 8 (2): 159–62.

Lewis, J. (2002) 'Gender and welfare state change', *European Societies* 4 (4): 331–57.

Lewis, J. (2003) 'Economic citizenship: a comment', *Social Politics* 10 (2): 176–85.

Lewis, J. and Giullari, S. (2005) 'The adult worker model family, gender equality and care: the search for new policy principles and the possibilities and problems of a capabilities approach', *Economy and Society* 34 (1): 76–104.

Lewis, S., Izraeli, D. and Hootsmans, H. (eds) (1992) *Dual Earner Families. International Perspectives*, London: Sage.

Lewis, S. (1996) 'Rethinking employment: an organizational culture change framework', in S. Lewis and J. Lewis (eds) (see Bibliography).

Lewis, S. and Lewis J. (eds) (1996) *The Work–Family Challenge: Rethinking Employment*, London: Sage.

Lewis, S. and Taylor, K. (1996) 'Evaluating the impact of family friendly employment policies. A case study', in S. Lewis and J. Lewis (eds) *The Work–Family Challenge. Rethinking Employment*, London: Sage.

Lewis, S. (1997) ' "Family friendly" employment policies: a route to changing organizational culture or playing about at the margins?', *Gender, Work and Organization* 4 (1): 13–23.

Lewis, S. (1998) 'Work–family arrangements in the UK', in L. den Dulk, A. van Doorne-Huiskes and J. Schippers (eds), *Work–Family Arrangements in Europe*, Amsterdam: Thela-Thesis.

Lewis, S. and Cooper, C. (1999) 'The work–family research agenda in changing contexts', *Journal of Health Psychology* 4 (4): 382–93.

Lewis, S., Kagan, C. and Heaton, P. (2000) 'Dual earner parents with disabled children. Patterns for working and caring', *Journal of Family Issues* 21(8): 1031–60.

Lewis, S. (2001) 'Restructuring workplace cultures: the ultimate work–family challenge?', *Women in Management Review* 16 (1): 21–9.

Lewis, S. and Smithson, J. (2001) 'Sense of entitlement to support for the reconciliation of employment and family life', *Human Relations* 55 (11): 1455–81.

Lewis, S. (2003) 'The integration of paid work and the rest of life. Is post industrial work the new leisure?', *Leisure Studies* 22: 343–55.

Lewis, S. and Cooper, C. (2005) *Work–Life Integration: Case Studies of Organisational Change*, Chichester: Wiley.

Lewis, S., Das Dores Guerreriro, M., and Brannen, J. (2005) 'Case studies in work–family research', in M. Pitt-Catsouphes, E. Kossek and S. Sweet (eds) *The Work–Family Handbook: Multi-Disciplinary Perspectives and Approaches*, Mahwah, NJ: Lawrence Erlbaum Associates.

Lewis, S. and Cooper, C. L. (2005) *Work–life Integration. Case Studies of Organisational Change*, Chichester: Wiley.

Lewis, S. and Smithson, J. (2006) 'Final report. Gender, Parenthood and the Changing European Workplace (Transitions). A framework 6 EU Project', Brussels: European Commission.

Lewis, S., Gambles, R. and Rapoport, R. (forthcoming) 'The constraints of a "work–life balance" approach: an international perspective', *International Journal of Human Resource Management*.

Lima, Maria de Paz, Alves, P., Morais, F., Pires, L. and Freire, J., (1999) *Contuédos das Convenções Colectivas de Trabalho na Optica do Emprego e da Formação*, Lisbon: OEFP.

Lister, R. (2003) *Citizenship: Feminist Perspectives*, second edition, Basingstoke: Macmillan – now Palgrave Macmillan.

Lloyd-Jones, S. (1994) *Corporatism in Spain and Portugal: a Comparison*, Lisbon, Portugal: Contemporary Portuguese Political History Research Centre.

Lollivier, S. (1988) 'Activité et arrêt d'activité féminine: le diplôme et la famille', *Economie & statistique* (212): 25–9.

Lutz, H. (2002) 'At your service, madam! The globalisation of domestic service', *Feminist Review* 70: 89–104.

Lyonette, C., Crompton, R. and Wall, K. (forthcoming 2007) 'Gender, occupational class and work–life conflict: a comparison of Britain and Portugal', *Community, Work and Family* 10 (4).

Macek P., Flanagan, C., Gallay, L., Kostron, L., Botcheva, L. and Csapo, B. (1998) 'Postcommunist societies in times of transition: perceptions of change among adolescents in Central and Eastern Europe', *Journal of Social Issues* 54: 547–61.

Macura M., Kadri, A., Mochizuki-Sternberg, Y. and Lara Garcia, J. (2000) 'Fertility decline in the transition economies, 1989–1998: economic and social factors revisited', *Economic Survey of Europe 2000 No. 1*, New York and Geneva: United Nations.

Macura M., Mochizuki-Sternberg, Y. and Lara Garcia, J. (2002). 'Eastern and Western Europe's fertility and partnership patterns: selected developments from 1987 to 1999', in M. Macura and G. Beets (eds), *Dynamics of Fertility and Partnership in Europe: Insights and Lessons from Comparative Research* 1, New York and Geneva: United Nations.

Macura M. and MacDonald, A. (2003) 'Fertility and fertility regulation in Eastern Europe: from the socialist to the post-socialist era', in I. E. Kotowska and J. Jóźwiak (eds) *Population of Central and Eastern Europe. Challenges and Opportunities*, Warsaw: Institute of Statistics and Demography, Warsaw School of Economics.

Major, V. S., Klein, K. J. and Erhart, M. G. (2002) 'Work time, work interference with family, and psychological distress', *Journal of Applied Psychology* 87 (3): 427–36.

Martin, J. (1998) 'Politique familiale et travail des femmes mariées en France. Perspective historique: 1942–1982', *Population* (6): 1119–54.

Maruani, M. (2000) *Travail et emploi des femmes*, Paris: La Découverte.

Maruani, M. (2002) *Les mécomptes du chômage*, Paris: Bayard.

Math, A. and Meilland, C. (2004) *Family-related Leave and Industrial Relations*, Dublin research report for the Foundation for Improvement of Living and Working Conditions. European Centre for Industrial Relations. www.eiro. eurofound.ie/2004/03/study/index_2.html

McDonald, P. (1997) *Gender Equity, Social Institutions and the Future of Fertility*, Canberra: The Australian National University: Working Papers in Demography.

McDonald, P. (2000a) 'Gender equity in theories of fertility transition', *Population and Development Review* 26 (3): 427–39.

McDonald, P. (2000b) 'Gender equity, social institutions and the future of fertility', *Journal of Population Research* 17 (1): 1–15.

McDonald, P. (2002) 'Sustaining fertility through public policy: the range of options', *Population* 57 (3).

McDonald, P. (2005) *Fertility and the State: the Efficacy of Policy*. Available at: http://iussp2005.princeton.edu/download.aspx?submissionId=50830.

McDowell, L. (1997) *Capital Culture: Gender and Work in the City*, Oxford: Blackwell.

McDowell, L., Perrons, D., Fagan, C., Ray, K. and Ward, K. (2005) 'The contradictions and intersections of class and gender in a global city: placing working women's lives on the research agenda', *Environment and Planning A*, 37 (3): 441–61.

McDowell, L., Ward K., Fagan, C., Perrons, D. and Ray, K. (2006) 'Connecting time and space. The significance of the transformation in women's work in the city', *International Journal of Urban and Regional Research* 30 (1): 141–58.

McLaughlin, K., Osborne, S. P., and Ferlie, E. (2002) *New Public Management: Current Trends and Future Prospects*, London: Routledge.

McMahon, M. (1995) *Engendering Motherhood*, New York: Guildford Press.

Ménahem, G. (1988) 'Activité féminine ou inactivité: la marque de la famille du conjoint', *Economie et statistique* 211.

Menahem, G. (1989) 'Les rapports domestiques entre femmes et hommes s'enracinent dans le passé familial des conjoints', *Population* 3.

Metcalfe, B. and Afanassieva, M. (2005) 'Gender, work and equal opportunities in Central and Eastern Europe', *Women in Management Review* 20 (6): 397–411.

Moen, P. (ed.) (2003) *It's About Time: Couples and Careers*, Ithaca and London: Cornell University Press.

Morgan, K. J. (2002) 'Forging the frontiers between State, Church and Family: religious cleavages and the origins of early childhood education and care policies in France, Sweden and Germany', *Politics and Society* 30: 113–48.

Moss, P. and Deven, F. (eds) (2000) *Parental Leave in Europe: progress or pitfall? Research and Policy Issues in Europe*. Brussels: NIDI/CBGS.

Možný, I. (2002) *Sociologie rodiny*, Praha: SLON.

Možný, I. and Rabušic, L. (1999) 'The Czech family, the marriage market and the reproductive climate', in J. Večerník and P. Matějů (eds) *Ten Years of Rebuilding Capitalism*, Prague: Academia.

Nakano, Glenn (1992) 'From servitude to service work: historical continuities in the racial division of paid reproductive labour', *Signs* 18 (1): 1–43.

Nicole-Drancourt, C. (1991) *Le labyrinthe de l'insertion*, La Documentation française.

Nolan, P. and Salter, G. (2002) 'The labour market: history, structure and prospects', in P. Edwards (ed.) *Industrial Relations: Theory and Practice*, Oxford: Blackwell.

Nussbaum, M. (2003) 'Capabilities as fundamental entitlements: Sen and social justice', *Feminist Economics* 9: 33–59.

Oakley, A. (1974) *The Sociology of Housework*, London: Martin Robertson.

OECD (2001a) 'Balancing work and family life: helping parents into paid employment', in *Employment Outlook*, Paris: OECD.

OECD (2001b) *Employment Outlook 2001*, Paris: Organization for Economic Cooperation and Development.

OECD (2001c) *Starting Strong. Early Childhood Education and Care*, Paris: OECD.

OECD (2002) *Employment Outlook*, Paris: OECD. http://www.oecd.org

OECD (2002a) *Employment Outlook*. Paris.

OECD (2002b) *Babies and Bosses: Reconciling Work and Family Life*. Vol. 1, *Australia, Denmark and the Netherlands*. Paris.

OECD (2004) *Babies and Bosses: Reconciling Work and Family Life*. Vol. 3, *New Zealand, Portugal and Switzerland*. Paris.

OECD (2005) *Babies and Bosses: Reconciling Work and Family Life*. Vol. 4, *Canada, Finland, Sweden and the United Kingdom*. Paris.

Orloff, A. (1993) 'Gender and the social rights of citizenship: state policies and gender relations in comparative perspective', *American Sociological Review* 58 (3): 303–28.

Parcel, Toby L. and Cornfield, Daniel B. (2000) *Work and Family: Research Informing Policy*, Thousand Oaks: Sage.

Parsons, T. (1949) 'The social structure of the family', in R. Anshen (ed.) *The Family, its Function and Destiny*, New York: Harper.

Pateman, C. (1989) 'The patriarchal welfare state', reprinted in C. Pierson and F. Castles (eds) (2001) *The Welfare State Reader*, Cambridge: Polity Press.

Perista, H. (2002) 'Género e trabalho não pago: os tempos das mulheres e os tempos dos homens', *Análise Social* 163.

Perlow, L. A. (1998) 'Boundary control: the social ordering of work and family time in a high tech organisation', *Administrative Science Quarterly* 43: 328–57.

Perrons, D. (2003) 'The new economy and the work–life balance: conceptual explorations and a case study of new media', *Gender, Work and Organisation* 10 (1): 65–93.

Perrons, D. (2005) 'Gender mainstreaming and gender equality in the new (market) economy: an analysis of contradictions', *Social Politics* 12 (3): 389–411.

Perrons, D., Fagan C., McDowell, L., Ray, K. and Ward, K. (eds) (2006) *Gender Divisions and Working Time in the New Economy: Changing Patterns of Work, Care and Public Policy in Europe and North America*, Cheltenham: Edward Elgar.

Peters, M., Vossen, I., Versantvoort, M., van der Lippe, T. and de Ruijter, J. (2005) *Time Use in a Life Cycle Perspective and the Role of Institutional Frameworks in the European Union*, Ecorys-NEI – ICS/Universiteit Utrecht.

Peters, P. and den Dulk, L. (2003) 'Cross cultural differences in managers' support for home-based telework. A theoretical elaboration', *International Journal of Cross Cultural Management*, 3 (3): 329–46.

Pfau-Effinger, B. (1999) 'The modernization of family and motherhood in Western Europe', in R. Crompton (ed.) *Restructuring Gender Relations and Employment. The Decline of the Male Breadwinner*, Oxford: Oxford University Press, pp. 60–79.

Pfau-Effinger, B. (2004) 'Socio-historical paths of the male breadwinner model – an explanation of cross-national differences', *British Journal of Sociology* 55 (3): 377–400.

Pfau-Effinger, B. and Geissler, B. (eds) (2005) *Care Arrangements and Social Integration in European Societies*, Berlin: Policy Press.

Philipov, D. (2003) 'Fertility in times of discontinuous societal change', in I. Kotowska and J. Jóźwiak (eds) *Population of Central and Eastern Europe. Challenges and Opportunities*, Warsaw: Statistical Publishing Establishment, pp. 665–89.

Philipov, D., Spéder, Z. and Billari, F. (2005) *Now or Later? Fertility Intentions in Bulgaria and Hungary and the Impact of Anomie and Social Capital*, Vienna: Vienna Institute of Demography: working papers.

Pierson, P. (ed.) (2001) *The New Politics of the Welfare State*, Oxford: Oxford University Press.

Plantenga, J. and van Doorne-Huiskes, J. (1992) *Gender, Citizenship and Welfare: a European Perspective*, Paper presented at the first European Conference in Sociology, Vienna.

Plantenga, J. and Remery, C. w.a.o. Helming, P. (2005) *Reconciliation of Work and Private Life: a Comparative Review of Thirty European Countries*. Downloadable at: http://europa.eu.int/comm/employment_social/gender_equality/docs/2005/reconciliation_report_en.pdf

Plantin, L. (2001) *Män, familjeliv och föräldraskap*, Umeå: Boréa.

PNE (2005) *Plano Nacional de Emprego*, Lisbon: DGEP, MSE.

Popay, J., Hearn, J. and Edwards, J. (eds) (1999) *Men, Gender Divisions and Welfare*, London: Routledge.

Popov A. A. and David, H. P. (1999) 'Russian Federation and USSR Successor States', in H. P. David (with the assistance of J. Skilogianis), *From Abortion to Contraception: a Resource to Public Policies and Reproductive Behavior in Central and Eastern Europe from 1917 to the Present*, Westport, CT: Greenwood Press, 223–77.

Portugal, S. (1995) 'As mãos que embalam o berço: um estudo sobre as redes informais de apoio à maternidade', *Revista Crítica de Ciências Sociais* 42.

Rabušic, L. (2001a) *Kde ty všechny děti jsou? Porodnost v sociologické perspektivě*, Sociologické nakladatelství (SLON). Edice Studie. Praha.

Rabušic, L. (2001b) 'Value change and demographic behaviour in the Czech Republic', *Czech Sociological Review* 9 (1): 99–122.

Rapoport, R. and Rapoport, R. N. (1971) *Dual Career Families*, London: Penguin.

Rapoport, R., and Rapoport, R. N. (1975) 'Men, women and equity', in *The Family Coordinator* October: 421–32.

Rapoport, R., Bailyn, L., Fletcher, J., and Pruitt, B. H. (2002) *Beyond Work–Family Balance: Advancing Gender Equity and Workplace Performance*, San Francisco: Josey-Bass, London: Wiley.

Rebelo, G. (2002) *Trabalho e igualdade. Mulheres, teletrabalho e trabalho a tempo parcial*, Oeiras: Celta Editora.

RFV (2004) *14 Flexibel föräldrapenning – hur mammor och pappor använder föräldraförsäkringen och hur länge de är föräldralediga*, Riksförsäkringsverket.

Rose, G. (1993) *Feminism and Geography: the Limits of Geographical Knowledge*, Cambridge: Polity.

Rose, N. (1989) *Governing the Soul*, London: Routledge.

Rostgaard, T. (2002) 'Setting time aside for the father: father's leave in Scandinavia', *Community, Work and Family* 5 (3): 343–64.

Rothstein, B. (1998) 'Varifrån kommer det social kapitalet ?', *Socialvetenskaplig tidskrift* 5 (2–3).

Rubery, J., Ward, K., Grimshaw, D. and Beynon, H. (2003) *Time and the New Employment Relationship*, Manchester School of Management, UMIST (University of Manchester Institute of Science and Technology).

Rubery, J., Ward, K., Grimshaw, D. and Beynon, H. (2005) 'Working time, industrial relations and the employment relationship', *Time & Society* 14 (1): 89–111.

Rychtaříková, J. (2003) 'Trajectories of fertility and household composition in the demographic profile of the Czech Republic', *Population and Environment* 24(3): 225.

Sainsbury, D. (ed.) (1994) *Gendering Welfare States*, London: Sage.

Sainsbury, D. (1996) *Gender, Equality and Welfare States*, Cambridge: Cambridge University Press.

Sainsbury, D. (2001) 'Gender and the making of welfare states: Norway and Sweden', *Social Politics*, 8 (1): 113–43.

Sardon, J. P. (2004) 'Evolution démographique récente des pays développés', *Population* 2: 305–60.

Schaapman, M. (1995) *Ongezien onderscheid: Een analyse van de verborgen machtswerking van sekse*, Den Haag: Ministerie van Sociale zaken en Werkgelegenheid/ VUGA.

Schrimsher, K. P. (2004) 'Career commitments: women and men law school graduates', in Nancy E. Sacks and Catherine Marrone (eds) *Gender and Work in Today's World*, Westview Press.

Schweitzer, S. (2002) *Les femmes ont toujours travaillé: Une Histoire du travail des femmes aux 19ème et 20ème siècles*, Paris: Odile Jacob.

Seccombe, W. (1993) *Weathering the Storm*, London and New York: Verso.

Sevenhuijsen, S. (2002a) 'Caring in Third Way: the relation between obligation, responsibility and care in Third Way discourse', *Critical Social Policy* 20 (1).

Sevenhuijsen, S. (2002b) 'A third way? Moralities, ethics and families: an approach through the ethic of care', in A. Carling, S. Duncan and R. Edwards (eds) *Analysing Families*, London: Routledge.

Skinner, C. (2003) *Running Around in Circles: Coordinating Childcare, Education and Work*, Bristol: Policy Press.

Sleebos, J. (2003) *Low Fertility Rates in OECD Countries: Facts and Policy Responses*, OECD Working papers n°15, Directorate for Employment, Labour and Social Affairs.

Smithson, J. (2000) 'Using and analysing focus groups: limitations and possibilities', *International Journal of Methodology: Theory and Practice* 3 (2): 103–19.

Smithson, J. (2005) 'Full-timer in a part-time job: identity negotiation in organisational talk', *Feminism and Psychology* 15 (3): 275–93.

Smithson, J. (2006) 'Using focus groups to study work and family', in M. Pitt-Catsouphes, E. E. Kossek, and S. Sweet (eds) *The Handbook of Work and Family: Multi-disciplinary Perspectives and Approaches* (forthcoming) (see Bibliography).

Sobotka, T. (2004) *Postponement of Childbearing and Low Fertility in Europe*, Amsterdam: Dutch University Press.

Stanley, K. (ed.) (2005) *Daddy Dearest? Public Policy and Active Fatherhood*, London: ippr.

Stloukal, L. (1996) 'Eastern Europe's abortion culture: puzzles of interpretation', Paper presented at the IUSSP seminar *Socio-culural and political aspects of abortion in a changing world*, Trivandrum, India 25–28 March 1996, in T. Sobotka, 2004: *Postponement of Childbearing and Low Fertility in Europe*, Amsterdam: Dutch University Press.

Stolle, D. and Lewis, J. (2002) 'Social capital – an emerging concept', in B. Hobson, J. Lewis and B. Siim (eds) *Contested Concepts in Gender and Social Politics*, Cheltenham: Edward Elgar.

Sullivan, O. and Gershuny, J. (2001) 'Cross-national changes in time use', *British Journal of Sociology* 52 (2): 331–47.

Thompson, P. and Warhurst, C. (eds) (1998) *Workplaces of the Future*, Basingstoke: Macmillan – now Palgrave Macmillan.

Torres, A. C. and Silva, F. V. D. (1998) 'Guarda das crianças e divisão de trabalho entre homens e mulheres', *Sociologia, Problemas e Práticas*, 28.

Treas, J. and Widmer, E. D. (2000) 'Married women's employment over the life course: attitudes in cross-national perspective', *Social Forces* 78 (4): 1409–36.

Tyrkkö, A. (1997) 'Anpassning mellan arbetsliv och familjeliv i Sverige och i Finland', in J. Näsman (ed.) *Dilemmat arbetsliv – familjeliv i Norden*, Köpenhamn: Socialforskningsinstitutet 97:5, Nordiska Ministerrådet.

UNDP (2005) *Human Development Report 2005*, New York and Oxford: Oxford University Press.

Valcour, P. M. and Batt, R. (2003) 'Work–life integration: challenges and organizational responses', in P. Moen (ed.) *It's About Time*, Ithaca and London: Cornell University Press.

Van den Bogard, J., Collins, I. and Van Iren, A. (2003) *On Linking the Quality of Work and Life*, Publication of the Netherlands Ministry of Social Affairs and Employment.

Van de Kaa, D. J. (1996) 'Anchored narratives: the story and findings of half a century of research into the determinants of fertility', *Population Studies* 3: 389–432.

Van de Kaa, D. J. (1997) 'Options and sequences: Europe's demographic patterns', *Journal of the Australian Population Association* 1.

Van de Kaa, D. J. (1998) *Postmodern Fertility Preference: from Changing Value Orientation to New Behaviour*, Canberra: The Australian National University: Working papers in demography.

Velho, G. (1994) *Projecto e Metamorfose*, Rio de Janeiro: Zahar.

Večerník, J. (1999) *Communist and Transitory Income Distribution and Social Structure in the Czech Republic*, Helsinki: UNU/WIDER.

Wajcman, Judy (1998) *Managing like a Man: Women and Men in Corporate Management*, Cambridge, Polity.

Wall, K. (1997) 'Portugal: issues concerning the family', in J. Ditch et al. *Developments in National Family Policies*, European Observatory on Family policies, DGV/University of York, pp. 213–49.

Wall, K. (coord.) (2000) *Famílias no Portugal Contemporâneo. Relatório Final*, Lisbon: CIES-ISCTE e ICS.

Wall, K. (2001) *Family Life and Family Policies in Portugal – Developments in the Late Nineties*, Lisbon: ICS-UL/European Observatory on the Social Situation, Demography and Family.

Wall, K., José, J. S. et al. (2001) *Care Arrangements in Multi-career Families*, Lisbon: ICS-UL.

Wall, K. and Guerreiro M. D. (2005) 'A divisão familiar do trabalho', in K. Wall, (org.) *Famílias em Portugal*, Lisbon: ICS.

Wall, K. (2006) 'Attitudes face à Divisão Familiar do Trabalho em Portugal e na Europa', in K. Wall, L. Amâncio and A. Ramos (eds) *Atitudes Sociais dos Portugueses: Família e Género*, Lisbon: Imprensa de Ciências Sociais.

Warren, T. (2003) 'Class and gender-based working time? Time poverty and the domestic division of labour', *Sociology* 37 (4): 733–52.

Webster, J. (2004) *Working and Living in the Knowledge Society: the Policy Implications of Developments in Working Life and their Effects on Social Relations*, Report for the project 'Infowork', Dept. of Sociology, Trinity College, Dublin.

West, C. and Zimmerman, D. (1987) 'Doing gender', *Gender and Society* 1 (1): 125–51.

White, M., Hill, S., McGovern, P., Mills, C. and Smeaton, D. (2003) 'High-Performance management practices, working hours and work–life balance', *BJIR* 41 (2): 175–95.

Williams, F. (2004) *Rethinking Families*, London: Calouste Gulbenkian Foundation.

Williams, J. C. (1991) 'Domesticity as the dangerous supplement of Liberalism', *Journal of Women's History* 2 (3): 69–88.

Williams, J. C. (2000) *Unbending Gender*, New York: Oxford University Press.

Wood, S., Menezes, L. and Lasaosa, A. (2003) 'Family friendly management in Great Britain. Testing various perspectives', *Industrial Relations* 42.

Woodward, K. (ed.) (2000) *Questioning Identity: Gender, Class, Ethnicity*, London: Routledge.

Yeandle, S., Wigfield, A., Crompton, R. and Dennett, J. (2003) *Employers, Communities and Family-Friendly Employment Policies*, Bristol: Policy Press.

Index